For
Dummies™

BESTSELLING
BOOK SERIES

Lotus Notes® R5
For Dummies®

Cheat Sheet

D1408076

Navigating among Do...

To Go To This	Use This	Or This
Next unread document	Tab or F4	
Previous unread document	Shift+Tab or Shift+F4	
Next document	Enter	
Previous document	Backspace	

Working with Documents

To Do This	Try This
Read selected document	Press Enter or double-click document
Delete selected document	Press Delete or choose Edit⇨Clear
Clear document from screen	Press Esc or right double-click document
Edit document	Press Ctrl+E or double-click open document
Send a message	Choose Actions⇨Send, or click Send button
Forward a document	Choose Actions⇨Forward
Send a memo when you're in another database	Choose Create⇨Mail⇨Memo
Update a view	Press F9 or choose View⇨Refresh

Selecting Text

To Select This	Do This
A word	Double-click it
Next several words (Edit mode)	Ctrl+right-arrow key
Previous several words (Edit mode)	Ctrl+left-arrow key
All text in current field	Edit⇨Select All
A large chunk of text	Position cursor at beginning, Shift+click at end of chunk
From cursor to beginning of field	Shift+Ctrl+Home
From cursor to end of field	Shift+Ctrl+End

For Dummies®: Bestselling Book Series for Beginners

BESTSELLING
BOOK SERIES

Lotus Notes® R5
For Dummies®

Cheat Sheet

Getting Help Quickly

To Do This	Use This
Get help on current task	F1
Find a help topic	Help⇨Help Topics
Get help on error messages	F1 when message appears

Using the Universal Navigator

To Do This	Use This Universal Navigator Icon
Open the Admin Client (See note below)	
Open the Designer Client (See note below)	
Go to the Web page you visited before the current one	
Go to the Web page you visited after the current one	
Stop the Web action you just started	
Refresh the current Web page	
Search the Web	
Open a URL	

Note: The admin and designer icons will not be visible unless they have been activated by your administrator.

Hungry Minds™

For Dummies®: Bestselling Book Series for Beginners

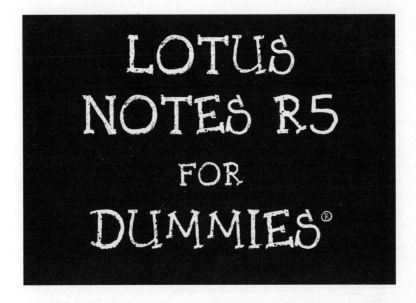

LOTUS NOTES R5 FOR DUMMIES®

**by Stephen Londergan
and Pat Freeland**

Hungry Minds™

Best-Selling Books • Digital Downloads • e-Books • Answer Networks • e-Newsletters • Branded Web Sites • e-Learning

New York, NY ◆ Cleveland, OH ◆ Indianapolis, IN

Lotus Notes R5® For Dummies®

Published by
Hungry Minds, Inc.
909 Third Avenue
New York, NY 10022
www.hungryminds.com
www.dummies.com

Library of Congress Catalog Card No.: 99-61892

ISBN: 0-7645-0320-0

Printed in the United States of America

10 9 8 7 6

1O/QW/RR/QR/IN

Distributed in the United States by Hungry Minds, Inc.

Distributed by CDG Books Canada Inc. for Canada; by Transworld Publishers Limited in the United Kingdom; by IDG Norge Books for Norway; by IDG Sweden Books for Sweden; by IDG Books Australia Publishing Corporation Pty. Ltd. for Australia and New Zealand; by TransQuest Publishers Pte Ltd. for Singapore, Malaysia, Thailand, Indonesia, and Hong Kong; by Gotop Information Inc. for Taiwan; by ICG Muse, Inc. for Japan; by Intersoft for South Africa; by Eyrolles for France; by International Thomson Publishing for Germany, Austria and Switzerland; by Distribuidora Cuspide for Argentina; by LR International for Brazil; by Galileo Libros for Chile; by Ediciones ZETA S.C.R. Ltda. for Peru; by WS Computer Publishing Corporation, Inc., for the Philippines; by Contemporanea de Ediciones for Venezuela; by Express Computer Distributors for the Caribbean and West Indies; by Micronesia Media Distributor, Inc. for Micronesia; by Chips Computadoras S.A. de C.V. for Mexico; by Editorial Norma de Panama S.A. for Panama; by American Bookshops for Finland.

For general information on Hungry Minds' products and services please contact our Customer Care Department within the U.S. at 800-762-2974, outside the U.S. at 317-572-3993 or fax 317-572-4002.

For sales inquiries and reseller information, including discounts, premium and bulk quantity sales, and foreign-language translations, please contact our Customer Care Department at 800-434-3422, fax 317-572-4002, or write to Hungry Minds, Inc., Attn: Customer Care Department, 10475 Crosspoint Boulevard, Indianapolis, IN 46256.

For information on licensing foreign or domestic rights, please contact our Sub-Rights Customer Care Department at 212-884-5000.

For information on using Hungry Minds' products and services in the classroom or for ordering examination copies, please contact our Educational Sales Department at 800-434-2086 or fax 317-572-4005.

For press review copies, author interviews, or other publicity information, please contact our Public Relations Department at 317-572-3168 or fax 317-572-4168.

For authorization to photocopy items for corporate, personal, or educational use, please contact Copyright Clearance Center, 222 Rosewood Drive, Danvers, MA 01923, or fax 978-750-4470.

Hungry Minds™ is a trademark of Hungry Minds, Inc.

About the Authors

Stephen Londergan has been on the Lotus Notes and Domino bandwagon since 1989, and this is his eighth book about it. He lives near Boston with his wife Robyn and three children, Mike, Richard, and John.

Pat Freeland is an independent Notes Application Developer and the author of several books and magazine articles about Notes and other applications. He lives in Hingham, Massachusetts, with his wife Vicki, his daughter Cavi, and his son Michael.

Dedication

As Tennyson said, "Ah, why should life all labour be?" I'm not sure why either, but I dedicate this book to my family.

— Stephen Londergan

To John and Karline, my parents-in-law, with love. For your love and generosity, for allowing me to be part of your family, and for making it possible to have Vicki in my life, I am truly grateful.

— Pat Freeland

Authors' Acknowledgments

Thanks to Susan Pink, for her patience, perseverance, and perspicacity; to David Hamilton for his vigilance and his verifications; and to all the IDG people with whom we did not deal directly, but who helped put this book into production.

Publisher's Acknowledgments

We're proud of this book; please send us your comments through our Online Registration Form located at www.dummies.com.

Some of the people who helped bring this book to market include the following:

Acquisitions, Editorial, and Media Development

Project Editor: Susan Pink
(*Previous Edition: Shannon Ross*)

Acquisitions Editor: Sherri Morningstar

Technical Editor: David Hamilton

Editorial Manager: Mary C. Corder

Editorial Assistants: Alison Walthall, Paul E. Kuzmic

Production

Project Coordinator: Valery Bourke

Layout and Graphics: Linda M. Boyer, Kelly Hardesty, Angela F. Hunckler, Brent Savage, Jacque Schneider, Janet Seib, Michael A. Sullivan, Brian Torwelle

Proofreaders: Kelli Botta, Vickie Broyles, Laura L. Bowman, Nancy Price, Ethel M. Winslow, Janet M. Withers

Indexer: Sharon Hilgenberg

Special Help
Suzanne Thomas

Hungry Minds Technology Publishing Group: Richard Swadley, Senior Vice President and Publisher; Mary Bednarek, Vice President and Publisher, Networking; Joseph Wikert, Vice President and Publisher, Web Development Group; Mary C. Corder, Editorial Director, Dummies Technology; Andy Cummings, Publishing Director, Dummies Technology; Barry Pruett, Publishing Director, Visual/Graphic Design

Hungry Minds Manufacturing: Ivor Parker, Vice President, Manufacturing

Hungry Minds Marketing: John Helmus, Assistant Vice President, Director of Marketing

Hungry Minds Production for Branded Press: Debbie Stailey, Production Director

Hungry Minds Sales: Michael Violano, Vice President, International Sales and Sub Rights

Contents at a Glance

Cartoons at a Glance

By Rich Tennant

page 115

page 7

page 35

page 245

page 287

page 161

Cartoon Information:
Fax: 978-546-7747
E-Mail: richtennant@the5thwave.com
World Wide Web: www.the5thwave.com

Table of Contents

Introduction

• •

*Y*our company just decided to use Lotus Notes. Suddenly, you're faced with the prospect of interacting with fellow human beings by means of your computer, instead of by paper and the telephone. The prospect of going online may be as frightening as being forced to sit through Acts III & IV of *Hamlet* at your local high school. Or perhaps you've been online forever (you trendsetter, you), but now you're going to start using Lotus Notes — and that's a new program to you.

Who needs Notes anyway? For what seems like ages, you've been sending memos on paper, and calling people in distant offices, jotting little notes to yourself as you talk, and then filing these shreds of paper in the In box on your desk. Company policies, sales projections, marketing strategies, and other miscellaneous information are right at your fingertips — until the cleaning crew arrives and cleans your desk. Now where *is* that sales sheet from last quarter?

And how often have you been frustrated and delayed by something silly, such as having to make copies of a memo you want to send to 25 people? Ensuring that up-to-date information is available to everyone who needs it is a big, time-consuming, and not-altogether-enticing task.

So who needs Notes? You may not know it yet, but *you* do! Notes can make your life easier with a capital *E!* Notes is the program to use when you begin to realize that there *has* to be a better way — a way to do your work more efficiently, a way to communicate and share information with people more quickly.

Notes is a program for getting information into the hands of the people who need it . . . and also for keeping that same information out of the hands of the people who shouldn't see it (no matter how much they want to snoop). With Notes, you don't have to worry about silly things such as what kind of computer people have, or where they are, or what kind of network or modem they use.

Yeah, sounds great. But is it worth it? Do you have all kinds of time to invest in learning this (allegedly) wonderful program? Fear not. The book you're holding in your hot little hands can get you up and running as quickly as possible.

This book is for anyone who's using or planning to use Lotus Notes and Lotus Domino. You might be a relative Notes novice (or even a computer neophyte). Or maybe you're a cc:Mail jock who's about to launch into the wonderful world of Notes. Either way, you've come to the right place.

About This Book

We know that you're busy and that you hate to read computer manuals. So we designed this book to tell you just what you need to know to get rolling as quickly and as painlessly as possible.

Among other things, this book contains the following:

- ✔ How to send an electronic message to one person or to a group of people — forget the copy machine, interoffice envelopes, and the like

- ✔ How to read, reply to, and (occasionally) ignore all the e-mail you receive

- ✔ How to organize, print, save, and forward messages

- ✔ How to read and contribute to Notes databases, and how to store information in those databases so others can see it

- ✔ How to hide sensitive and confidential information from prying eyes

- ✔ How to create attractive documents

- ✔ How to communicate with the office from your house or a hotel room

- ✔ How to cruise the Internet without leaving your chair (or Notes, for that matter)

You have a choice: Either read this book from cover to cover (not necessarily in one sitting!) or choose the particular topics that interest you and read just those parts in the order that makes the most sense for you. Both approaches give you the information you need. In general, the concepts are straightforward, so you won't have any trouble jumping from chapter to chapter or from section to section.

We strive to avoid techno-babble and "geek speak" as much as we can. If a particular term is unfamiliar to you, you can always check the glossary at the end of the book. You can also use the Index and Table of Contents to find more information about a particular concept.

Foolish Assumptions

Without so much as a phone call, we're making the following assumptions about you, dear reader:

- You want to know *what,* but not necessarily *why.* We leave the why to the computer nerds and concentrate on what's important to getting you working with Notes ASAP.

- You have access to a computer on which someone has already installed Lotus Notes Release 5.

- You're willing to send a check for $357 to your beloved *Lotus Notes R5 For Dummies* authors. (Just kidding, although tips, in either cash or securities, are always appreciated.)

Conventions Used in This Book

If we want you to type something, we put it in bold, like this: **Type this** and then press Enter. (In this case, you type "Type this" but not "and then press Enter." But you probably already figured that out.)

Sometimes, we refer to text that you see on-screen. When we refer to a message just as it appears on the monitor, it looks like this: *Some words on your screen.* If the text is longer than a few words, we write it like this:

```
This is a computer message exactly as it appears on-screen.
```

We frequently tell you to make menu selections or use the SmartIcons (special Notes buttons). When we tell you to click a SmartIcon, we include a picture of that SmartIcon in the margin. We present menu commands like this: Choose File⇨Database⇨New. You simply click the first menu and then, from the drop-down list, click the second one and so on. Or you can press Alt (on your keyboard) and, simultaneously, the underlined letter.

If a dialog box appears when you use a command, we reproduce it right in the book (in brilliant black and white) and tell you how to use it.

How This Book Is Organized

The arrangement of the chapters in this book reflects the order in which most people become familiar with the various aspects of Notes.

Part I: Get Rolling with Notes

In the first part of the book, we get the inevitable definitions out of the way and then jump right into getting Notes set up on your computer. Reading Part I is like finding out what all those dials on the dashboard do before you try driving a car.

Part II: It's a Mail Thing

The second part of this book deals with the things you use Notes for the most: sending, receiving, and working with e-mail and memos.

Part III: Delving into Databases

The chapters in the third part of this book show you how to get at your company's databases, how to read and create documents, and how to create your own databases. You also find some other cool things to expand your already dazzling command of the program.

Part IV: Making Notes Suit You!

Eventually, everyone wants to type special characters (such as the copyright symbol, ©), modify the style of paragraphs, customize and personalize the way Notes works, use Notes with other programs, search for information, or manage their bookmarks. When that time comes for you, peruse Part IV.

Part V: Worldwide Notes

When you're ready to move into high gear and take your Notes knowledge with you into the 21st century, turn (without delay) to Part V. In this part, we show you how to take Notes with you on your business trips, how to hop from Notes straight onto the Internet, and how to get Notes talking to the other programs and places where you store information.

Part VI: The Part of Tens

Every single one of the books in the . . . *For Dummies* series has a Part of Tens. Why should this book be any different? In this part, we present an assortment of useful factoids. This treasure trove of tips includes ten cool tricks you can use to impress your friends, ten things you should never, ever do, and other cool tidbits. The Part of Tens in this book is nowhere near as exciting as The Part of Tens in Dr. Ruth's *Sex For Dummies,* but it'll hold your interest.

Glossary

We finish up the book with a glossary of the terms and concepts explained throughout the book.

What You're Not to Read

We, of course, consider every last word in this book to be informative, insightful, and often quite humorous, and we can't think of a reason why you wouldn't want to read every one of the scintillating sentences contained herein. You, on the other hand, probably have better things to do. So we've marked the especially trivial details with a special Technical Stuff icon, so you know what you can (and can't) skip.

Icons in This Book

We've scattered scads of little pictures (we call them *icons*) amongst the pages of this book. Read on to see what each icon signifies.

This icon alerts you to information that's especially interesting to, uh, *nerds.* You know, the kind of people who always kept your high-school math classes late because they were asking so many questions? In some high schools, this person was all too often the victim of something known as a *wedgie,* but that's a separate book. We're not saying a bunch of football players will give you a wedgie if you read these sections, but then again. . . .

This icon tells you that some little shard of knowledge is coming your way to make your life with Notes just a bit easier. Definitely worth reading.

As you stumble along the pathway of life, these little commandments are things that you should never forget. For example, you should always . . . well, it had something to do with, ummm. . . . We'll come back to this later.

Ignore these at your own peril. You've been warned.

Where to Go from Here

Get going; you have a lot of reading to do. Don't be afraid to experiment, and remember to check out the Notes Help feature early and often.

Part I
Get Rolling with Notes

The 5th Wave · By Rich Tennant

Andy soon began to think he shouldn't have opted for the cut-rate Web hookup after all.

In this part . . .

*W*hen you tackle a new program, the best thing to do first is read the basic information about how the program works. (Of course, most people install the program, make lots of mistakes, get mad, and finally, after sputtering and fuming, turn to the instructions.)

Notes is a powerful and complex program. The chapters in this part prepare you to use Notes to its full potential without wasting a lot of time, developing bad habits, or cursing the program because you can't figure out how to do something.

So, here in the first part of the book, we present the information you need to know before getting started. We have attempted to avoid technobabble whenever possible, but sometimes knowing the official terms actually helps. If you call your administrator and say, "The thingie next to the hinkyminky returns a box that says something when I clunk it," you can bet two things: You haven't been helpful — and therefore the administrator can't help you — and you've provided the administrator with some comic relief.

Chapter 1

Just What Is Notes, Anyway?

*L*otus Notes is a computer program that enables you to communicate and interact electronically with other people. You can use Notes to send people e-mail and to share other kinds of information, such as word processing documents, spreadsheets, Web pages, and other good stuff.

If you're a loner who doesn't like to talk to people or if you think that information is power and you'd rather not share, well, then, you probably won't like Notes. If, on the other hand, your work entails interacting with other people and you want (or need) to share information with coworkers, customers, and the like, you'll be a Notes junkie in no time, sharing information and interacting with people in ways you probably haven't yet imagined.

The ultra-cool thing about Notes is that it's easy to use. You get to jump on the *electronic superhighway* (bet you haven't heard that expression before) with little or no knowledge of the messy underside of computers. If you find expressions such as *local area network, ISDN,* and *HTML* scary (or even downright boring), Notes is the program for you! Even if you still think *Java* has something to do with coffee, you'll be able to use Notes.

With Notes, you can concentrate on the important things — such as sending flattering e-mail to your boss, responding to your customers, and sounding lofty and knowledgeable at meetings.

And what's better, you don't even have to be at the office to participate in the aforementioned technological fiesta. If you have a modem or can connect to the Internet, you can do all your work from home, the hotel, or even from an airplane — although you better get the boss's permission first!

What Is Groupware?

Groupware is a new kind of software that lets you work together with a group of other people. Groupware is different than, say, a spreadsheet program, such as Lotus 1-2-3, or a word processor, such as Microsoft Word. In programs like 1-2-3 and Word, the work you do is yours and yours alone; you store the files that you create on your own computer's hard disk, and no one else can see them.

Groupware, on the other hand, lets you share information with other people, by putting the information you create in a centralized and shared location. Lotus Notes is a kind of groupware, just like Microsoft Word is a kind of word processor. (Incidentally, Notes is the oldest groupware program of all; it has been around since 1989!) Groupware won't make you a better golfer or help you win friends and influence people (use Dale Carnegie for that), but it can help you do the following:

- ✔ Send e-mail.
- ✔ Create databases and fill them with information that you, everyone, or only people you choose can see and edit.
- ✔ Be sure that the same information on a particular subject is available to everyone who needs it — regardless of where they are and without having to worry about what kind of computer or network they use.
- ✔ Allow people to communicate as quickly as possible, whether the communication is gossip, news, or vital corporate data (assuming you can tell the difference).
- ✔ Be sure that the forms and documents your organization uses are standard so that you all seem organized, even if you're not.
- ✔ Provide a central place to look for everybody's daily calendar of appointments.
- ✔ Keep information in a safe and readily available place, rather than in piles on everyone's desk.
- ✔ Prevent prying, nosy, unauthorized busybodies from rummaging around in places where they have no business.
- ✔ Save trees.

✔ Combine information, graphics, text, and tables from different places, such as spreadsheet programs, word processors, and even the World Wide Web and other parts of the Internet.

✔ Store information and e-mail for users who are only occasionally connected.

I mail, you mail, we all mail e-mail

Unless you've been living under a rock, you've heard of e-mail, and you probably know that the *e* stands for *electronic*. So, take away the *e* and you have *mail,* and that's all there is to it.

Most people prefer e-mail to p-mail *(p* for *paper)* because e-mail is so fast; you can get a five-page e-mail to a coworker in Japan in just a few minutes. The post office can't compete with that! Plus, you don't need to hunt for stamps or walk down to the mailbox. You send e-mail right from your desk, without even leaving your chair. Just put a name at the top of a memo and click the Send button. Put several names at the top of the memo, and the memo goes to everyone. (Of course, there is the *little* matter of someone buying a computer for everyone, connecting them all together, and then buying Lotus Notes. But that's probably somebody else's headache.)

In Lotus Notes, the e-mail you send goes to everyone you address it to and to *only* those people. If you write a nasty note about the boss and send it to a friend two floors down, you don't have to worry that the boss will see it — unless your (former) friend decides to forward it to the boss or print it and hang it on the bulletin board.

Notes, unlike some other e-mail systems we could mention, enables you to add text enhancements (such as boldface, italics, and underlining), change colors and fonts, and add tables, links (whatever that means), and graphics. Instead of sending messages that make people yawn, your messages can make people sit up and take notice — just like the one in Figure 1-1.

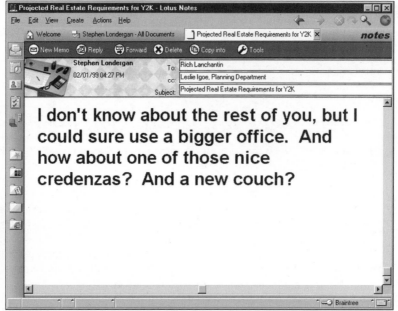

Figure 1-1:
You can
send short
memos like
this to many
people
quickly and
easily, with-
out leaving
the comfort
of your
chair.

And, barring the rare (and expensive) system breakdown, you can be confident that your Notes e-mail message will be delivered. Contrast this assurance with a memo slipped into a company mailer and left to languish in the quagmire of interoffice mail. Figure 1-1 shows a memo addressed to Rich Lanchantin, with a carbon copy (cc) to Leslie Igoe and a whole group of people called the Planning Department. All these people will receive the memo in time to act on the schedule changes.

With the year 2000 just around the corner, more and more people around the world are hooked up with all sorts of e-mail programs. Using Notes, you can send an e-mail message to your buddy working down the hall, a friend who works at another company, your cousin who's studying art in Paris, or even your kid who's at home using America Online. In other words, you can use Lotus Notes to send e-mail to anybody, anyplace, anytime. Any questions?

Databasically

The most important concept in Notes is the database. In fact, the entire program is organized around databases. A *database* is just a bunch of information grouped together. The L. L. Bean catalog is really a database — it's organized in a particular order, with the name, description, picture, and price of each item kept nice and neat. But the only way to find an item in the L. L. Bean catalog is to turn the pages and let your fingers do the walking. That's where electronic databases are much more useful.

When you use Notes, you create *documents,* such as memos, company policy statements, sales records, or listings of baseball statistics. These documents are all stored in databases with other documents. You can select information from that database without ever turning pages or scanning long lists. Ask your database to show you all sales contacts in Alabama, for example, and — as quick as you can say "How y'all doin'?" — the list of Alabama good ol' boys (and girls) appears on-screen.

A good example of a Notes database is a *discussion database,* which is the electronic equivalent of the backyard fence. You can express your opinion on a particular subject by composing a main document. Then someone in the Singapore office might compose a reply to your statement telling you that you're all wet. Someone else in Stockholm can compose a response to that response, telling the Singapore person to lay off you. And so on. Others might sound off their opinions by writing entries to the discussion database. People anywhere and everywhere in your organization can respond to these opinions.

You can write your opinion by using Lotus Notes working in Windows, for example, while one person's response is created on a Macintosh and others use UNIX. Everyone can read all the documents, regardless of what kind of computer the documents were composed on. You can all share not only your highly sought-after opinions, but also drawings, enhanced text, Excel spreadsheets, and Web pages. You might even find that some people who are responding don't use Lotus Notes at all, but are instead using a Web browser (such as Microsoft Internet Explorer or Netscape Communicator).

In Notes, databases contain *views.* Views contain *documents.* Documents contain *fields.* And fields contain individual pieces of *data.* See, the whole concept is based on data, and that's why they call it a *data*base. Don't let all these new words bog you down. We get into what these terms mean for you and how you can put them to good use in other chapters. For now, we just want to give you the big picture.

You Can't Be All Things to All People

Notes is groupware with amazing e-mail, database, and Internet capabilities. But, for all its power and glory, Notes does have some limitations.

What Notes isn't

Notes is a database program, that's for sure. But it isn't a true relational database. *Relational databases* allow you to enter data in a field in one database and then use that same field in another database. Notes can't do that. Unless you're a database design jockey, you probably don't give two toots about whether a database is relational. But the fact that Notes isn't relational translates into some good news and some bad news for you.

The good news is that Notes is not rigid. Unlike other databases, Notes doesn't require you to set the size of a field and then limit entries in that field to your specified maximum size. (*Fields,* as you may or may not yet know, are the little bits of information, such as a person's last name, that make up a document.)

For example, in other programs, you would have to decide how many characters a Last Name field would accept. Suppose that you allow 15 characters, and then you hire John Jacob Jingleheimerschmidt. You would either have to be satisfied with "J J Jingleheime," or you would have to go through the nail-breaking procedure of redesigning the database. With Notes, you just type away, secure in the knowledge that Notes will take anything and everything you type.

Because it isn't rigid, Notes allows you to create rich text fields. A *rich text field* is a field in which you can add such fancy stuff as character formats (boldface and italics, for example), embedded word processing documents, bits of Web pages, or maybe even video clips and pictures of your (no doubt lovely) children.

So, what's the bad news? If you use your computer to track customer orders and you have 19,200,675 orders to track, using Notes is kind of like using a screwdriver to bang a nail — it's not the best tool for that job. Applications that require the care and management of millions and millions of records usually *don't* belong in Notes.

Not only is Notes not a relational database, it's also not the program to use for *transaction-based systems,* such as airline ticketing. Imagine lots of travel agents in lots of different cities selling lots of tickets for a particular flight and recording the data on their own copy of a reservations database. Later, at departure time, a huge crowd of people appears, all with tickets for the same seat on the same plane. When companies need *immediate* sharing of information everywhere, they typically use a rig of terminals connected to a single gigantic computer somewhere. Notes allows periodic, but not immediate, sharing of updates to databases.

But don't worry — whether you use Notes probably isn't your decision, anyway. Let the geeks down in the MIS department decide when to use Notes and when not to. Just make sure that you tell them to buy lots of copies of this book — whatever they decide!

What Notes is

Notes is a truly useful and powerful program because of its capability to send e-mail *and* create databases of all sorts that every person in the organization can share, add to, and read. Sure, you can use other programs for e-mail, and some even let you share information. What sets Notes apart from the crowd is its capability to do it all.

Rich text fields and other Notes fields have an advantage over those in regular databases: They don't have a field size limit. In other database programs, changing the size of a field in a large database can be a heck of a lot of work and, if not executed correctly, can corrupt your database. Notes, on the other hand, doesn't care whether you put one word or a whole book in a field.

Fields in other databases are, in a word, *blah.* No boldface, no variety in fonts, and no possibility for attachments or embedded objects. Not so with rich text fields, because they contain more than just information. Rich text fields can contain anything your heart desires, setting them apart from the mundane, educating and exciting readers, and allowing you to show yourself to be the creative genius that you are.

With Notes, you can create databases for any of the following uses:

- ✔ **Reference:** Members of your organization seeking knowledge can find what they need to know, contributed by those who have knowledge to share — from each according to his or her ability, to each according to his or her need. Kind of brings a tear to your eye.

- ✔ **Workflow:** Those charged with a broad task can record the individual assignments and proclaim the completion of each, documenting both progress and completion. "Well done, old chap!"

- ✔ **Calendars:** You and your colleagues can easily schedule appointments and meetings with one another.

- ✔ **E-mail:** All the people in the organization can communicate privately or publicly with anyone they choose.

- ✔ **World Wide Web:** People can browse a database containing Web pages and other types of information from the Internet — even if they are not connected or don't have Web browser software.

- ✔ **Fax:** You and your coworkers can distribute valuable data stored in your organization's databases to a needy and grateful public.

This, then, is Notes. More than just a program, more than just a database, e-mail program, or Web browser — Notes is a dynamic tool for sharing knowledge throughout the organization. And remember, knowledge *is* power.

What Makes Notes So Special?

A few additional features that distinguish Notes from mere e-mail programs or database programs are its capabilities to make compound documents and to replicate databases.

Compound documents feel the power

You've heard of compound fractures, right? Well, compound documents are nothing like them. That doesn't clear things up? Well, how about this: Normally, when you're busy using Notes, you're typing a memo or filling in a form or writing some text to be included with other similar entries in a database. Sometimes, however, you need to put more than just text in your document.

To emphasize a point you're making about sales figures, you might want to include a spreadsheet you created in Lotus 1-2-3, a graph you made in Microsoft PowerPoint, and even a related Web page you found on the Internet. So you copy and paste all these items into your document.

The result is a *compound document* containing data, graphics, or other stuff from other places. Figure 1-2 is a simple example of a compound document containing a small spreadsheet and a table. (We discuss compound documents in greater detail in Chapter 12.)

Replication explanation

Replication is what makes Notes the great program that it is. Oh sure, other programs allow you to send e-mail, but they don't replicate. Remember that your mail database is only *one* kind of database that you use in Notes. Chances are that other people in your organization have created other databases. *Replicas,* copies of those databases, may be on many of your organization's servers around the world. This magic is how your colleague in France can see what you've been working on. He looks at a *copy* of the database in question on his server in Paris while you look at a copy of the very same database on your server in, say, Chicago.

One example of this technological feat is a database listing each employee's name, employee number, location, shoe size, and other important data. At each location, these replicas are updated as people are hired or fired or change their shoe sizes. Obviously, employees at each location enter different information into the database. *Replication* enables Notes to include all the information on all the databases.

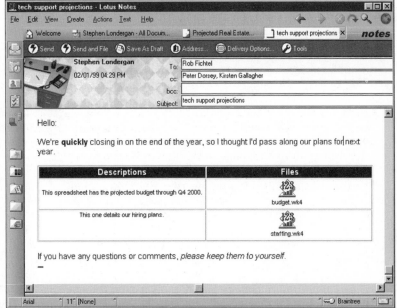

Figure 1-2:
An example of a compound document that has a table, a couple of spread-sheets from Lotus 1-2-3, and some bold and italicized text.

When the replication is complete, all replicas have the same information, so up-to-date information is available everywhere. Every so often, the server in France "talks to" your server in Chicago so that the two servers can synchronize their copy of the database. That way, the Chicago server ends up with the documents that your French colleague has been composing, while at the same time, the server *en France* gets the documents you've been adding to the database. Pretty cool, *non?*

Replication is also the process by which remote workstations update their own copies of databases, such as your e-mail. So, when you take your laptop on a trip to Denver, you can *replicate* with the server back at the home office, too. How often this technological feat occurs is a decision that the laptop owner makes. In a database that has a rapid turnover of information, such as your e-mail or a database of news articles from the Internet, replicating several times a day may be necessary. A database that doesn't change often, such as one listing corporate policies, may replicate only once or twice each week.

Who's the Boss?

Notes uses computers all hooked together in a network. In some ways, a *network* is like a department in a corporation because it has individual workers and someone in charge. The individual computers need to be connected to a sort-of *boss* computer to be able to work together. No doubt your boss serves the same vital role in your department.

Servers with a smile

The computer in charge of a Notes network is called the *server*. The server acts as a central, shared computer for the others, storing the mail databases for all the people whose computers are hooked to it and regulating the flow of information. (It might also store other databases, besides just e-mail.)

Around 1997, Lotus started calling its servers by a new name: *Domino* (as in "we just got a new Domino server" or "Domino servers are really cool"). Don't let the vocabulary get in your way. Your server does the same thing, whether it goes by the name of Domino or Notes.

The server is usually a more powerful computer with more storage than the ones connected to it, and it's often housed in a physically secure and remote location. Is this beginning to sound like your boss — powerful, having the best equipment, remote, and in charge? The server might also be like your boss in that it's not where the regular work in Notes is performed. The actual work is performed on the individual computers connected to the server.

In large organizations, many servers (all around the world), each with their own bunch of attached computers, are connected together over the company-wide network.

Down by the workstation

In the wonderful world of Notes, your computer is known as a *workstation*. Workstations are where real people perform real work. Workstations usually contain the Notes program files for each individual user (known as a *client*) and also any databases that the users create for their own personal use.

Not all workstations are always connected to a server. For example, if you go on a business trip and take your laptop with you, you would need a pretty long network cable to connect directly to the office, unless your business trip takes you to only the parking lot. When you use your computer to connect to the server by phone line and modem, your computer is called a *remote workstation*. Some workstations are both LAN (local area network) and remote. If you have a laptop, you can hook it to the LAN when you're at the office and then use its modem for a remote hookup when you're on the road.

No matter how fast your modem is, using Notes on it is slower than using Notes on the network. So plan on taking extra time with the modem and be sure that your teenager won't need the phone for a while.

User ID — Your Key to Notes

When you were born, the hospital gave your mother a copy of your birth certificate. When you graduated from high school, you got a diploma. And when you learned to drive, you got a driver's license. When you start using Notes, someone gives you what's known as a *user ID*.

Don't expect to get a copy of Notes, install it on your computer, and then be able to tap into the nerve center of your company. Even if you're the company president and have a fistful of Notes disks, even if you *do* lunch rather than eat it, even if you have the fanciest car in the lot, until you get that user ID, you don't have a prayer of being able to use Notes.

Your user ID is the key that gives you access to your own mail database and other databases in the company. Figure 1-3 shows some information about a user ID. To you, this might look like only a series of numbers and letters, but to the servers, it's what makes you a legitimate user of Notes in your organization.

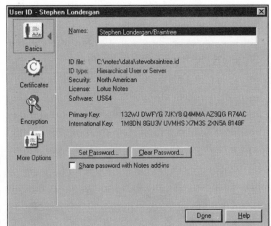

Figure 1-3:
A sample
user ID.

Those last three words are very important, by the way. Your user ID makes you a member of *your* organization. You can't sneak into your competitor's offices down the street and use your user ID in their Notes network, because your user ID is created by and recognized only by your own organization.

Keep a copy of your Notes user ID on a floppy disk so that you can copy it back to your hard disk if you accidentally delete your Notes program files or if you experience the heartbreak of computer failure. Remember, if your computer breaks down, your user ID enables you to use another person's computer as if it were your own. For this reason, you should keep your Notes user ID in a secure place (under lock and key). If you're lucky, the folks down in MIS might have a backup copy, but check with them before relying on them!

When push comes to shove, your user ID is just another (small) file on your computer. You need your user ID each and every time you use Notes. Most people keep their user ID file on their hard disk. If you want to use your computer at home to do some work, you must make a copy of your user ID file and bring that copy home with you. You can't use Notes without that user ID. Never, ever — no fooling.

Chapter 2

Getting Acquainted with Notes and Domino

....

In This Chapter

▶ Starting and stopping the program

▶ Facing the Notes interface

▶ Getting smart about SmartIcons and bookmarks

....

So, your company just got Lotus Notes, and you're all excited about using this powerful, state-of-the-art program that you've heard so much about. Or maybe you aren't so thrilled because your boss announced that you had to start using Notes, and you're not exactly overjoyed at the prospect of cozying up to yet another software program. In either case, the good news is that figuring out how to set up, start, and stop the program isn't all that difficult.

We've made the assumption in this chapter that your Lotus Notes software has already been installed on your system; contact your administrator (in a hurry) if that's not the case.

As we note in Chapter 1, around 1997, Lotus started calling its servers by a new name: *Domino*. So your server may be called either Domino or Notes.

Starting the Program

First things first: To start the program, double-click the Notes program icon. Where is this mysterious Notes icon? Well, that depends on where the person who installed the program put it. The icon you're trying to find looks like Figure 2-1. We can't say exactly where it appears on your computer, because its location depends on whether you're using Windows 95, Macintosh, or whatever. If you're using Windows 95, for example, you can find the Lotus Notes program icon in the Folder named Lotus Applications, which is in turn found in the Programs menu, all of which is available through the Start menu (phew!).

Figure 2-1:
The Notes
program
icon.

When you finally find the icon, double-click it to start the program.

Understanding the Workspace

Now that Notes is running, how do you get started? At the starting gun, you see something that looks like Figure 2-2 — this is your *workspace*. Although it took a minute to get here when you started Notes the very first time, this screen is what you'll see from now on whenever you start the program. You need to know about the following main elements of the Notes workspace:

- ✔ Bookmarks
- ✔ Menus
- ✔ SmartIcons
- ✔ Task buttons
- ✔ Universal navigation bar
- ✔ Welcome page

What's on the menu?

The menus work exactly the way you would expect them to. You're probably already familiar with many of the options available on the Notes menu because many are the same as the options in other programs. For example, you save a document in Notes the same way that you save a spreadsheet in Lotus 1-2-3, which is the same way that you save a document in Microsoft Word.

If you're a mouse user, you can click any menu item to open it. If you don't like to (or downright refuse to) use the mouse, you can press Alt and then use the right- and left-arrow keys to select the menu you want. (Press Enter when the item is selected.) You can use the same strategy to choose an item in a menu; use the arrow keys to select the item you want and then press Enter.

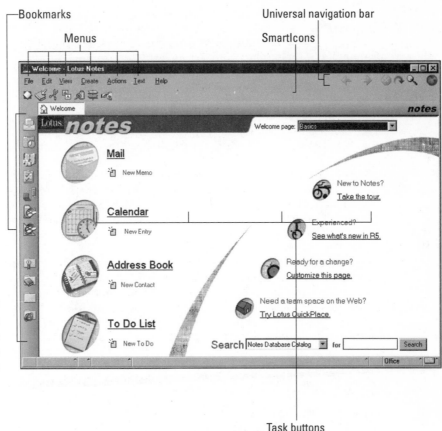

Bookmarks

Menus

Universal navigation bar

SmartIcons

Figure 2-2:
The Notes
workspace.

Task buttons

Note that some of the words in the menus are gray and others are black. You can choose only the black items; menu options that appear gray aren't appropriate for whatever you're doing. For example, if you're in the middle of editing a document and you take a look at the Edit menu, you find that the Select by Date option appears dimmed, indicating that you can't select by date (whatever that means!) while you're editing a document.

Wise up with SmartIcons

If you've ever used any other Lotus program, you probably recognize the row of small pictures that stretches across the top of the screen; these pictures are what Lotus calls *SmartIcons*. SmartIcons are just a way for you to execute certain commands quickly — without having to use the menus.

For example, if you want to print the document that's on-screen, you *can* choose File⊃Print, but an easier and faster approach is to click the Print SmartIcon, which is shown in the margin. (Lotus probably doesn't like to admit it, but their SmartIcons are an awful lot like the buttons found on the Microsoft toolbar. Or maybe the Microsoft buttons are an awful lot like the Lotus SmartIcons. . . .)

Some SmartIcons are obvious — or relatively obvious, anyway. For example, you can probably guess that you use the SmartIcon that looks like a small jar of library paste to paste from the Clipboard.

 Some of the SmartIcons aren't so obvious, though. What about the sixth one in from the left — the one with red and green arrows that sort of looks like a traffic sign? (Incidentally, this is one of the Help SmartIcons, called Help Guide Me.) Fear not, befuddled reader — you don't have to be an Egyptologist to use SmartIcons.

If you can't guess what a SmartIcon does, just point to it and then wait a second or two. A cute little balloon appears to tell you what's what — as in Figure 2-3. (Okay, so even some of the balloon hints don't make sense, but a lousy hint is better than no hint, right?) If you want to see the SmartIcon hints on your Mac, you have to choose Balloon Help⊃Show Balloons (the little question mark in the upper-right corner of the screen).

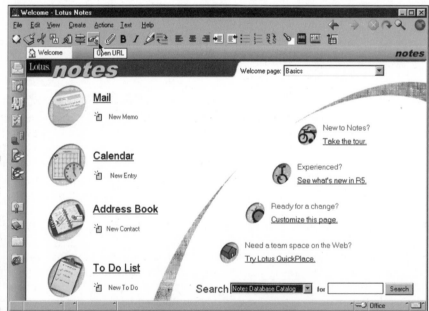

Figure 2-3:
Get a hint
for any
SmartIcon
by putting
the mouse
pointer on it
and waiting
a moment.

Notes has more SmartIcons up its sleeve than it appears — in fact, probably more than you'll ever use. Because so many SmartIcons are available, Lotus has collected them into bunches, which they refer to as *palettes.* The idea here is that the SmartIcons you use when you read a message, for example, are probably not the best ones to have around when you compose a message. So don't be surprised if you notice the SmartIcons changing. The SmartIcon palette you see in one context (such as reading your e-mail) will be different from the one you see in another context (such as setting up your modem).

Betting on bookmarks

Bookmarks are your way to remember a particular Web page, Notes document, view, or database. Notes is preloaded with a bunch of bookmarks for you. As you use Notes more and more, and as you develop your own favorite places to go, you can add your own personal bookmarks, too. Figure 2-4 shows the bookmarks you get by default. The bottom line: Use Bookmarks to get back quickly and easily to some place that you've been before.

Opening a bookmark

When you want to open a bookmark, just click it. For example, if you, Jane Q. Public, want to read your mail, click the first icon in the bookmark bar. Presto, there's your mail.

What happens, *exactly,* when you click a bookmark depends on what kind of bookmark it is. Some might open a particular Notes database, such as the one for your Mail. Others might open a particular document in a Notes database, others may open a Web page, and still others might open a list of even more bookmarks.

If you're not sure what a bookmark is going to do before you click it, treat it like it was a SmartIcon — put your mouse pointer on the bookmark without clicking it. As you can see in Figure 2-5, Notes doesn't waste any time and shows you a hint about what the bookmark is going to do or where it's going to go.

Creating bookmarks

Suppose that you've opened a Web page or maybe a Notes database. It's really cool, and you want Notes to remember it for you so that you can easily get to it again. We're doing exactly that in Figure 2-6, and you can do the same. (Note the mouse pointer, which is just above the Favorite Bookmarks folder in the figure.)

Replicator

To Do

Address Book

Calendar

Mail

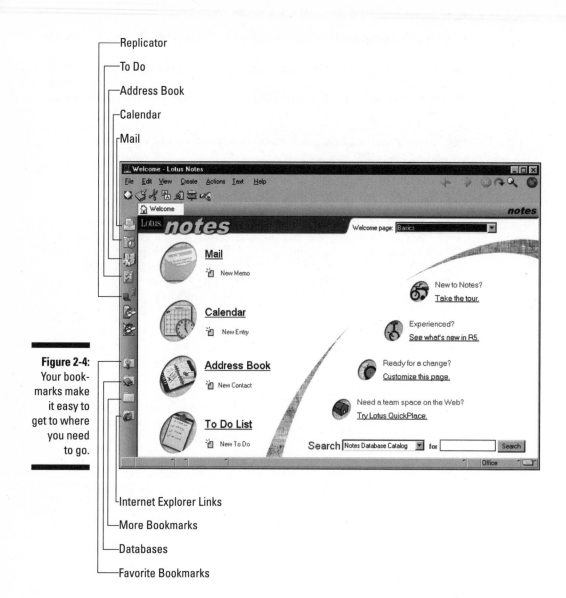

Figure 2-4:
Your book-
marks make
it easy to
get to where
you need
to go.

Internet Explorer Links

More Bookmarks

Databases

Favorite Bookmarks

1. **Point to the task button for the thing you want to bookmark.**

2. **Click and drag the task button over into the bookmark bar.**

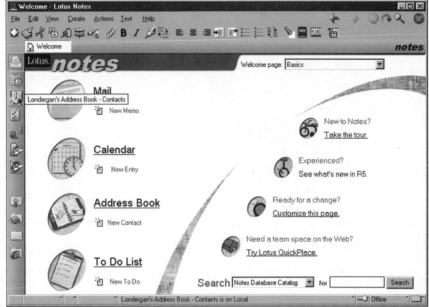

Figure 2-5:
You can get hints for bookmarks, too.

Deleting bookmarks

Use the following steps to remove a bookmark you no longer need:

1. **Point to the bookmark you want to delete.**

2. **Press and hold down the right mouse button.**

3. **Choose Remove Bookmark from the pop-up menu.**

Creating bookmark folders

If you want a new place to put bookmarks, you need to create a new bookmark folder. Use the following steps to do so:

1. **Point to a place in the bookmark bar where there is room for your new folder.**

2. **Press and hold down the right mouse button.**

3. **Choose Create Folder from the pop-up menu.**

4. **In the Create Folder dialog box, type the name of the new folder.**

5. **Click OK.**

Bookmark bar

Moving bookmarks

If you decide that you are unhappy with a bookmark's location, you can move it to another place on the bookmark bar or into one of the bookmark folders. Use the following steps to move a bookmark:

1. **Point to the bookmark you want to move.**

2. **Press and hold down the left mouse button.**

3. **Drag and drop the bookmark to its new location in the bookmark bar.**

Deleting bookmark folders

Use the following steps to remove an entire bookmark folder:

1. **Point to the bookmark folder in the bookmark bar.**

2. **Press and hold down the right mouse button.**

3. **Choose Delete Folder from the pop-up menu.**

Think long and hard before you delete a bookmark folder because doing so also removes all the bookmarks inside the folder, too.

Try out the task buttons

Have you noticed that as you open different databases, documents, and Web pages, you get a task button for each? Figure 2-7 shows what your screen might look like after you've opened several different things.

Use these buttons to switch from one window to another and to close the window altogether.

Switching windows

It's easy to switch from one open window to another because all you have to do is click the task button you want.

Figure 2-7:
Everything
you open
has its own
task button.

Closing a window

It's just as easy to close a window because all you have to do is click the little X in the right corner of the task button for the window you want to close, and it's history. (If you have the window open, you can also close it by pressing Esc, or by choosing File⇨Close.)

You don't have to switch to a window before you close it.

Wise up with the universal navigation buttons

Have you asked yourself what those buttons are in the upper-right corner of the screen? Have you asked yourself what they are used for? How often do you talk to yourself?

The buttons in the upper-right corner are collectively known as the universal navigation bar. *Universal* in that the buttons are always in the same place and always work the same way. *Navigation* as in they help you move around and get someplace. *Bar* as in they aren't arranged in a *pile*, right? Table 2-1 explains what each of the buttons does.

Table 2-1		The Universal Navigation Bar
Button	*Name*	*What You Do with It*
●	Open URL	Enter the address of the Web page you want to open
🔍	Search	Find something
↻	Refresh	Reload the current window
⊗	Stop	Stop loading a Web page
⇨	Next	Go to the next thing you've visited (click the drop-down arrow to see all the places you can go)
⇦	Previous	Go to the previous place you've been (click the drop-down arrow to see all the places you can go)

Places you've never been before

Bookmarks certainly provide an easy way to open documents, databases, and Web pages. But the day will come when you want to go someplace you haven't been before. Maybe your company has a new Notes application that you need to check out, or perhaps you want to open a new Web page. It's easy to do, but how you do it depends on where you're trying to go.

Opening a new database

To open a new database, choose File⇨Database⇨Open (or press Ctrl+O), and then use the Open Database dialog box to tell Notes the server and database you're after, as shown in Figure 2-8.

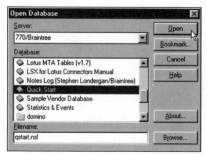

Figure 2-8: Opening a new database.

After you find the database you want to open, select its name in the Database list, and then click the Open button.

You can use the Bookmark button in the Open Database dialog box to add the selected database to your bookmarks for future reference. Doing so adds the database to your bookmarks *without* opening the database at the same time.

Opening a new Web page

To open a new Web page, click the Open URL button in the navigation bar, and then type the Web page's address in the URL field. (This elusive field appears directly under the Open URL button after you click it.) Press Enter, and Notes opens the Web page you've requested.

Although Notes automatically bookmarks any database you open in the Bookmark bar's Databases folder, you have to add a bookmark manually for any Web page you want to remember.

Using the Welcome page

As you can see in Figure 2-9, the Welcome page has a bunch of buttons and things you can click. Most of these are shortcuts to bookmarks and menus. They're always available, and you may find that they are an easy way to accomplish something.

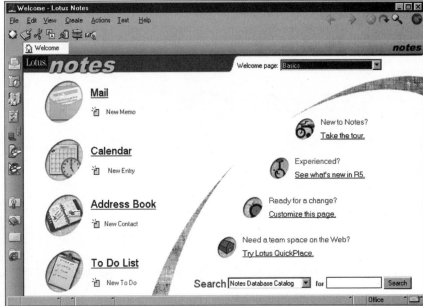

Figure 2-9:
The
Welcome
page.

The Welcome page shown in Figure 2-9 is the default page that you get when you install Notes. Because the important buttons tell you exactly what they are going to do — such as New Memo and New Contact — there's no need to describe them in mind-numbing detail.

You can customize the Welcome page so that it shows you exactly what you want. Hey, you can even replace it altogether and see your Headlines, instead. Take a look at Chapter 14 if you want to know how to do that.

Multitasking (Easier Than It Sounds)

One of the advantages to using Windows, OS/2, or a Macintosh is that these operating systems can multitask. *Multitask* is a $25 computer word for an operating system that can run more than one program at the same time.

What does that mean to you? Suppose that you're using Notes to read e-mail. After you finish reading your e-mail, you have to do some work in your spreadsheet program. Sure, you *could* exit Notes and then start Excel, but what happens when you want to check your e-mail again in half an hour? Are you going to shut down Excel, start Notes, and then, after you've read your new e-mail, shut down Notes to start Excel again? Of course not! You're going to multitask. (Sounds exciting, doesn't it?)

If you want to leave your Notes session temporarily in order to start a different program, don't exit Notes. Leave Notes up and running while you work in your other programs. You'll find that you can switch between the programs much more quickly and easily. Most people leave Notes up and running all day.

The cool thing about leaving Notes running while you're in another program is that Notes can notify you when you've received new mail, even though you're typing a letter in WordPerfect or doing something else. You might occasionally hear a sort of "beep beep beep" message, which is the Notes way of telling you that you have new mail.

If you want to get the "beep beep beep — New mail has been delivered to you" message while you're using some other program, you have to leave Notes running in the background. You will *not* get this notification if you shut down Notes as soon as you're finished with it.

The way you switch from one active program to another depends on the operating system you use:

- ✔ **In Windows:** Press Ctrl+Esc to get the Start menu, choose the program you want to switch to, and click OK. (Or, if the other program is already running, press Alt+Tab to switch to it.)

- ✔ **On a Macintosh:** From the Application menu, choose the program you want to switch to. To start a new program, choose Finder from the Application menu and then start the program as you normally would.

When the Time Comes to Say Good-Bye

When you're finished using Notes (is it time to go home already?), exit Notes the way you exit any other program. The easiest way to tell Notes that you're finished is to choose File⇨Exit. Depending on your operating system, you may have other, snazzier ways to end the program. For example, with Windows 95, you can press Alt+F4 to exit Notes.

Part II
It's a Mail Thing

The 5th Wave   By Rich Tennant

"WELLL, I'M REALLY LOOKING FORWARD TO SEEING THIS WIRELESS DATA TRANSMISSION SYSTEM OF YOURS, MUDNICK."

In this part . . .

When you know what Notes is and what it isn't and can use random bits of Notes terminology to the amazement of your friends and coworkers, you're ready to actually send a message. Maybe you can already read a message that someone sends you. Then again, maybe you have 50 important messages crowding your mail database, the boss is drumming her fingers, and here you are reading this little introduction.

The chapters in this part explain the e-mail functions of Notes and make you wonder why the heck any office ever bothers with photocopies and phone calls.

Chapter 3

Gotta Get My E-Mail

· ·

In This Chapter

▶ Opening your mail database

▶ Rearranging your e-mail in the navigation pane

▶ Reading and sorting your e-mail in the view pane

▶ Discovering what all those icons mean

▶ Glimpsing the action bar

▶ Closing your mail

· ·

*Y*our regular mail arrives in a mailbox at the end of your driveway, but your e-mail arrives in your Inbox on your computer. (Actually, although you read your e-mail while sitting at your computer, your e-mail messages are usually saved on the server computer, and are not stored on your own system.)

May I Have the Envelope, Please?

 The easiest way (although many other ways exist) to open your mail is to click (just once) on the Mail icon in the bookmark bar. Up springs something that looks very much like Figure 3-1. There, in a list, is your very own, personal, for-your-eyes-only e-mail.

 We should mention right up front that nobody but you can open *your* mail database. (And you can't open anyone else's, either. Not that you would even think of doing such a thing.)

Navigation pane   View pane   Preview pane   Action bar

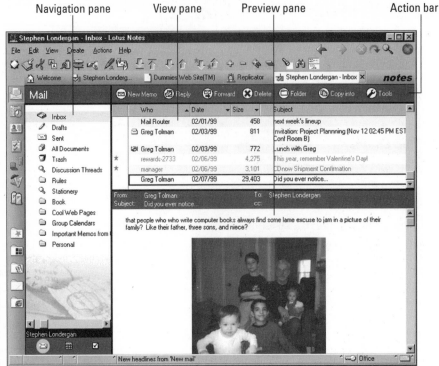

Figure 3-1:
Your e-mail
database
looks a lot
like this one.

Actually, as Figure 3-1 shows, more than just your mail is on-screen when you open your e-mail database. In fact, the screen is divided into four parts:

✔ The first pane (as you can see in the figure) is called the *navigation pane.* You use this pane to move amongst the folders and views in your mail.

✔ On the right side of the screen is the *view pane.* This pane provides a summary of the messages in whichever folder you've selected in the navigation pane.

✔ Beneath the view pane is the *preview pane,* which displays an actual e-mail message, sent to you by an actual person. (If your mail database doesn't show the preview pane, choose View➪Document Preview➪ Show Preview.)

✔ Last, but not least, is the *action bar,* which is just a bunch of buttons that let you do things to your mail.

A rose is a rose is a memo is a message! The words *memo, document, message,* and even *e-mail* are often used interchangeably. In Notes, they all mean the same thing.

Onward, upward, and e-ward! Get ready to see how you can adjust the panes, rearrange your messages, and (most importantly) read your messages.

Having it your way

Although the action bar at the top of the screen isn't going anywhere, you can choose a few different ways to arrange the rest of your e-mail database.

When you choose View⇨Document Preview⇨ Arrange Preview, the dialog box looks like the accompanying figure.

Choose the layout that turns you on and click OK.

May we suggest that you try each of the Layout options in the Preview Pane dialog box to find out which one works best for you?

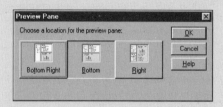

The Navigation Pane

The navigation pane lets you sort and otherwise rearrange the messages in your mail database. Each item in the navigation pane is called a *folder*. For example, the Inbox folder shows you all the messages that have been sent to you (and not the messages you've sent to other people); the Drafts folder shows messages you started to create but never bothered to send.

The navigation pane contains eleven important folders — listed, for your browsing convenience, in Table 3-1.

Table 3-1		Eleven Important Folders in Your Navigation Pane
Folder Icon	*Folder Name*	*What the Folder or View Contains*
	Inbox	Messages sent to you
	Drafts	Messages you have composed but haven't mailed yet
	Sent	Messages you wrote and sent to other people

(continued)

Table 3-1 *(continued)*

Folder Icon	Folder Name	What the Folder or View Contains
	All Documents	Pretty obvious
	Trash	Messages that will be deleted
	Discussion Threads	Messages listed together based on their subject
	Rules	Optional instructions for your mail to automatically move certain messages to certain folders
	Stationery	Sort of like a reusable template for documents that you send again and again
	Other Folders	A list of other folders, if you've created any
	Group Calendars	The schedule for other people, displayed together
	Other Views	Other views of your mail, if you've created any

You may, of course, find other items listed in the navigation pane, such as *Agents* and *Design*. You use the Agents folder to create a little miniprogram in your mail database. You use the Design folder to change the ways your mail database works.

To see what's in one of those folders, just click the folder you want. Don't be surprised if a few folders are empty!

The View Pane

The view pane presents you with a summary of the documents in a given folder. When you press the up-arrow and down-arrow keys (↑ ↓), the selection bar moves from one message to the next. (The *selection bar* is that big black outline that highlights the message in the view pane.) And, as you press ↑ and ↓, you also see a preview of that document in the preview pane (if you have the preview pane open).

Each row of information in the view pane represents an individual message. Each message is divided into columns of information, such as the name of the person who sent the message, the date when it was sent, and the subject of the message. Aside from just looking at the pane to see who sent you what messages, you can do a few other things, described in the following section.

Changing the column width

Sometimes, the contents of a column are wider than the column itself, which means you can't see all the information. This problem (unlike world hunger) is easily remedied because you can change any column's width, right here and right now. In fact, we're doing so in Figure 3-2.

To change a column's width, move your mouse so that the pointer is on the horizontal line representing the right side of the too-narrow column. When you get the mouse right where you want it, the pointer changes to a two-headed monster, as you can see in Figure 3-2. Then all you do is drag the column to its new size. Easy, huh?

Sorting your mail

Did you notice in Figure 3-2 that the headings for the Who column and the Date column have little triangles in them? Columns with triangles are set up to *sort on-the-fly,* which is a fancy way of saying (no, this doesn't involve an airplane) that you can re-sort the documents by clicking the column heading.

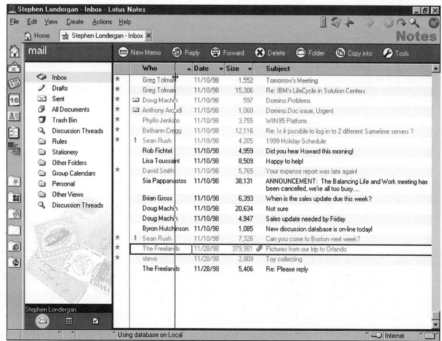

Figure 3-2:
You can easily make a column bigger or smaller by dragging its right edge.

For example, if you want to rearrange the documents in this column so that they're listed from newest to oldest, click the word *Date* in the column heading. Before your very eyes, the documents rearrange themselves. Click the word *Date* again, and the documents shuffle into the opposite order — oldest to newest. You can do the same thing with the Who and the Size columns to realphabetize the documents based on the person's name or to sort by document size.

Anytime you see a little triangle in any column heading in any database, you know now that you can click the heading to rearrange the documents listed in that column.

Reading your mail

As you press the ↑ and ↓ keys to move the selection bar in the view pane, the Preview pane changes to give you a preview of what's in each message.

But when you want to read the message in its entirety, you can either double-click the message in question or highlight it with the selection bar and press Enter. Bye-bye panes; the document you selected fills the screen. After opening a document, use the ↑ and ↓ keys (or the vertical scroll bar) to move through the body of the document.

Closing a message

When you finish reading your message, you can close it and return to the view pane by doing one of the following:

✔ Press Esc.

✔ Click the little x in the document's Task button.

✔ Choose File⇨Close.

Or you can move immediately to another message:

✔ Press Enter and the next message appears.

✔ Press Backspace and the preceding message appears.

✔ Press Tab to move to the next unread message or press Shift+Tab to move to the previous unread message, if you have one.

✔ Press F4 to see the next unread document or press Shift+F4 to see the previous unread document.

If you're getting a little worried about remembering all these options, don't bother trying. Choose the one that works best for you and forget the others. Enter and Backspace are pretty easy to remember.

If you're especially observant, you may have noticed that, before you opened the document, it had a little star next to it in the view pane, but now it has none. You may have noticed also that the name of the document in the view pane changed colors after you opened it. It used to be red, but now it's black. What gives?

Notes keeps track of which documents you have read and which you haven't. If a document in the view pane has a star next to it and is red, you know that it's brand-spanking-new — or at least that you haven't read it yet. On the other hand, if the document in question doesn't have a star and is black, you *have* read it.

R-E-D documents haven't been R-E-A-D.

Aren't those pictures just the cutest things . . .

Gaggles of little icons inhabit the view pane, and each icon tells you something about the message beside it. So what could be more appropriate, at this point in the book, than to include a table explaining what all these icons mean? Enter Table 3-2, stage left.

Table 3-2	Icons in Your Mail Database
Icon	*What It Means*
🖼	A message you sent
🖹	A message you've saved, but have not sent yet
❗	A message that has been marked as High Importance — probably from your boss
📎	A message that has an attached file or an embedded object

That Distracting Preview Pane

At the bottom of the screen, the preview pane shows you the beginning of whichever message you've highlighted with the selection bar. You really can't do much with the preview pane, other than read the document displayed there.

If you don't want to see a preview of each document in the preview pane, you can always choose View⇨Document Preview⇨Show Preview. Each time you select this command from the menu, Notes switches back and forth between opening and closing the preview pane. Some people prefer to keep the preview pane closed all the time.

The Action Bar

Last, but not least, the *action bar* is that strip of big buttons at the top of your mail database window. These buttons aren't much different from SmartIcons; if you see one you want to use, just click it. As you may notice, the buttons change depending on what you're doing. (In other words, the buttons you see in the action bar while you're previewing a message are different from the ones you see while you're reading a message.)

Get Me Outta Here!

When you want to close your mail and return to the Notes workspace, choose File⇨Close or press Esc. You may have to choose this command twice if you're reading a message when you decide to close your mail. The first time closes your message; the second time closes your mail database.

Chapter 4

Making a Message

*H*ooray! You opened your e-mail database and read all your messages. You called your boss back to confirm that power lunch (so what if you had to use the telephone because you didn't know how to use Notes to answer an e-mail?), and you didn't miss that emergency 3:00 staff meeting. Still, a few messages remaining in your e-mail deserve an answer — and maybe the phone isn't the best way to respond. Perhaps you even want to compose a few messages of your own. It's time to get on board the Notes e-mail wagon.

The purpose of this chapter is not to turn you into a Shakespeare or a Hemingway. What you say in your memos is up to you. We just want to give you some pointers so that your message gets where you want it to go.

Good Memo Manners

The following news will probably come as no surprise: You shouldn't use e-mail for some things. The following messages are simply not appropriate for e-mail:

> ✔ Vicki and I are giving a little wedding for our daughter next week. Can you make it? Bring your own champagne.

- ✔ I'm sorry your parakeet died; hope it wasn't anything serious — or catching.

- ✔ Hey, J. B. Here are a few suggestions about how to get this company turned around. First, fire all your vice presidents.

- ✔ Smedley, you're fired. Be out of your office in five minutes. We've already hired a replacement.

- ✔ Fire! Everyone leave the building as quickly as possible!

- ✔ Don't you think the president is a jerk? I sure do. What a moron! I could do the job better than that idiot.

- ✔ I just found out that Rogers is making $90,000.

Each of the previous points may have its place in some form of communication, but not in e-mailed memos. Before you put fingers to keyboard, pause to ponder the following points:

- ✔ At times, more formal styles of communication (such as paper documents) are more appropriate than e-mail.

- ✔ At times, talking face-to-face is preferable to e-mail.

- ✔ Don't go over your boss's head in writing if you wouldn't consider doing so under other circumstances.

- ✔ Resist the temptation to include the whole world in your cc: list.

- ✔ A message could be delivered almost instantly, but this doesn't mean everyone is going to read it instantly.

- ✔ Although Notes is a secure e-mail system (a message goes only to the person you address it to), nothing prevents that person from sending your message on to other people.

- ✔ If you have composed a nasty-gram, sleep on it before sending it.

- ✔ Rogers is making only $70,000.

Sending an e-mail to too many people is called *spamming,* as in: "Jim really spammed his complaints around, huh? What an idiot! I wonder how soon he'll get fired?" Don't include too many people in your cc: lists — you may end up overloading (or at least slowing down) the mail server.

Your New Outgoing Memo

So you're ready to compose an actual, honest-to-goodness, real-life memo? One of the nice things about Notes is that you can always compose a new mail message, anytime and anywhere. You may be reading a discussion database or looking at your company's phonebook database when the urge to write an e-mail strikes you. No matter where you are or what you're doing, a new e-mail message is just a menu choice (or mouse click) away.

When you want to write a new e-mail message, choose Create⇨Mail⇨Memo, or click the New Memo icon in the Create Bookmark folder. The blank memo form in Figure 4-1 appears. If you're one of those people who has trouble writing, think of writing a memo as filling in the fields in a record in a database.

As you can see in Figure 4-1, your new memo has four parts:

- ✔ **Action bar:** Buttons you can use while composing your memo
- ✔ **Your name:** Whatever that may be
- ✔ **Addresses and Subject fields:** Where you enter the names of your memo's recipients and a short description of the memo
- ✔ **Body:** Where you type the body of your message

Writing a new message involves three basic steps:

1. **Figure out the people to whom you'll be sending your message.**

2. **Type the body of the message.**

3. **Save the message, or send it, or both.**

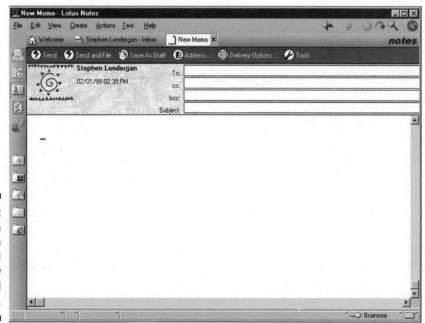

Figure 4-1:
The form you use to create and send a new mail message.

The fine print

At this point, we think it's a good idea to tell you that what you're reading here may not be true for you. Or this section may be true, but later in the book you may notice that what we describe is not what you see on your screen. If you find a discrepancy between what you're reading and what you're seeing, one of the following excuses could apply:

✔ Your company's Notes administrator could have altered the memo form to customize it for your organization.

✔ Your company may not be set up to use Notes mail — some people use Notes for its

database capabilities but use a separate program to send e-mail. If this is the case, you probably want to stop reading this chapter and skip ahead to Chapter 5.

✔ Your company may not be using a Web browser for your mail. That's okay because it only means that some of the buttons may be in different places.

✔ You can't always believe everything you read.

Before we get carried away explaining each of these three steps in mind-numbing detail, allow us to mention that you can simply enter a recipient's name in the To: field, type something in the body, and then click the Send button (up there in the action bar) to dispatch your message.

Step 1: Addressing a message

In the simplest case, you know the name of the person (or persons) to whom you'll be sending a memo (or memos), so you simply type the name (or names) in one or more of the address fields. As you may have noticed in Figure 4-1, you have three address fields: *To:*, *cc:*, and *bcc:*. What's the difference, you ask?

✔ **To:** This field is where you enter the name of the primary recipient of your memo. If you're sending your memo to more than one person, separate each name with a comma.

✔ **cc:** This field is where you enter the name of anyone to whom you want to send a *carbon copy* of your memo. Again, if you have more than one name, separate each with a comma.

✔ **bcc:** Use this field to send a *blind carbon copy* of the memo — that is, to send someone a copy without the rest of the recipients knowing about it. Imagine, for example, that you send a memo to a coworker asking him or her to do a certain job. You want your manager to know that you've made the request, but you don't want the coworker to know that your manager is aware of what's going on. Send the memo To: the coworker with a bcc: to your manager. When your coworker receives the message, the bcc: field won't be visible, so your secret is safe. Your coworker won't know that you sent a copy of this same message to your boss. Pretty devious, huh?

Of course, spelling is important, so you want to be pretty careful to spell the names correctly. Fear not, though; if you misspell a name, Notes may be able to catch your mistake and let you correct it. You may also notice that, as you type a recipient's name, Notes does its best to help you get it right. If you're typing a name and want to accept the guess that Notes offers, just press Enter to accept the suggestion.

If you're not sure how to spell a person's name, Notes provides an easy way for you to find out. You can use the Address button on the action bar, and let your fingers do the walking.

You have at least two directories full of e-mail addresses available — your very own *personal* name and address book and your company's *public* directory. These are the two databases that Notes uses when you click that Address button. Each of these databases contains the e-mail addresses of various people. Your personal N&A book may have the names of your friends (usually people who don't work at your company), and the public directory has the names of everyone at your company. (Find out more about your N&A book and directories in Chapter 8.)

When you click the Address button, you see the dialog box in Figure 4-2. Use the Look in drop-down list at the top left of this dialog box to select either your personal N&A book or the company's public directory.

Figure 4-2:
Use this
Select
Addresses
dialog box
to choose
the names
of people
you want to
send your
memo to.

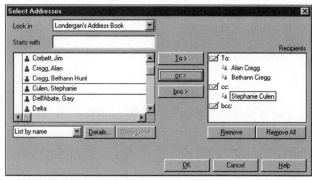

On the left side of the Select Addresses dialog box, you see the names of the people who are listed in your personal N&A book or the public directory, whichever you chose. If you want to send your memo to someone on this list, select that person's name and then click the To:, cc:, or bcc: button, depending on how you want the message to be addressed. When you do, the name of the person you selected appears on the right side of the dialog box, inside the Recipients window. (If you make a mistake, use the Remove or Remove All button to start over.)

The simplest way to find a particular person in the list is to use the scroll bars. If lots and lots of people are listed, you can type the first letter (or first few letters) in the Starts with field.

If you are a mouse aficionado, drag a name from the left window into the appropriate field in the Recipients window.

When you've finished using the Select Addresses dialog box to choose your recipient names, click OK.

After choosing the recipients' names, be sure to type a brief description of what your memo is about in the Subject field. Keep your description short and make it interesting. What you enter here shows up in the view pane of your recipient's mail.

Step 2: Writing the body of the message

And now on to the important stuff. You've typed (or chosen) all the names of the people who will (soon) be receiving your little pearl of wisdom. You get to say whatever it is that you want to say in the body of the message.

You can enter any text you want, and you can get as fancy as you want, too. You can make the text **bold** or *italicized,* or even change the font and size. Because the body of an e-mail is what's known as *rich text,* you can make its contents pretty elaborate. In addition to all these crazy things you can do with the text, you can even include other cool features such as files and objects. Read more about that in Chapter 12.

Step 3: Adding a special touch

Before dispatching a message, you can ask for some special delivery options. When you're finished with the body field, consider the Delivery Options button up there in the action bar, which leads inevitably to the dialog box shown in Figure 4-3.

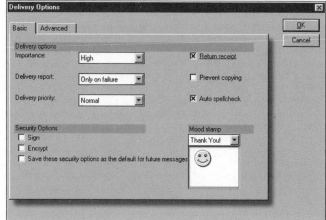

Figure 4-3:
Use these
options to
do some
special
things with
your
outgoing
message.

Importance

You have three settings for your message's importance: Low, Normal, and High. As we discuss in Chapter 3, Notes flags messages that have been marked as high importance with a special red icon in your recipients' mail. Use this feature if you want to alert your recipient to an especially important or urgent message.

Mood stamp

The Mood stamp list is a way to get in touch with your (electronic) inner child. This is the 90s, after all. A *mood stamp* is a picture that Notes adds at the top of a message, so that your reader knows what frame of mind you were in as you sent the message. A message with a mood stamp is also marked as such in the view pane of the recipient's mail database.

You have eleven mood stamps to choose from; try each to see what they look like. The Joke selection (see Figure 4-4) is useful if you want to send a message that's just a little sarcastic, and you need to make sure that your reader realizes that, yes, you were just kidding! If you don't want any mood stamp in your outgoing message, choose Normal.

Delivery report

The four choices regarding a Delivery report are: Only on failure, Confirm delivery, Trace entire path, and None.

- ✔ **Only on failure** is a good choice if you can assume that no news is good news. In other words, Notes informs you only in the event that your outgoing message couldn't be delivered for some reason.

- ✔ **Confirm delivery** is the choice for you if you're a little less of an optimist. In this case, Notes tells you exactly when and where your message was delivered.

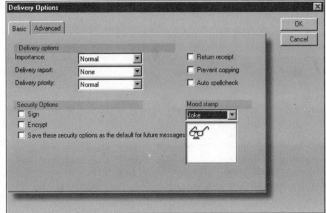

✔ **Trace entire path** tells you where (and at what times) your message stopped on its way to your recipient. (You probably don't care.)

✔ **None** means that you're throwing caution to the wind, and don't care to know whether your message gets delivered or not.

If you do choose a Delivery report option other than None, you'll receive the report back (as an e-mail message to you) as soon as the message you sent arrives. When that will be depends on your network and on your network administrator. If your recipient is far away, it may take a few hours or maybe an entire day for the message to get delivered. Check out Figure 4-5 to see an example Delivery report.

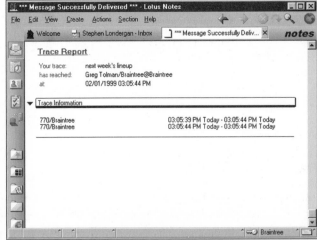

Figure 4-5:
A Delivery
report tells
you when
your mes-
sage arrived
at its
destination.

Delivery priority

Your next decision in the Delivery Options dialog box relates to how quickly you want Notes to deliver your message:

- ✔ **Low** sends the message late at night, when the network isn't so busy.
- ✔ **Normal** sends the message as soon as possible, based on the mail delivery schedules your administrator has crafted.
- ✔ **High** sends your message right now — step aside, coming through!

If you're sending a huge attachment in an e-mail message, consider marking it as Low priority. The message won't be delivered until you're home fast asleep, but it'll probably cost your company less money to send it late at night. Maybe this is a way to earn that Employee of the Month award!

Sign

The company president calls you and complains about a memo you sent demanding shorter working hours and a raise for the whole department. Try as you might, you can't remember sending a memo like that. Are you losing your marbles? Memory blackout? That may be, but it's more likely that someone sent a memo in your name. A mischievous Notes administrator, for example, may be able to figure out how to make a message look like it came from you, even when it didn't.

The way to avoid being blamed for messages that aren't really from you is to *sign* them. You sign messages for the same reason that you sign checks or official documents: to show that they're really from you. You don't need to sign a meet-me-for-coffee memo, but when you send a message with crucial or sensitive information, you may want Notes to prove that the message really came from you.

We're talking computers here — obviously you can't scratch your signature on the screen at the bottom of a memo. (Well, actually, you can, but we don't think your boss would appreciate it.) You sign a message by checking the Sign field on the Delivery Options dialog box.

The signature you use in Notes is even more difficult to forge than your own John Hancock, because it's a numeric computer code added to the message when you send it and checked by the recipient's computer when the message is opened. The memo doesn't have an actual signature on it, but this message appears at the bottom of the screen:

```
Signed by Alan Dunkel/Eastisle on 07-11-99 08:30:46, according
to Eastisle.
```

Encrypt

Sure enough, the world is crawling with busybodies, bad guys, and spies — and you may be sending your messages over less-than-secure media. If you use a modem, you're sending your messages over phone lines, where a person up to no good might be able to read them. This is no problem for your meet-me-for-coffee messages, but if you send a message that includes information such as sensitive corporate data, employee performance appraisals, or really, really good gossip that you don't want anyone else to read, you had better *encrypt* it.

Encrypting a message is easy. Notes does all the work to scramble the body of a message so that only the people you send it to can read it. From the time the message leaves your mail database until the recipient opens it, the message is encrypted. So, if some low-life snooper does intercept your message, the only things he or she will be able to read are the addresses and the subject line.

To encrypt a message, click the Delivery Options button in the action bar. Click the Encrypt check box at the bottom of the Delivery Options dialog box, and click OK to close the dialog box when you're finished.

When you send an encrypted message, Notes does the scrambling for you — behind the scenes. When the recipients open the message, they'll see the plain text just as you wrote it. Only the intended recipients with the proper user IDs can read the encrypted part of the message. The only one who will see the actual jumbled-up version is the poor spy who intercepts the message in transit.

If you're sending e-mail to a person who uses a different e-mail program, or if you're sending your message through the Internet, you should check with your company's Notes administrator to see if you'll be able to encrypt it.

Think about it — who can read your e-mail if it's open and visible on your screen and you're away from your desk? If you guessed "anyone who walks near your computer," you might have a bright future in the spy business because you're absolutely right. If you leave a highly sensitive message visible and go for a cup of coffee, forget about your bright future in the spy business. The message is decrypted while it is open. So when you leave your desk, close the message and then press F5 to disable your access to Notes. That way, the next time you try to use Notes, you'll have to enter your password — and so will anyone else. Get it? To find out how to set a password, check out Chapter 14.

Return receipt

If you use the Delivery Options dialog box to request a Return receipt, Notes notifies you when the recipient *reads* your message. This is different from a Delivery report, which tells you when the message arrived in the recipient's mail database. Request a Receipt report to prevent the "I never saw your message" excuse; use Delivery reports to eliminate the "I never got your message; the network must have lost it" excuse.

If you're sending a message to someone who doesn't use Notes, or if your message is going through the Internet, you may not be able to get a Receipt report.

Prevent copying

Should you choose Prevent copying, you can be certain that the person who receives your message will not be able to forward it to anyone else. In fact, they won't even be able to Edit➪Copy your memo to the Clipboard, in case they're intent on a little illicit Edit➪Pasting. The Prevent copying option ensures that what you say to one person doesn't get spammed all over your company.

When you're finished with the delivery options, click OK to get back to your document. In most cases, after you make up your mind vis-à-vis these options, you then click the Send and File button.

If your head is spinning from all these delivery options, you may be happy to read that you need to use them only under special circumstances. In fact, for most messages, you'll blow right by the delivery options, without a second thought. What a relief!

If you find that you are always visiting the Delivery Options dialog box to set a particular mood stamp or to change the delivery priority to high or whatever, you can check the "Save these security options as the default for future messages" check box. That way, any new messages you create will have the same security settings. Of course, you can always change your mind by returning to the Delivery Options dialog box to change a setting or to turn off the Save these security options check box.

Step 4: Sending the message

After successfully choosing the address and entering the text of your message, you're ready to dispatch your message. When the time comes to let 'er rip, choose Actions➪Send, or click the Send button on the action bar. Off the memo goes, with barely a whisper.

If you change your mind and decide not to send a message (what were you thinking?), press Esc and then choose Discard Changes. If you want to send your message later, and just save it for now (maybe you want to take a little break first), click the Save As Draft button in the action bar.

What happens when you send your memo? It gets handed off to your mail server, the computer down in the basement that's responsible for shuttling the message to its recipients. And you? You're right back where you were when you started composing the message in the first place. Rest assured that Notes will deliver your memo to the recipients; Notes notifies you if, for some reason, it can't deliver your message.

The only possible downside to using Actions⇨Send is that the memo is *not* saved for you. The memo goes to the recipients all right, but you'll have no record of what you sent. This is why you might consider using Actions⇨ Send and File (or clicking the Send and File button in the action bar) to dispatch your documents. This choice really does two things: saves your message and sends it. That way, you get a record of what you sent.

When you choose to send and file your message, you get the dialog box in Figure 4-6. Click the folder into which you want to save your outgoing message and then choose Add.

Figure 4-6:
Choose
Send and
File to save
a copy of
your
outgoing
message in
your own
database.

When you're not sure about which folder to save your message in, adding it to your Inbox folder is always a safe bet. And remember that no matter where you put your message, you'll always be able to find it in the All Documents view.

Working in Your Mail Database

Way back at the beginning of this chapter, we discussed how you can compose a new mail memo anytime, anywhere. That's nice, of course, but the times you're most likely to want to work with mail are when you're right in your mail database. For example, you may want to open your mail database to do the following:

 ✔ Read the messages that have been sent to you

 ✔ Reply to messages you have received

 ✔ Forward documents to other interested parties

 ✔ Search for old messages

 ✔ Manage, organize, and delete messages

We discussed how you read your messages in Chapter 2, so jump right in and see what this replying business is all about.

Replying

By way of setting the stage, imagine that you open your mail database and you read an incoming message in which a colleague asks you for directions to your house. Being the responsive and social sort of person that you are, you reply to her straight away. You have two options:

 ✔ You can reply to her directly by choosing Create⇨Reply or by choosing Reply from the drop-down menu that appears when you click the action bar's Reply button.

 ✔ Better yet, forward her document back to her by choosing Create⇨ Reply with History or by choosing Reply with History from the drop-down menu that appears when you click the action bar's Reply button.

In either case, Notes starts you off with a new memo and automatically fills in the mail address of the person who sent you the request in the first place.

When you Reply with History, Notes includes a copy of the original memo in the memo you're sending back, which is a nice way to remind the person what you're talking about. All too often, you'll receive memos in which authors expound on some topic, leaving you without the faintest idea of what they're talking about or why they're talking about it. (Or consider the e-mail that arrives, containing just the word "No." No *what*? No bananas? No to your request for a raise? No way to know what they're talking about?) To prevent this situation and to keep your technological reputation on the up-and-up, always use Reply with History, so that your readers know of which you speak. Figure 4-7 shows a sample Reply with History.

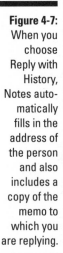

Figure 4-7:
When you
choose
Reply with
History,
Notes auto-
matically
fills in the
address of
the person
and also
includes a
copy of the
memo to
which you
are replying.

After clicking either of the Reply options, you are free to alter the address fields. Perhaps you want to invite someone else over? Type whatever you want in the Body field and then Send or Save the message as you would any other outgoing memo.

If you have received a memo that's addressed to more than one person, use the Reply to All and Reply to All with History buttons to include everybody in your response.

Forward, ho!

In addition to replying to a message, you can forward a message. Perhaps you get a message asking about some company policy, but you're not the right person to ask. Just forward the misdirected document to the right person by clicking the action bar's Forward button. Forwarding mail is also a common way for your manager to get you to do things: (Someone asks your boss a question, and now all of a sudden it's your problem?) Or, if you get a message (or see a document in a database), and you think that your pal should know about it, forward it!

If you're forwarding a document to someone, it's considered proper (thank you, Emily Post) to include a cc: to the person who sent the document in the first place. That way, the original author knows that you're not going to reply directly.

Other kinds of mail documents

Look in the Create menu of your mail database, and you see that Notes has a few other mail forms available to you. Face it, an e-mail message is an e-mail message, but these other, extra-special forms were created with a few special purposes in mind:

- ✔ **To Do:** Use this form for yourself as a reminder for something you need to do or to assign a task (via e-mail) to somebody else. To Do's that you create or receive have check marks next to them in the view pane of your mail database. (Of course, just because you send a To Do to somebody doesn't mean said person is going to actually do it!)

- ✔ **Calendar Entry:** Use this form to schedule a meeting, which will appear on your (you guessed it) calendar. Check Chapter 6 to find out how to use your calendar.

Chapter 5

Managing Your Mess(ages)

● ●

● ●

*A*fter you read your messages, then what? Do you have to do anything with them? Can you keep them, or do they disappear after you read them?

No, yes, and no. Any other questions? End of chapter.

The truth is, you don't have to do anything with memos after you've read them. They just continue to pile up in your e-mail Inbox the same way that stuff accumulates in the in-basket on your desk. E-mail doesn't automatically disappear after you read it. It would be awfully irresponsible of Notes to delete messages that you may need later.

This chapter deals with the various things that you can do with a message or a group of messages after you have read them.

The Scrap Heap of History

To keep a message, you need to do absolutely nothing. Unless you specifically decide to delete a message and (more importantly) then punch the proper keys to delete it, Notes saves it in your mail forever and ever. But every message you keep is that much more disk space you're using on your Domino server, so you should seriously consider deleting most of your messages.

Selecting messages

Before you choose any command that does something to a document, you have to tell Notes which document (or documents) will be affected by the command you're about to choose. If you want to do something to just one document, well, then, selecting it is easy. You either click the document in question with the mouse, or you use the up-arrow and down-arrow keys to select it in the view pane. Either way, when the selection bar is highlighting the document you want, you're in business.

If you need to select more than one document, highlight the first document and press the spacebar. (Watch for a little check mark to appear to the left of the document in the view pane.) Then you highlight the next document and press the spacebar again. Then you high-light the next document in the view pane, and press the . . . you get the idea.

If you want to select multiple documents with the mouse, click right where the check mark will appear — in the column immediately to the left of the message(s).

If you change your mind, you can use the same technique (with the mouse or the spacebar) to *de*select a message.

If everyone in your organization kept those three-year-old memos that Joann sent to brag about her new baby, your company would have to keep buying more hard disks for your Domino servers, and those people who happen to share your mail server would run out of disk space, and everyone would notice that the database was getting slower and s-l-o-w-e-r. This might explain why someone in your office is constantly sending out messages asking people to clean out their e-mail databases.

You should find out what the policy is in your organization about the maximum size of mail databases; you can also check out Chapter 7 for some tips on how to archive messages you don't need anymore.

 How can you find out how large your mail database is? Open your mail and choose File⇨Database⇨Properties. When you click the Info tab (the one with the small letter *i* in a circle) in the Database infobox, you see something remarkably like Figure 5-1. Note that this irresponsible blot on society has an e-mail database that is almost 13MB and has over 300 documents!

Figure 5-1:
The Database infobox tells how big the database is: in this case, a whopping 13MB.

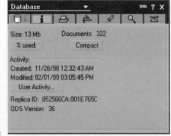

The most sensible course of action is to delete all memos you won't need again as soon as you've read them. If you don't delete memos right away, you have to go back through your database every so often and delete the old messages.

To delete a message, do any of the following:

✔ While the memo is open on-screen, press Delete. Doing so puts the memo in the trash bin, and then automatically opens the next memo in the database. (Pressing Delete doesn't actually delete the message; it only puts the message in the trash bin.) If you open the memo again, the word *[Deleted]* appears in the title bar.

 ✔ In the view pane, select the document you want to delete and either press Delete or click the Delete button on the action bar. This also marks the message for deletion, without actually deleting it. You can tell that the message has been marked for deletion because a little trash can appears next to it in the view pane.

✔ Highlight a message and press the spacebar or click in the far left column. A check mark appears next to the highlighted memo. This is the best way to select a bunch of memos for eventual deletion. After you check all the memos that you want to delete, press Delete or click the Delete button in the action bar. Again, you know that the messages have been queued for deletion, because a little trash can appears next to them in the view pane.

✔ Select the message(s) you want to delete, and then choose Actions⇨ Folder⇨Move To Folder. Select the Trash folder from the Move To Folder dialog box, and then click the Move button.

✔ Drag the message from the view pane and drop it on the trash bin in the navigation pane.

If you change your mind and decide that you don't want to delete a message after all, now is the time to act! All you need to do is

1. **Open the trash bin (by clicking it in the navigation pane).**

2. **Highlight the message (use the spacebar to select a bunch of them, if you want to rescue more than one).**

 3. **Choose Actions⇨Restore, or click the action bar's Restore button.**

   Presto! The message (or messages, if you selected more than one) go back to their original folders.

If you change your mind about deleting a message, you can always open the Trash folder to get it back.

A message that has been marked for deletion doesn't get removed from the database until you do one of the following:

- ✔ Press F9 or click the action bar's Refresh button to update the database.
- ✔ Close the database.

- ✔ Open the trash bin and then either choose Actions⇨Permanently Remove or click the Permanently Remove button in the action bar.

No matter which of these three methods you use to empty your trash bin, you always get one last chance to change your mind, using the dialog box in Figure 5-2. If you want to keep the messages that you've marked for deletion, choose No, and you'll be happy to find the messages still saved in the database.

Figure 5-2:
When you
finally
decide to
empty your
trash bin,
you get one
last chance
to change
your mind.

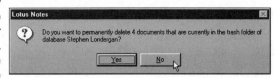

Another way to save server disk space is to *archive* messages. This is a way to take old messages and move them from your mail on the server to a special database on your computer. Check out Chapter 7 to find out how to archive.

The easiest and fastest way to delete a document is to highlight it in the view pane, press Delete, and then press F9.

Fun with Folders

Of course, you aren't going to delete *all* your messages; therefore, those that you keep ought to be arranged in some sort of system. Depending on the folder you're using, all your memos might be arranged by date or by the person who sent them, but those arrangements may not be particularly useful for your day-to-day work. If you're not happy with the folders that are already in your database, you're just going to have to find out how to create your own.

Creating a new folder

When you want to add a new folder to your mail, follow these steps:

1. **Choose Create⇨Folder.**

2. **Name your new folder by entering it's name in the Folder Name field at the top of the Create Folder dialog box (shown in Figure 5-3).**

3. **Click OK.**

If that seems easy, it's because, well, creating a folder *is* easy. As soon as you click OK, your new folder is visible in the navigation pane — probably at the bottom of the list of folders.

You can put folders inside other folders. If you want your new folder to be inside another folder, select the existing folder in the Create Folder dialog box. In Figure 5-3, the new folder (named Personal) will go inside the Cool Web Pages folder.

Figure 5-3:
Use the
Create
Folder
dialog box
to put a new
folder in
your mail
database.

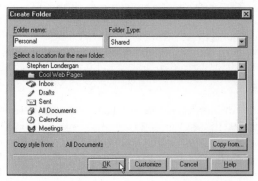

Putting a document in a folder

To put a message (or a bunch of messages) in a folder, select the message(s) and choose Actions⇨Folder⇨Move to Folder. Select the folder name from the Move to Folder dialog box and click Move. You can also use your mouse to put a document into a folder: Just drag and drop the message (or messages) from the view pane to the desired folder in the navigation pane.

One of the coolest things you can do for your mail is set up Rules so that incoming mail from a certain person or a particular subject is automatically added to a particular folder. Take a look at Chapter 7 if the idea of creating a Rule turns you on.

Opening a folder to see what's in it

To open a folder with the mouse, just click the folder you want in the navigation pane. You can also choose View⇨Go To and choose the folder from the Go To dialog box.

Deleting a folder

If you no longer need a certain folder that's in your mail, select the folder in the navigation pane and choose Actions⇨Folder Options⇨Delete Folder. Bye-bye!

Note that deleting a folder does not delete the documents in that folder.

Oh Where, Oh Where?

Folders are a great way for you to make some sense of the piles and piles of e-mail you receive every day, and folders can certainly help you find a particular message when you need it. But what about when the boss calls and asks you to find some memo she sent you last month about one of your company's clients? You look in all the likely folders and don't find anything on that client, but you know that you *never* delete messages about clients.

Rest assured that, if you didn't delete the message, it's still there — somewhere. Hunting down a particular message can be a chore, unless you know who sent you the message. If you do, just switch to the folder that is most likely to contain the message you're trying to find (if all else fails, use the All Documents folder) and then sort the messages in the folder by name. Just click the little sort arrow in the Who column heading.

When you sort the folder based on the Who column, all the messages from each person are listed together, which makes it easier to find a document from a particular person. Use the arrow keys and PgUp and PgDn to move through the documents in the view pane.

If you want to jump right to the messages from a particular person, rather than having to scroll down through the alphabet, use Quick Search. With the Message selector in the view pane, type the name of the person you're looking for. As soon as you start typing a name in the view pane, the Starts With dialog box appears, as you can see in Figure 5-4. Enter the name you're trying to find and click OK. Notes quickly takes you to the first message from that person.

Figure 5-4:
Use the
Starts With
dialog box
to find a
message
quickly.

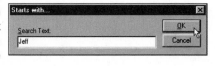

You have to sort the messages in the view pane before you can use Quick Search. If you don't know the name of the person who sent the message you're trying to find, you just have to hunt a little harder and look through a lot more messages.

You can create a Full Text Index for your mail database so that you can search the contents of the documents very quickly. We have an entire chapter about indexing a database — Chapter 16.

All the News That's Fit to Print

Lotus Notes and Domino are supposed to rocket you into the information age and eliminate the use of paper. Sadly, the world hasn't reached that goal yet — we're still using enough paper to bury the Empire State Building every year. So it stands to reason that, sooner or later, you're going to want to print one of your e-mail messages.

You can print a single document, such as the one you happen to be looking at on your screen or the one currently highlighted in the view pane, or you can select a bunch of documents in a view and print them all.

If you want to print the document that's visible on-screen, choose File➪Print and watch for the dialog box in Figure 5-5.

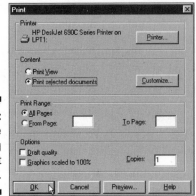

Figure 5-5:
Use the
Print dialog
box to print
your e-mail.

Despite all the buttons and fields on the Print dialog box, you don't have too many decisions to make. In fact, you're probably interested only in entering the print range (whether you want to print the entire document or just some of the pages), and View options (whether you want to print the document you have selected or, instead, print the contents of the view pane). If you choose Print Selected Documents, the *contents* of the selected messages are printed. If you choose Print View, Notes prints exactly what you see in the view pane — only the summary columns.

Assuming that you choose Print Selected Documents, and assuming that you are printing more than one message, you have to decide how Notes should separate one printed message from the next, using the Customize button on the Print dialog box. Your choices for Document separation are

✔ **On a New Page:** Each document starts on a new page.

✔ **Page Break:** Each document starts on a new page.

✔ **One Blank Line beneath the Previous Document:** Between each document, Notes prints a line.

✔ **Immediately beneath the Previous Document:** Each document follows the one before it, with no separation.

If you choose On a New Page, you may also decide how to number the pages, assuming that you *are* numbering the pages (see Chapter 12). Select the Starting with Page Number 1 check box, and each new first page is number 1. Otherwise, the first page of each new document gets the next consecutive page number. Check out Chapter 11 for more information about printing documents.

Whether you choose to use the Customize button or not, there ain't nothin' gonna come outta that printer until you click the Print dialog box's OK button.

Chapter 6

Calendars and Schedules

● ●

In This Chapter

▶ Trying out the calendar in Notes

▶ Keeping track of your appointments and meetings

▶ Working with group calendars

● ●

Did you know that your calendar is built right into your e-mail, so it's always available to you? Even if you are accustomed to keeping track of your meetings and appointments in one of those leather-bound, take-it-with-you calendar books, there are some really cool reasons why you should use Notes for all of your scheduling needs:

✔ Keeping track of your calendar in Notes means that all your information is on the computer and you can view it by the day, week, fortnight, or month.

✔ If you use a PalmPilot or IBM WorkPad, you can even carry your calendar with you in your shirt or blouse pocket.

✔ If your organization uses shared calendars, you can easily use Notes to see other people's calendars and check their free time — and let them do the same to you.

✔ You can use a feature of Notes called delegation to let your assistant schedule meetings for you (if you're lucky enough to have an assistant, that is; otherwise, you're on your own).

✔ You can print your calendar in a variety of ways.

✔ You don't have to buy any fancy leather covers for your Notes calendar or worry about a monogram.

Using Your Calendar

You'll most likely use your calendar in two ways: You'll read it to see where you're supposed to be, and you'll respond to invitations from your friends and colleagues. But before you can reach out and touch your calendar, you have to open it.

Opening your calendar

Just as there are many ways to skin a cat (such a pretty image), there are a few ways to open your calendar. The following list below presents them, in no particular order:

- ✔ Click the task bar's Calendar icon.
- ✔ Click that big Open Calendar button on the Welcome page.

- ✔ If you've already opened your mail, click the Calendar icon at the bottom of the navigation pane.

Looking at your calendar

After you have your calendar open, you'll find that you can look at it in lots of different ways, and you can do lots of things with it. Before you rush off, though, it's worth a minute to look at the big picture, as shown in Figure 6-1.

As you can see in Figure 6-1, when you open your calendar, you get a special set of buttons to use to change the way the calendar is presented. For example, if you click the little round 14 button, the view switches to show fourteen day's (that is, a fortnight's) worth of the calendar. Click the 1 button, and you get one whole day's worth.

The buttons in the lower-right corner of the calendar help you switch to the next or previous screen's information. If you have the calendar displaying one day at a time, the left arrow shows you the previous day, and the right arrow shows you the next day. If you were looking at the calendar one whole month at a time, those buttons switch to a different month, not a different day.

No matter what, the middle button always takes you to today.

To switch to a different month, click the little arrows in the upper-right corner of the calendar. You can also click on a day in the monthly calendar to go right to that day.

Scrolls to the preceding or next month   Changes how much of your calendar you can see

Changes the displayed dates

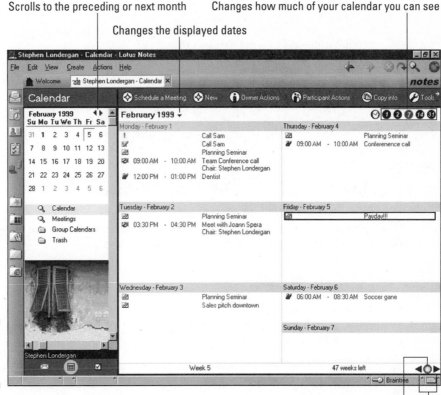

Figure 6-1:
Your
calendar.

Goes to today's entries

Scrolls to the preceding or next page

More than meetings

Your Notes calendar includes more than just meetings. You can find up to six kinds of things in your calendar:

✔ **To Dos:** Your tasks.

✔ **Appointments:** Places that you need to go or meetings that you have to attend, but to which you don't need to invite other people — such as a dentist's appointment, or a meeting with your parole officer. Use appointments to keep track of personal scheduled items, and also so that your colleagues know *not* to book you for meetings at those times.

✔ **Meetings:** Just like appointments, except they include other people from the office. You probably have to go to too many meetings, but you use this calendar item to keep track of those you can't avoid!

✔ **Anniversaries:** Birthdays, holidays, wedding anniversaries, and so on, Anniversaries are one-day affairs that repeat from one year to the next. (Listing an anniversary in your calendar does *not* prevent people from inviting you to a meeting on that day.)

✔ **All Day Events:** Affairs that can span multiple days, such as an out-of-town meeting. If you list an event on your calendar, people will not be able to invite you to a meeting.

✔ **Reminders:** Sort of like a to do. A reminder entry is something you want to remember to do at a particular time on a particular day.

Adding stuff to your calendar

To add a new item to your calendar, you can either click New on the Calendar's action bar, or you can choose Create➪Calendar Entry. What you do next depends on the type of entry you're creating.

Adding an appointment

To record an appointment on your calendar, open your Calendar and choose Appointment from the New menu. See Figure 6-2 for a sample appointment — and notice that it has two tabs. The first tab contains the appointment's Basic information, and the other tab has some options.

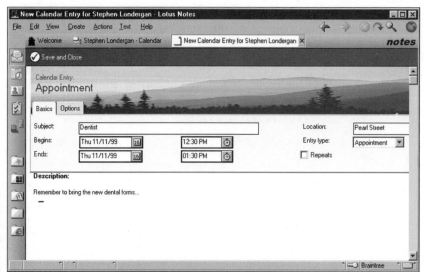

Figure 6-2:
Scheduling
an
appointment.

To schedule an appointment, fill out the following fields:

- **Subject:** Type some words describing the appointment.

- **Begins** and **Ends:** Use these fields to enter the length of the appointment. You can type the time and date, or you can click the calendar and the watch pictures next to each of these fields.

- **Location:** You want to remember where you're supposed to be, right?

- **Description:** You may enter any text — or nothing — in this area of the form.

- **Pencil in:** Click this check box on the Options tab if you want your colleagues to still be able to invite you to meetings during the time you have scheduled for the appointment.

- **Mark Private:** This button prevents people from seeing what you're doing at the time of the appointment. Other people will be able to tell that you are busy, but the details of your activity will not be available to them.

- **Notify Me:** Check this field if you want Notes to warn you of the appointment, so that you don't forget to go. (How could you forget to go to the dentist, anyway?) If you do choose to be notified, use the Alarm Settings button to determine exactly when and how you'll get the warning.

- **Categories:** Optionally, you can type (or choose) a category for the appointment in this field.

If you double-click a particular time on your calendar, Notes will start a new calendar entry for you, and automatically fill in the start time.

Click the action bar's OK button when you finish setting the options on the Appointment form.

Adding a meeting invitation

To schedule a meeting that includes other people, click the Calendar action bar's Schedule a Meeting button. As you may notice in Figure 6-3, the Meeting form is like the Appointment form, with a few extra tabs and fields to handle the names of the other people who'll be attending.

Each person whose name you list in either the Invite, CC, or BCC fields on the form's Meeting Invitations & Reservations tab receives an invitation to your meeting. You can check your meeting entry later to see who has responded yea or nay. Notes won't schedule the meeting, however, until *all* required people accept your invitation.

The hardest part of scheduling a meeting has always been finding a time that's convenient for everybody — but no more! If you click the action bar's Scheduler button, Notes peruses the individual calendars of each person listed in the Invitee fields, finds a time at which they are *all* available, and changes the date and time of your meeting accordingly. How cool!

When you invite people to a meeting, they each receive an e-mail message from you detailing the meeting. They can then respond, letting you know whether or not they plan to attend your little get-together. These responses are sent back to you as e-mail messages, and arrive in your inbox.

If your administrator has configured your system appropriately, you can also use the Reserve Rooms and Reserve Resources section of the New Calendar Entry form to book a room or resource (maybe an overhead projector?) for the meeting.

Click the action bar's Save and Send Invitations button when you finish with the form, and then sit back and relax as Notes sends each person you invited a message with the details of your little get-together.

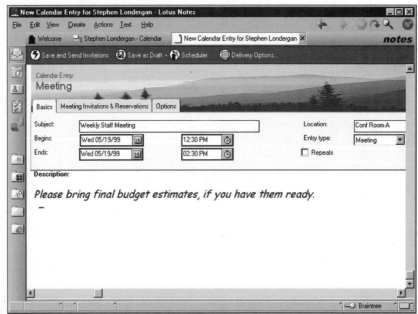

Figure 6-3:
Meetings
include
other
people.

Use the Repeats check box on any of the Calendar forms if the item that you're scheduling will occur more than once.

Adding an anniversary

To record an anniversary in your calendar, click the Calendar action bar's New button, and then choose Anniversary. As you can see in Figure 6-4, the New Anniversary form has fewer fields than the other calendar forms; whatever you type in the Subject field will be what shows up on that day in your calendar.

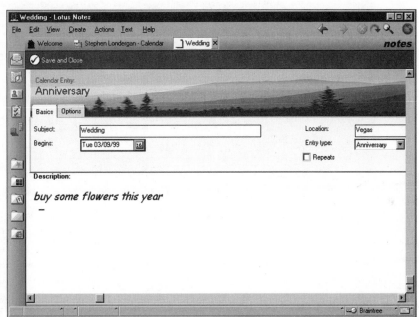

Figure 6-4:
A new anniversary.

You'll probably want to use the Repeats check box on the New Anniversary form, because anniversaries, by their very nature, happen more than once. For example, suppose you want your wedding anniversary to appear every year on your calendar (not that you would ever forget that auspicious day). You would type something like 11/9/87 in the Begins field, and then click the Repeats check box so that you can then tell Notes how often to repeat the anniversary on your calendar. Click the Save and Close button when you finish with the New Anniversary form.

Adding a reminder

To add a reminder to your calendar, click the Calendar action bar's New button, and then choose Reminder. Type a brief description in the Subject field, and then choose the date and time when you want to be reminded. Figure 6-5 shows a sample New Reminder form.

You can rush right ahead and click the Save and Close button when you finish with the New Reminder form. However, you might also consider the Options tab if you want to mark the document Private or set up an Alarm for the reminder.

Figure 6-5: Scheduling a reminder is like tying a string around your finger.

Adding an event

To record an event in your calendar, click the Calendar action bar's New button, and then choose Event.

An *event* is just a day-long affair, and it can last more than one day. Therefore, using the Event form is a lot like using the Appointment or Meeting form to schedule yourself for a meeting or an appointment that lasts the whole day.

You may want to use the Repeat Options dialog box if the event is more than one day long, as you can see in Figure 6-6. Click the action bar's Save and Close button when you finish the form.

Figure 6-6:
Use the
Repeat
Options
dialog
box to
automatically
enter multiple
items on
your
calendar.

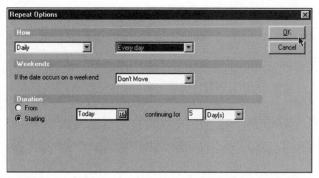

Responding to an invitation

Being the popular and gregarious sort that you are, you will no doubt be
invited to lots and lots of meetings. Figure 6-7 shows a sample invitation
(notice the special buttons in the action bar).

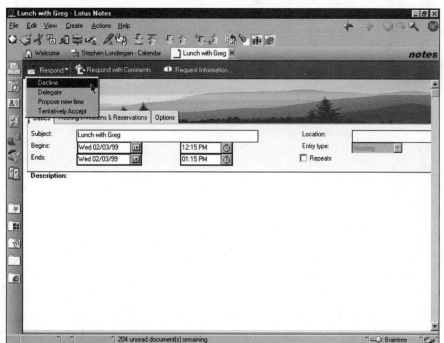

Figure 6-7:
An
invitation.

When you receive such an invitation for a meeting, use the Respond buttons in the message's action bar to let the person know whether or not you're coming. As you can see in Figure 6-7, you can respond five different ways:

- ✔ **Accept** means you will be there, with bells on. Accepting a meeting both saves the invitation on your calendar, and sends a message to the meeting's chairperson so that they know you'll be there.

- ✔ **Decline** means you ain't goin'. (Sorry!) The meeting chairperson gets a note saying so, too.

- ✔ **Delegate** (our favorite) lets you suggest that someone else should attend in your place.

- ✔ **Propose New Time** means that you would love to go to the meeting but you would like to propose that the meeting be held at a different time because you're busy at the proposed time.

- ✔ **Tentatively Accept** means that you'll be there, but that the time of the meeting will *not* be marked as busy on your schedule. (In other words, you can schedule a different meeting that conflicts with this one.)

Okay, you now know that no matter which way you choose to respond to an invitation, the person who sent you the invitation in the first place gets a message back from you. Use the action bar's Respond with Comments button if you want to add anything (condolences, perhaps, if you need to decline) to the message.

You can also use the action bar's Check Calendar button to take a look at your calendar before you decide if you'll accept the invitation. When you click the Check Calendar button, Notes opens your calendar, and displays the day in question. Once you're done looking, press Esc to close your calendar, return to the invitation, and use the Respond menu to Accept, Decline, and so on, the invitation.

Use the Invitees tab on a new invitation to see who else got invited to the meeting.

Managing your calendar

It's a sad fact that the meeting and appointments you track in your calendar aren't cast in the proverbial concrete. Before long, you'll need to change the time or date of a meeting. Fortunately, your calendar already has what it takes to make sure the people you've invited get notified of your decision to reschedule, or maybe even to cancel, a meeting.

You may have already noticed Owner Actions and Participant Actions in the calendar's action bar. These buttons help you manage meetings. It stands to reason that these buttons apply only to items already on your calendar, right? (You can't cancel a meeting if you haven't scheduled it in the first place!)

If it's your meeting

If you are the owner of the meeting, which means you are the person who scheduled the meeting and sent out the invitations, you can do five things to an item on your calendar:

- ✔ **Reschedule** lets you change the time and date of the meeting. After you choose the new time and date, Notes automatically sends each person you've invited a notice — which the person may have to decline, if he or she is busy.

  When you need to reschedule a meeting, let Notes find a time that's open and convenient for your invitees — make sure to use the Check Schedules button on the Reschedule Options dialog box.

- ✔ **Cancel** does three things. First, it removes the meeting from your calendar. Second, it removes the meeting from your participants' calendars, too. Third, it sends each person an e-mail to notify them that the meeting has been canceled. (Is anything sweeter than the feeling you get when you find out a meeting has been canceled?)

- ✔ **Confirm** just sends a message to your participants to confirm the meeting's date and time. It's sort of an optional reminder; you never have to send confirmations.

- ✔ **View Participant Status** is a quick way to see a list of all the people you invited, and whether or not they have agreed to attend.

- ✔ **Send Memo to Participants** is a quickie way to start a new e-mail message, preloaded with the addresses of the people you've invited to the meeting.

If it's not your meeting

If you are a participant, which means you are a person who was invited to a meeting and agreed to attend, you have three things you can do with a meeting:

- ✔ **Decline** lets you change your mind, in the case of a meeting you previously agreed to attend. When you decline, Notes sends an e-mail to the person who invited you to warn him or her that you won't be able to attend, after all.

- ✔ **Delegate** lets you send someone else in your place. (Lucky you!)

- ✔ **Propose New Time** means you still *want* to come, but you can't come to the meeting at its original time or date. When you propose a new time, Notes sends a message to the meeting's chairperson with your alternative time and date.

Setting Up Your Calendar

What's known in the trade as your Calendar Preferences document controls many of the finer points concerning the way your calendar functions. You can change your Preferences by opening your calendar, and then either choosing Preferences from the action bar's Tools button, or choosing <u>A</u>ctions⇨ Tools⇨<u>P</u>references. In either case, you're presented with the dialog box shown in Figure 6-8.

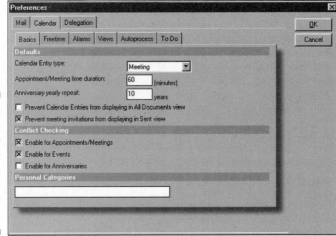

Figure 6-8:
Configure
your
Calendar
options
with the
Preferences
dialog box.

As you can see in Figure 6-8,, the Preferences dialog box is divided into three main tabs (Mail, Calendar, and Delegation), each of which is further divided into tabs of its own. (The ins and outs of the Mail Preference options are covered in stunning detail in Chapter 7, so we'll focus here on just the Calendar and Delegation Preferences.)

Calendar preferences

The Preferences dialog box has a lot to ask you. You've seen that it's divided into three main tabs — Mail, Calendar, and Delegation. You'll also find that each of the dialog box's main tabs is further divided. For example, when you click the Calendar tab, you get six more tabs: Freetime, Alarms, Entries, Views, Autoprocess, and Misc.

My favorite calendar entry

As you see in Figure 6-8, nine fields show up when you click the Basics tab in the Calendar Preferences dialog box. These values tell Notes how, in general, you would like your calendar to behave. More specifically:

✔ **Calendar Entry Type** is handy if you tend to enter one type of calendar entry more than any other.

✔ **Appointment/Meeting Time Duration** tells Notes what to make the default duration for new calendar entries.

✔ **Anniversary Yearly Repeat** is the default value for when a new anniversary document recurs.

✔ **Display Calendar Entries in All Documents View** should be turned off if you don't want the All Documents view in your mail to be cluttered with calendar items.

✔ **Display Meeting Invitations in Sent View** should be turned off if you want to hide the meeting invitations you've sent from the Sent view in your mail.

✔ **Conflict Checking** warns you, as you enter a new calendar entry, if you have something booked at the same time. You should probably turn this on for meetings and appointments, but turn it off for anniversaries, because an anniversary usually isn't scheduled at a particular time and doesn't prevent you from scheduling a meeting.

✔ **Personal Categories** is used to set up the choices you'll have on your calendar forms to categorize the new meeting, appointment, and so on.

When can you meet?

The second tab on the Preferences dialog box pertains to your Freetime options. These options list each day of the week, with two time ranges associated with each day.

Notes uses Freetime to know when you are generally available. If, for example, a colleague who is looking to schedule a meeting with you uses the Scheduler button on her New Meeting form, Notes tells her that you are free to meet during any time that (a) is not already booked on your calendar with a different meeting, and (b) falls within the Freetimes you have set on this dialog box.

Suppose that you are lucky enough to work only four days a week, Monday through Thursday. You should change the Freetime settings so that Notes knows you aren't available on Fridays. (Just un-check Friday in the dialog box.) After you do that, Notes won't let anyone propose to meet with you on that day. If you always leave early on Tuesdays, for example, you would change the second date range for Tuesday.

By default, Notes assumes that you don't work on Saturdays and Sundays — or at the very least, that you're not generally available to meet on those days. If that is not the case, check Saturday or Sunday in the dialog box.

The settings on the Freetime dialog box are just suggestions for Notes. Even when you say that you are generally unavailable on Fridays, another person could still invite you to a meeting on that day — and you could still agree to attend.

By default, all the people in your organization can use their Scheduler button when preparing a New Meeting form to see whether you are available to meet at a particular time and on a particular date. If the idea of all those people looking over your shoulder gives you the willies, enter their name (or names) in the Only the Following Users Can Request My Free Time Information field.

When people check out your free time information (by clicking the Scheduler button on their New Meeting form), remember that they see only when you are and are not available. The Scheduler button *never* shows them where you'll be or what you'll be doing.

Setting alarm defaults

Let's face it, the whole idea behind the calendar is to make you remember that you have to be someplace, or do something, or see somebody. That's great if you remember to look at your calendar, but what if you spend a given morning slaving away on a new memo and you forget to even look at your appointments for the day? That's where alarms come in. When you enable alarms, Notes warns you of an impending meeting or appointment by beeping at you and showing you the name of the appointment. (As you've seen, you have the option of turning on an alarm for each type of calendar entry form.)

The Alarms tab on the Calendar Preferences dialog box lets you decide, for those entries in which you've chosen to be reminded by an alarm, what sound will play, when the alarm will go off, and so on. The Alarms dialog box is shown in Figure 6-9.

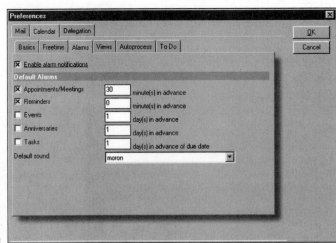

Figure 6-9:
Turn on alarms, and you'll never be late for a meeting again!

If you want to use alarms, the first thing you need to do is click Enable Alarms Notifications. You can then choose the type of calendar entries that will get an alarm and the amount of warning you'll get before the event or appointment.

Just like the Freetime settings discussed previously, remember that the Alarms settings in the Calendar Preferences dialog box are default values. That means you can override them on any particular calendar entry.

Show me

If you look closely at Figure 6-10, you'll see that the fields in the Views tab of the Calendar Preferences dialog box tell Notes how much of the day to show on the calendar. If you work in the evening, for example, you could change these settings so that your calendar automatically displays times from 4 p.m. to midnight, instead of the default values of 7 a.m. to 7 p.m. The Time Slot Interval determines how many time slices are shown on your calendar each day.

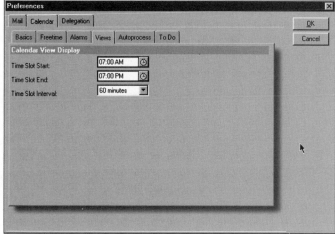

Figure 6-10:
The View settings in the Calendar Preferences dialog box.

Automatic replies

Figure 6-11 shows the Autoprocess tab on the Calendar Preferences dialog box. In the typical course of events, a person decides to schedule a meeting, and enters your name as one of the invitees. Notes sends you a new invitation, so that you can let that person know whether or not you're coming. You open the invitation, take a look at your calendar, decide if you are free and whether you want to go, and then you accept, decline, or delegate the invitation. Sounds like a lot of work, right?

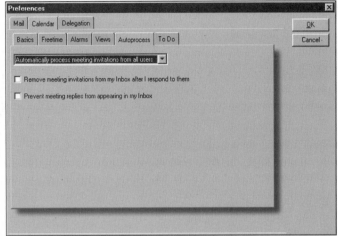

The autoprocess settings take care of some of that for you. If for example, you always agree to attend the invitations from your boss (which we suggest you do), Notes can be set to automatically accept invitations from him or her. You can autoprocess invitations in four ways. You choose which one from the drop-down box in the dialog box:

- ✔ **Do Not Automatically Process Meeting Invitations** is the default value, and it means Notes will not reply on your behalf to meeting invitations. You have to look at each one, manually.

- ✔ **Automatically Process Meeting Invitations from All Users** tells Notes to automatically enter meetings on your calendar, if you are available, and to automatically respond to the person who invited you. (You still have to manually review requests that conflict with meetings you've already scheduled, but when your schedule is open, Notes automatically books you.)

- ✔ **Autoprocess Meeting Requests from the Following Users** tells Notes to automatically book you for meeting requests from just a few, select people (like you, boss, remember?).

- ✔ **Forward Meeting Requests to the Following Person** lets you duck the meeting invitation altogether (our favorite), and instead forward the invitation to a colleague.

Use the Remove Meeting Invitations from My Inbox after I Respond to Them check box if you don't want old invitations to appear in your mail's Inbox folder. Similarly, use the Prevent Meeting Replies from Appearing in My Inbox field if you prefer to keep them from cluttering the Inbox folder.

Letting other people into your calendar

You may, or may not, want other people to be able to view your calendar — not to just check your free time, but to be able to actually open your calendar and see where you're going, at what time you'll be there, and with whom you'll be meeting. Think long and hard about giving anyone the right to do this!

Who gets to open and read your calendar? The Delegation tab of the Calendar Preferences dialog box gives you three choices:

- To let everyone see your calendar, click the Everyone Can Read My Calendar button on the Delegation tab of the Calendar Preferences dialog box.

- To let no one see your calendar, click the Only the Following People/Groups Can Read My Calendar button, but *leave the names drop-down list empty*.

- To give just a few people permission to see your calendar, click the Only the Following People/Groups Can Read My Calendar button, and then type the names of the people, or the names of the groups of people, in the drop-down list.

Even if you are allowing everyone to view your calendar, you can always hide a particular entry by using the Mark Private field, which is included on every Calendar entry form.

Similarly, you may, or may not, want other people to be able to manage your calendar, which means they can reply on your behalf and confirm your attendance at a meeting:

- In the extremely unlikely event that you want anyone in your organization to be able to manage your calendar, click the Everyone Can Manage My Calendar button.

- To let no one manage your calendar, click the Only the Following People/Groups Can Manage My Calendar button, but *leave the names drop-down list empty*.

- To give just a few people, or maybe just one person, permission to manage your calendar, click the Only the Following People/Groups Can Read My Calendar button, and then type the name or names in the drop-down list.

Click the OK button when you finish with the Calendar Preferences dialog box.

Group Calendars

Group calendars are a quick and easy way to see an overview of several people's calendars, all lumped together. You might use a group calendar to manage an entire department's appointments, or anytime you need to see more than one person's calendar at the same time.

Creating a group calendar

Before you can view a group calendar, you have to create a group calendar document in your mail database, as follows:

1. **Open your calendar or mail.**
2. **In the navigation pane, click the Group Calendars folder.**

3. **In the action bar, click the New Group Calendar button or choose Actions⇨New Group Calendar.**
4. **In the Title field, type the name by which the group calendar will be known.**
5. **In the Members field, type the names of the people whose calendar you want to view.**

   Click the drop-down arrow at the bottom of the field to choose the names from the public directory.

6. **Click the OK button to create the new group calendar.**

Opening a group calendar

After you have created a group calendar document, use it to easily open a collective view of the member's calendars. To see a group's calendar, use the following steps:

1. **Open your calendar or mail.**
2. **In the navigation pane, click the Group Calendars folder.**
3. **In the view pane, select the group calendar you intend to open.**
4. **Open the group calendar by either double-clicking it or pressing Enter.**

A group calendar shows you a collective, day-by-day representation of the schedules for the people who are members of the group. As you can see in Figure 6-12, each person's schedule is broken into hour-long blocks.

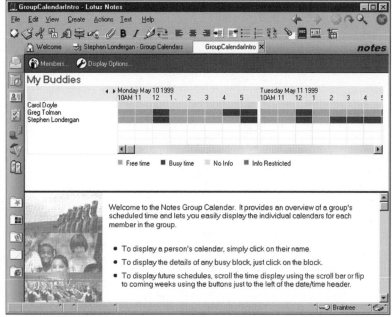

Figure 6-12:
Group
calendars
let you see
more then
one schedule
at the
same time.

Notes tell you whether the person is busy or available during a given hour by coloring the corresponding block: green when the person is free, or blue when the person is busy. You can see the details of a person's schedule by clicking the block.

You must be listed in the person's delegation profile before you can add a person to your group schedule.

Chapter 7

Making the Most of Your Memos

In This Chapter

▶ Including other files in your memos

▶ Making and hiding sections

▶ Using custom forms

*I*n the age of power ties, power lunches, and power lifting, it just stands to reason that you can write power memos. After you receive your tenth meet-me-for-coffee-at-10:00 memo, you may find yourself saying: "There must be more to memo writing than this. I'm getting wired from all this caffeine."

Well, you can do *plenty* more with memos than just arrange meetings. With your dazzling memos, you can be the talk of the office, a legend among your coworkers.

Enclosed Please Find

One reason for writing a memo is to discuss some information that already exists. For instance, you may want to get some feedback on a report that you're writing in Microsoft Word. Do you have to retype the entire report into your Notes memo? No way, José! This is the '90s! Notes, being the high-tech marvel that it is, comes to the rescue. You have several options for getting around the chore of retyping the report.

Why, I oughta paste you

If you've spent any time copying and pasting in other programs, you're familiar with the Clipboard. When you choose the Edit⇨Copy command, your computer holds the information you've selected in the Clipboard so that you can Edit⇨Paste it into other files, documents, or applications. The simplest way to get information from a separate program into Notes is to use the Clipboard.

Suppose you're preparing a memo about a section of a report written in Microsoft Word. Copy and paste that section from the report right into your memo and then add your own comments in and around the pasted text. Of course, you can also paste an entire file, unless it's too big to fit in the Clipboard.

Attaching attachments

If you write a paper memo that explains a report, you may decide to paper clip the report itself to the memo so that the recipient can see what you're writing about. That's what a Notes *attachment* is: a file attached to a memo. Figure 7-1 shows an e-mail message that includes a file attachment. A keen observer may notice that the attachment takes the form of an icon, which usually tells the recipient what program you used to create the attached file.

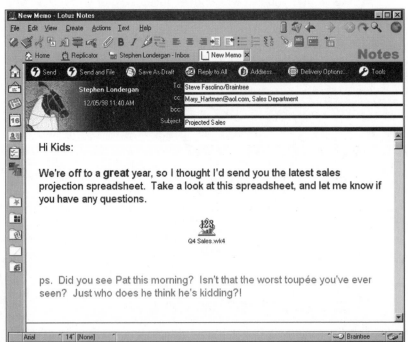

Figure 7-1:
You can attach files to your e-mail messages.

Feel free to attach virtually any type of file to any Notes document — binary files, compressed files, executable files, graphics files, and any other file created in any another program. Keep in mind that attaching a large file makes the memo large and increases the size of your database.

To attach a file to a memo, put the cursor where you want to place the attachment and then select File⇨Attach or click the File Attach SmartIcon. The Create Attachment(s) dialog box in Figure 7-2 appears; use this dialog box to choose the files to attach.

In the File Name box, highlight the proper filename and press Enter or click Create. You can even attach more than one file at once if the files are in the same directory. Highlight the first file and then hold down the Ctrl key while you select the other files you want to attach. To select several consecutive files, highlight the first and then press the Shift key as you click on the last one; Notes selects all the files in between.

Imagine getting a memo with an attachment — and nothing else. What is it? What program did it come from? What are you supposed to do with it? Sensible questions all, and ones that you should answer for the recipient when you send an attachment with your memo. Don't leave the person guessing.

What should you do if you receive a message with an attachment? Well, you can

- ✔ **View it:** Take a little peek inside and see (or even print) the file's contents.

- ✔ **Launch it:** Open the document with the program that was used to create it in the first place (assuming that you have said program installed on your computer).

- ✔ **Detach it:** Put a copy of the file on your computer, to have for your very own.

Figure 7-2:
Use the
Create
Attach-
ment(s)
dialog box
to add a file
from your
computer to
a Notes
document.

When you double-click an attachment icon, you're presented with an Attachment infobox, like the one in Figure 7-3. Click the View, Launch, or Detach button, depending on what you want to do with the file.

Figure 7-3:
Use the
Attachment
infobox to
view,
launch, or
detach an
attached
file.

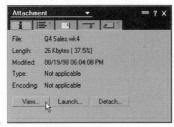

What a view!

If you click the View button, Notes shows you as much of the file as it can through the File Viewer. Figure 7-4 shows a spreadsheet attachment that's being viewed. You can view files from most popular computer programs; use the Print menu if you need to see the file on a piece of paper.

To view an attachment, you don't need to have the computer program that was used to create the attachment.

Choose File⇨Close or click the X in the window's upper-right corner to close the File Viewer and return to the document you were reading in the first place.

Let's do launch

If you choose Launch rather than View in the Attachment infobox, Notes starts the program that was used to create the attachment and automatically opens the attachment in that program.

To launch an attached file, you must have that file's program installed on your hard disk. If you don't have the program, you have to rely on the File Viewer to see what's in the file.

Detaching yourself

You may not want to view or launch the attached file. Instead, you may want to detach the file because

 ✔ You want to use the file later.

 ✔ You don't have the software required to launch the file.

 ✔ You want to put the file on a floppy disk to take to another computer.

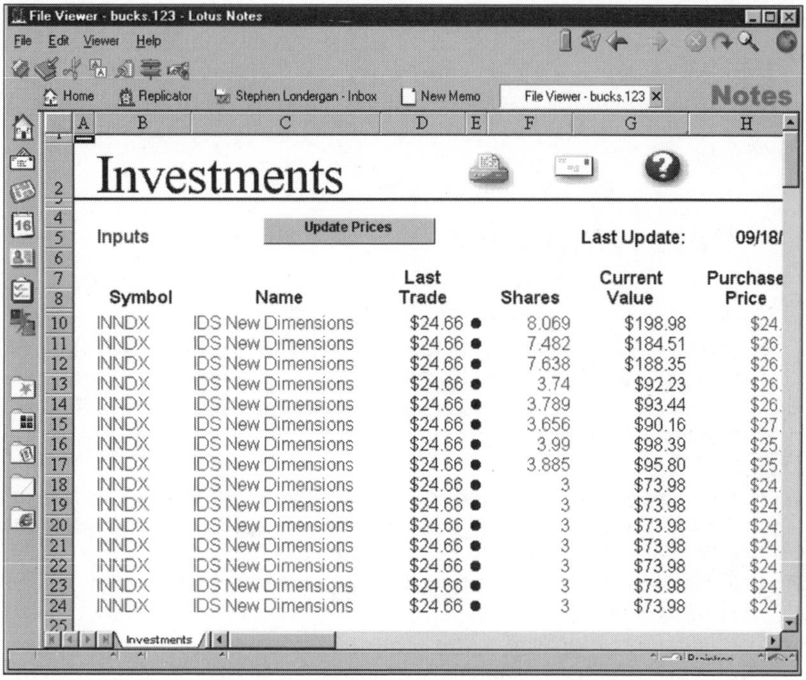

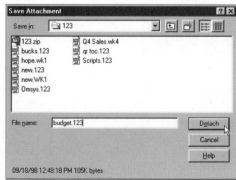

Figure 7-4: Use the File Viewer to see the contents of an attached file.

If you choose Detach from the Attachment infobox, you get the Save Attachment dialog box shown in Figure 7-5. Use this dialog box to tell Notes where on your hard disk you want to save the file and what you want to name it.

Notes (Windows, actually) relies on a file's *extension* (those three characters after the period) to know what kind of file it is, so you shouldn't change the file's extension.

Figure 7-5: When you detach an attachment, use this dialog box to tell Notes where to put the file.

Don't mention this to the folks at Lotus (we don't want to hurt their feelings), but it would be clearer if they had used the word *Save* rather than *Detach*, because the word *detach* may leave you with the mistaken impression that the file is actually removed from the memo. A copy of the file is saved to a disk, but the attachment remains attached to the memo in your mail.

Importing files

If you want the recipients of your message to see the contents of a file, rather than just a symbol, when they open your memo, attaching the file isn't such a hot idea. Rather, Import is the command to use, because it brings the contents of a file right into your message in readable form. *Importing* converts a file that was created in another program into a format that is readable in a Notes document.

You may not be surprised that the files you import have to be some sort of data file, with real words or numbers or graphics that people can look at. You can't, for example, import executable files (files ending with the extension EXE) because they are program files, not data files.

Place the cursor where you want the imported document to appear in your message, and then choose File⇨Import. The dialog box shown in Figure 7-6 appears.

Figure 7-6:
Use the
Import
dialog box
to put the
contents of
a file
directly
inside your
memo.

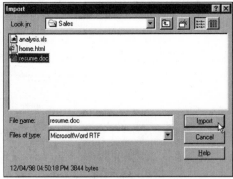

Use the Look in dialog box to tell Notes where to find your file. Then, in the Files of Type list box, select a file type (in Figure 7-6, we selected Microsoft Word RTF). Highlight the file you want to import, click Import, and as quickly as your hard disk can spin, you have the file in your Notes document.

Deciding what to do

Feeling a bit confused? Don't know whether to import or attach or use the Clipboard? Maybe the following list will help clear up your confusion:

- Use the Clipboard when you want to put only part of a file in a Notes document.

- Use the Clipboard if the recipient doesn't have the software necessary to open an attached file.

- Use the Clipboard if the recipient of your memo doesn't use Notes.

- Use File⇨Import when the readers don't need to have a copy of the file itself on their local disk.

- Use File⇨Import when you aren't sure whether the recipients have the software necessary to open the file you want them to see, and you can't use the Clipboard.

- Use File⇨Import when you need to include a file that's too large for the Clipboard, and you know that your memo's recipient doesn't use Notes.

- Use File⇨Attach when the file can't be imported, such as an executable file.

- Use File⇨Attach when you want the recipient to have an actual copy of the file to keep on a local disk.

Find out more about importing and exporting files in Chapter 16.

Creating Sections

Nothing's worse than receiving (or sending, for that matter) an e-mail that's too long. In this age of information overload, how many times have you been forced to wade through pages and pages of text, only to find that about half of it is irrelevant?

Well, we won't have any of that in Notes! By using a *section*, you make your messages easier to read. Sections let you make parts of your document *collapsible;* that is, your readers don't have to read a particular part if they don't want to.

Don't underestimate the power of readability. If you routinely send messages that are too long or too boring or have ugly fonts and colors, people won't read them. Some companies even offer classes in how to create interesting and readable e-mail!

To create a section, select the paragraph(s) that you want to be able to hide, and then choose Create➪Section. Faster than a New York minute, the paragraph disappears, and you see only the first line of the paragraph, as shown in Figure 7-7.

Notice the little triangle to the left of the first line of each paragraph? That triangle is the reader's cue that more is here than meets the eye. When you click the triangle, the section expands to display all the text; when you click it again, the section collapses and hides the words again.

Consider adding a title to your hidden section to make your document even more readable. Just type a heading before the section you want to hide, and then highlight both before choosing Create➪Section.

That's it! Sections are easy to make and use, and are invaluable for keeping messages readable and concise. Use the Section command whenever you want to make your documents more reader friendly. And remember that you can create a section in any database, not just in your e-mail!

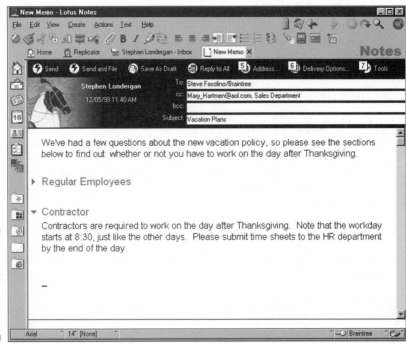

Figure 7-7:
Click the triangle next to a section to see its contents.

Mail Is More Than Just Memos

Most of the time when you use your e-mail database, you use the Create menu to write a memo. In some organizations, however, perhaps someone behind the scenes created special forms for everyone to use. For instance, suppose you need to order some staples. Or suppose that you need to reserve the conference room for your Monday morning poker game. Some genius may have already created a Staple Order Form or a Conference Room Reservation Form. Your company may also have forms for special announcements, special requests, status reports, or information sheets.

When you choose Create⇨Mail⇨Other, Notes presents you with a list of the custom forms that you can use for special occasions. The forms may even be addressed, so that you don't have to run around trying to find out who is in charge of ordering staples or reserving conference rooms or scheduling vacations.

This chapter presented some, but not all, of the things you can put in your e-mail messages. Because e-mail messages are really just documents in a database, check out Chapter 4 for more information about composing them.

Chapter 8

Mastering Your Mail

● ●

In This Chapter

▶ Sending mail to people who don't use Notes

▶ Following the rules

▶ Using your personal N&A book

▶ Going on vacation

▶ Creating reusable stationery

▶ Using some special delivery options

● ●

*L*ook at you! How you've grown! Why, it seems like it was only yesterday that you were learning how to create a memo and use the Trash folder, and now here you are! In this chapter, we present some pretty advanced mail options; in fact, you may never need to use any of them. But if you have the time to read about them, we have the time to explain them. So, without further ado. . . .

You Know, Not Everyone Uses Notes

As much as Lotus hates to hear it, not every person who uses e-mail uses Notes, so the day is going to come when you need to exchange e-mail with someone who doesn't use Notes at all.

Suppose that you want to send a message to your buddy. Addressing the message is easy: If his e-mail address is, say, `jmurphy@ravesoft.com`, you would enter exactly that in the To field of your memo.

To be able to send e-mail to someone on the Internet, your administrator must have installed some special software, known as an MTA, on the Domino server.

One of the nicest things about Notes e-mail is that it's pretty; you already know that you can use different fonts and colors and even include pictures in the body of a Notes e-mail message.

But here's the rub: When you send a message to someone who doesn't use Notes — especially someone with one of those .com e-mail addresses — there's a pretty good chance that your pretty fonts and colors and pictures will be lost in the translation. Rest assured, though, that the person will get your message okay and be able to read it. The message just won't have all that pretty formatting.

You can, however, get most of the formatting work you do in Notes to carry through so that the person who receives your pretty message *does* see the fonts and colors. It's a little work, though, so you have to make a decision.

Your decision is whether or not to bother. If you're happy just sending the text of the message, and you tend not to use different fonts and colors anyway, you can stop right here. If, on the other hand, you want your e-mail to include fonts and colors, you need to know about . . .

HTML mail

Perhaps you already know that HyperText Markup Language (HTML) has become the vernacular of the Internet. That is, HTML is a kind of programming language that Webmasters use to create Web pages. They use HTML so that they can be certain that their Web pages will look the same regardless of the type of computer, operating system, or Web browser being used.

The point — and there is a point to all this — is that you can use HTML to encode your e-mail messages, too. That way, the person on the other end gets to see your message's pretty fonts and colors, any pictures you have included in the body of the message, and so on. Before we see how to turn on the capability to encode your mail with HTML, there's one small issue: Not all mail programs can understand HTML mail. Fortunately, most do.

So that means you have to decide how you want your mail sent to people through the Internet. You can choose one of the following:

- ✔ **HTML** means that your message is automatically coded in HTML, your recipient uses an e-mail program that understands HTML, and your message arrives with special fonts and colors intact.

- ✔ **Plain Text Only** means that your message is sent in plain ASCII text, your recipient can use any e-mail program to read it, and your message arrives without any special fonts or colors or embedded pictures.

- ✔ **HTML and Plain Text** means that you aren't sure whether the recipient can read HTML-based mail, so Notes prepares and sends the person two copies of your message: a pretty, HTML-ised version *and* a plain text version. That way, if the recipient uses a mail program that can handle the HTML, your pretty message appears; but if the recipient's mail program can't handle HTML, your message can still be read.

If you choose the HTML and Plain Text method of sending mail, your recipients will get two versions of the message, but fortunately they'll never see two messages in their inbox. Their mail program sorts out which to use, and they'll see only that one.

Choosing your Internet mail format

To tell Notes how you prefer to have Internet mail encoded, choose File⇨Preferences⇨User Preferences. Then click the Mail and News tab on the User Preferences dialog box. As you can see in Figure 8-1, you can choose one of four settings in the Internet Mail Format field: HTML Only, Plain Text Only, HTML and Plain Text, and Prompt when Sending.

Figure 8-1: Use the Mail settings in the User Preferences dialog box to determine how your Internet-bound mail will be encoded.

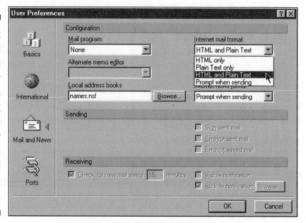

If you choose one of the first three selections in the Internet Mail Format field, you are telling Notes that you want all your outgoing Internet mail to be prepared that way. If, on the other hand, you choose the last option — Prompt when Sending — you're telling Notes that you would prefer to be asked how the message should be formatted each and every time you send an Internet message.

Click the OK button in the User Preferences dialog box when you're finished.

Choosing the encoding message for an individual message

If you use the User Preferences dialog box to set the Internet Mail Format field to Prompt when Sending, you better be prepared for the dialog box that's shown in Figure 8-2.

Figure 8-2:
Choosing
the
encoding
method for
an individual
message.

This dialog box appears when you click your new memo's Send button. As you can see in the figure, you can select one of the three options, which will be used as the encoding method *for that message*. In other words, you'll be asked again — and get to choose again — the next time you send a message.

Rules

Momma told you that you should always follow the rules, right? On the other hand, Katharine Hepburn was once quoted as saying "If you obey all the rules, you miss all the fun." Be that as it may, rules, as far as Notes is concerned, are a way to have Notes help you manage your mail.

For the sake of argument, suppose that you get a regular sales update e-mail every Thursday. And, for reasons known only to yourself, you always save these sales updates in a folder called (you guessed it) Sales Updates.

Using a rule, you can make it all happen automagically. A *rule* tells Notes what to do with certain incoming messages. For example, you could have a rule that always puts messages with a certain word in the subject field in a certain folder, or a rule that moves e-mail from a certain person directly into the Trash folder, or perhaps a rule that instantly changes the importance of any message you receive from your boss to High. Figure 8-3 shows the Rules view in your mail database. As you can see in the figure, you can have more than one rule.

Creating a rule

To create a new rule, click the action bar's New Rule button, which is found in the Rules view in your mail database. Figure 8-4 shows the New Rule dialog box.

As you can see from the figure, the New Rule dialog box is divided into three sections in which you determine whether the rule is enabled, on which messages the rule will act, and what the rule will do with the messages it chooses.

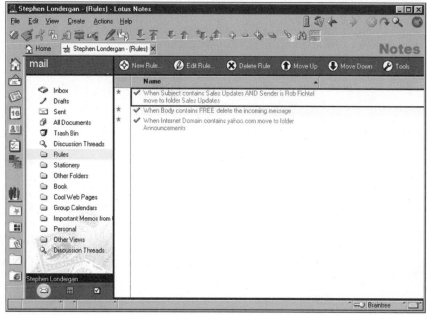

Figure 8-3:
Use rules to
help
manage
your mail.

In most cases, any rule you create will be turned on. You may, however, have a rule that you want to temporarily disable. The first field, at the very top of the dialog box, lets you decide whether the rule is being enforced. If you set the Rule Is field to On (which is the default), the rule does whatever you told it to do. On the other hand, if you use this same field to say that the rule is off, it doesn't do anything.

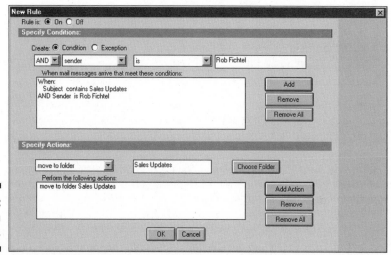

Figure 8-4:
Creating a
new rule.

Defining a rule's condition

The fields in the Specify Conditions section of the dialog box determine the messages to which the rule will apply. The basic idea is to use these fields to set up a criterion, and then to use the Add button to save the condition. Some rules may only one condition, such as "Subject contains Sales Updates." Others may be more complicated with more than one condition. For example, the example shown in Figure 8-4 has two criteria; the incoming message must have the words "Sales Updates" in the subject and the message must be from Rob Fichtel.

When you are defining the first field in the Condition section of the dialog box, you can choose from twelve different places to look:

- ✔ **sender** chooses messages by the name of the person who sent the message.

- ✔ **subject** selects messages based on what is in the subject of the message.

- ✔ **body** lets you find messages with a certain word or phrase in the body of the message.

- ✔ **importance** selects the message based on the importance that the sender chose for it (high/medium/low).

- ✔ **delivery priority** selects the message based on the delivery priority that the author assigned to the message.

- ✔ **to** selects the messages by the name of the person, or persons, in the message's To field.

- ✔ **cc** selects the messages by the name of the person, or persons, in the message's cc field.

- ✔ **bcc** selects the messages by the name of the person, or persons, in the message's bcc field.

- ✔ **to or cc** selects the messages by the name of the person, or persons, in the message's To or cc field.

- ✔ **body or subject** lets you enter a criteria that Notes will look for in both the subject and body of the messages.

- ✔ **Internet domain** lets you specify messages from a particular type of address on the Internet, such as `yahoo.com` or `aol.com`.

- ✔ **size** applies your rule to messages based on how big or small they are.

After you've told Notes where to look, you use the second drop-down field in the Specify Condition section of the dialog box to tell Notes what kind of comparison you're going to establish:

- ✔ **contains** means that the term you will enter in the third field can occur anywhere in the field you selected in the first field.

✔ **does not contain** means that whatever you chose in the first field can't contain what you'll enter in the third field.

✔ **is** means that whatever you chose in the first field must be exactly equal to what you'll enter in the third field.

✔ **is not** means that whatever you chose in the first field can't be what you'll enter in the third field.

Finally, use the third field in the Specify Conditions section to tell Notes what you're looking for. Just type the search term — the person's name, the word you want to find in the message body, the Internet domain, and so on — in the third field.

When you have defined the three parts of the condition, click the Add button to save the condition. (After you do that, you can use the Remove and Remove All buttons if you've made a mistake. You have to select the condition in the When Mail Messages Arrive that Meet These Conditions field to remove it.)

Defining a rule's action

After you tell Notes on which messages the rule will act, use the Specify Actions section of the dialog box to determine what Notes will do with those messages. This is the part of the dialog box where you tell Notes that you want the messages to be moved to a certain folder, deleted, and so on.

This section of the dialog box has two fields: The first tells Notes what you want to do to the messages, and the second tells Notes where to put them.

You can do four things with a message that meets the condition you established at the top of the dialog box:

✔ **move to folder** tells Notes to move the matching messages to the folder (the name of which you enter in the second field or use the Choose Folder button to select).

✔ **copy to folder** is like move to folder, except the message also remains in your inbox.

✔ **change importance to** marks the message's importance as high, medium, or low — regardless of how the sender set the message's importance.

✔ **delete** does exactly what it sounds like it does — it removes the matching message.

After you've defined the rule's condition and action, click the OK button at the bottom of the New Rule dialog box to save it. Your new rule will appear in the Rules view in your mail.

Managing rules

As you may have noticed back in Figure 8-3, the Rules view in your mail lists, in order, all the rules you have defined. You could have a few rules that both select the same message — maybe one does something with mail from stevo@tiac.net, and the other does something to all messages from the Internet domain tiac.net. Use the action bar's Move Up and Move Down buttons to determine which rule gets first crack at incoming mail.

You can also use the action bar's Edit Rule button if you need to change the rule's condition or action; use the Delete Rule button in the action bar to delete the thing altogether.

A new Rule applies to messages that arrive *after* you've created it, and it will *not* do anything to the mail you already have.

Your Personal N&A Book

Your personal name and addresss book is a special database that you already have, whether you realize it or not. You've probably noticed its bookmark.

Your personal N&A book is just a miniature version of the large public directory on the Domino server. Your personal N&A book makes your life easier in two ways:

✔ You can add contacts, which make addressing mail to certain people easy. This is especially helpful for people who have complicated addresses from other e-mail systems. These contact documents also give you a place to store information such as phone number and office address.

✔ You can also create groups, which are used to send a message to a bunch of people at the same time.

Adding a contact to your personal N&A book

To add a person to your personal N&A book, open it by clicking its bookmark, and then click the action bar's Add Contact button. Figure 8-5 shows the New Contact form.

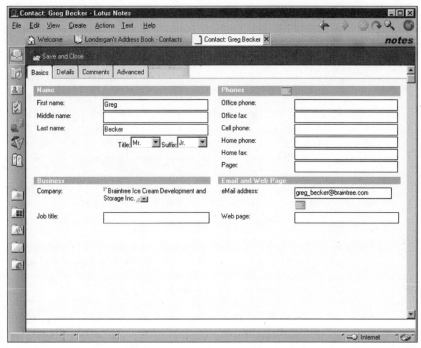

Figure 8-5:
Adding a
contact.

As you can see, you can use the Contact form to store such information as your friend's home address and zip code. That's all well and good, but if you're creating a contact to hold your friend's e-mail address, just concern yourself with the following fields:

- **First name/Last name** aren't for Notes; they're for you. These two fields are where you type the person's real, spoken name. What you type in these fields for the person's name is what you enter in the To field of a memo when you want to send the person e-mail.

- **Email address** is the most important field of all. In this field, type the exact e-mail address for the person you'll be sending mail to.

After you fill out the preceding fields, save the document by clicking the action bar's Save and Close button.

Creating a group in your personal N&A book

Friend, do you find yourself often sending a message to the same group of people? Are you getting sick of typing each person's name every time you want to send them all a memo? Well then step right up, because we have a trick that's guaranteed to make your life easier.

When you create a *group* in your personal N&A book, you can use the name of the group to send a message to that bunch of people. To add a group to your personal N&A book, open the database, click the Groups view, and then click the action bar's Add Group button. Then you fill in the form shown in Figure 8-6.

The most important (and only required) fields on this form are the Group Name and Members fields. In the Group Name field, you enter the name of the group, which can be any combination of letters and numbers. Because the Members field is a keyword field, you can click that little triangle next to the field to use the Names dialog box, as shown in Figure 8-7. This is a great way to make sure you spell all the names correctly!

Keep your group names short, so that they're easy to type and easier to remember.

In the Members field, you enter the names of the people whom you want to receive messages that you send to the group. You can put in as many names as you want, and you can include addresses of people who don't use Notes (as discussed in previous sections of this chapter).

After filling out these fields listed, click the action bar's Save and Close button. Then you can use the name of the group in any To, cc, or bcc field. That's all there is to it!

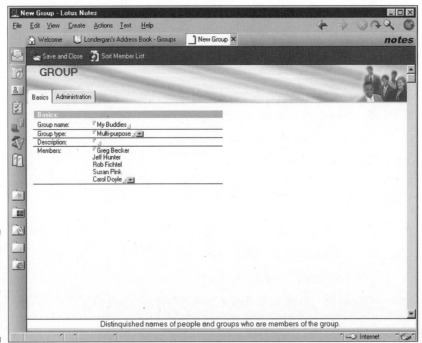

Figure 8-6:
Adding a
group to
your
personal
N&A book.

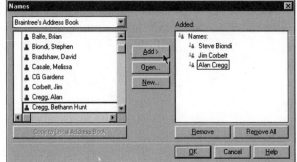

Figure 8-7:
Use the
Names
dialog box
to choose
names.

The Contacts and Group documents in your personal N&A book work only on your computer; your friend next door can't send a message to a group if it's defined in your personal N&A book. If everyone at your company needs to send mail to a certain group name, ask your administrator to add the group to the *public* directory.

I Need a Vacation

You work hard, and you certainly deserve a break. A week of fun and sun? Heading to Jamaica or the Bahamas? Great! Be sure to change the message on your office answering machine, so callers know that you're away from the office. You have to keep up your reputation for responsiveness, after all.

And while you're at it, set up your mail database so that Notes automatically replies to any mail you get while you're on the beach.

1. **Open your inbox.**

2. **Click the action bar's Tools button, and then select Out of Office.**

   Up pops the dialog box displayed in Figure 8-8, so you can tell Notes how you want to handle your mail while you're away.

3. **In the Leaving and Returning fields of the Dates tab, type the dates you'll be gone.**

   Notes automatically replies to any mail you receive during this period. You can also use the Book Busytime for these dates check box if you use group calendaring and you would like your schedule to reflect your imminent departure.

4. **Fill out the fields on the Basic Message, Special Message, and Exclusions tabs.**

   See the rest of this section for all that this step entails.

5. **Click the Enable button.**

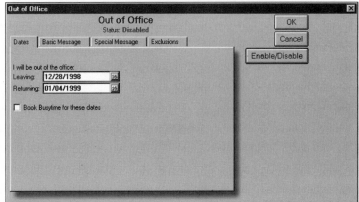

Figure 8-8:
Telling
Notes
you're
away.

Entering your profile involves answering three questions on the other three tabs of the Out of Office dialog box:

- ✔ What message should Notes send to most people?

- ✔ Which message should go to some special people?

- ✔ Which people shouldn't get one of these automatic replies?

On the Basic Message tab, type the subject and body of the message that you want Notes to automatically send to the majority of the messages you receive. Figure 8-9 shows a sample response, but feel free to say anything you want.

You may decide to send a different, special reply to certain people. Maybe you want a unique message for your boss or your coworkers? Enter the names of these special people on the Special Message tab.

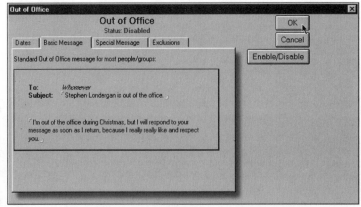

Figure 8-9:
This reply
goes out to
most
people.

Click the arrow next to the To field on the Special Message tab to choose people and group names from your personal N&A book.

Some messages may not deserve any response; use the Exclusions tab to tell Notes who doesn't get an automatic reply while you're away. As you can see in Figure 8-10, you can tell Notes to pretty much ignore messages from the Internet, or from a certain person, or addressed to certain groups, or containing a certain word or phrase in their subject.

Figure 8-10: Defining exclusions so that some messages don't prompt an automatic response while you're on vacation.

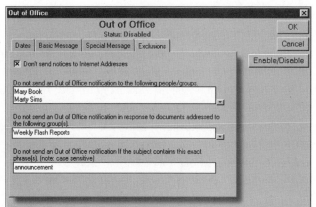

If you subscribe to any Internet-based mailing lists, be sure to include their name on the Exclusions tab. If you don't, every message you receive from the mailing list triggers one of your automatic responses, which might very well end up being sent to the whole list, over and over again.

When you finish entering your profile, click the Enable/Disable button on the action bar. Select the name of your home Domino server from the Server Name dialog box.

Don't forget to turn off your automatic replies after you return from your little vacation. When you're back at the office and ready to start replying to e-mail yourself, click the Disable button on the Out of Office dialog box so that Notes stops sending messages for you.

Reusing the Same Memo

If you find yourself regularly sending essentially the same memo to essentially the same people, you may want to create *stationery*. Then, next week, when the time comes to send your regular message again, you won't need to create a new message. Instead, you edit the stationery, which has the names, subject, and so on already filled in. And the week after that, you do the same thing. And the week after that, and the week after that. . . .

Creating stationery

Creating stationery is really just a matter of filling out the address fields (To, cc, bcc) and the Subject field, typing the part of the memo that's the same each time you send it, and then saving the document in a special way. Here are the nitty-gritty steps:

1. **Start creating a new memo.**

2. **Enter the appropriate names in the To, cc, and bcc fields and a topic in the Subject field.**

   Don't worry if this information will vary from time to time. You can change these fields each time you use this stationery to send a message.

3. **In the Body field of the stationery, enter the parts of the message that you want to send each week.**

4. **When you're finished, choose File⇨Tools⇨Save as Stationery and enter a name for your stationery document in the Save as Stationery dialog box.**

Don't get confused by the memo form you see when you create stationery. Despite all appearances to the contrary, you are not entering the text of a real e-mail. Rather, you are entering the parts of the message that you'll be sending on a regular basis *later*.

Using stationery

When the time comes to send an e-mail based on your stationery, open your inbox and click the action bar's Tool button. Then click the New Memo⇨ Using Stationery button.

Select the stationery you want to use and then add whatever you want to the To, cc, bcc, and Subject fields as well as to the body of the message. When you send your e-mail, Notes saves a *new* document in your mail database and leaves the stationery document just the way it was when you started — so you can use it again next time.

Special Options for a Message

Chapter 4 discusses such delivery options as importance, mood stamps, delivery reports, and delivery priority. You can find even more advanced options on the Advanced tab of the Delivery Options dialog box (see Figure 8-11).

If you need a response by a particular date, use the Stamp Message with a "Please reply by" Date field to warn your recipient. The date you enter in this field appears at the top of your e-mail, and the message you send is also placed in the recipient's To Do view.

As Figure 8-11 shows, you can do a favor for the people you're sending your message to by indicating that your message has an expiration date. Doing so helps the readers determine which messages to delete if they are cleaning up their mail database or mail archive.

When you use your mail database to create a reply to a message, Notes automatically puts the name of the person who sent you the e-mail in the first place in the To field. If you're sending a message but want replies to come back to someone other than you, use the Replies to This Memo Should Be Addressed to field to enter the name of the person who should receive replies to your message.

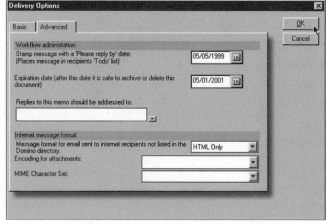

Figure 8-11:
The
Advanced
tab on the
Delivery
Options
dialog box.

Part III
Delving into
Databases

The 5th Wave   By Rich Tennant

©RICHTENNANT

CYBER Cafe

"Would you like Web or non-Web?"

In this part . . .

Important as it is, mail is only one part of the miracle that is Notes. The other work you do in Notes involves Notes databases. Your mail is contained in a database, so you already know a fair amount about how databases work in Notes (assuming you've read Part II, that is). The purpose of Part III is to let you peer into the heart of a database and discover what makes it tick.

The next chapters guide you through the maze of database features and then show you how you can add some touches of your own. *Caution:* Reading this part can cause you to use each database you encounter more efficiently, to tinker with various parts of a database, and to gain the skills that propel many database designers on to fame and fortune.

Chapter 9

It's Databasic

*W*e've said it before, and it deserves to be said again, "Notes is a database program." But what does that mean? In the simplest terms, a Notes database is nothing more than a collection of documents. But the unique nature of Notes enables you to share those databases and their documents with other Notes users just down the hall or scattered all over the world. In this chapter, we look under the hood of the average database and make sure that you can recognize what you see there. We also show you how to find and start databases.

A Notes database can be a directory of the people in your company, a series of hot sales leads, or a discussion forum in which people overcome their reluctance to express their opinions on any number of topics and respond to each others' opinions. One way or the other, Notes databases enable you to interact with people in ways you've never thought of — and with people you've never thought of, either.

How to Speak Database like a Native

You're much more comfortable in a country when you speak the language. The same is true when you enter the world of databases. So here's a list of the types of words you routinely hear from people who are fluent in the database language:

✔ A *database* is a collection of information. Most of the Notes databases you'll use aren't on your computer but rather on a Notes server somewhere.

✔ A *document* is what's in a Notes database. Notes documents are composed and saved by people, at least one of whom looks just like you. You can read and sometimes edit other people's documents.

✔ A *form* is a part of a database that you use to view, compose, and edit documents. Filling in a form creates a document.

✔ A *view* is a table listing the documents in a database. A view displays documents in a database, but not necessarily all of them. One database can have many views, so you may have one view that shows just your customers in California and another view that lists your customers by shoe size. Yet another view might display documents that have nothing to do with your customers, such as a list of companies that are hot sales prospects.

✔ A *field* is a place where you grow turnips. In a database, a field is a place where you enter data. When you're composing or editing a document, each field is marked by little L-shaped brackets or by a box in which you enter data or make choices. Notes boasts fourteen kinds of fields. You can consult the following list if anyone ever asks you what they are:

- Authors
- Check box
- Combo box
- Date/Time
- Dialog list
- Formula
- List box
- Names
- Number
- Password
- Radio button
- Readers
- Rich text
- Text

✔ The *data* is whatever information you or someone else entered into a field when composing or editing a document in a database.

So, putting it all together, you could open the Company Personnel *database,* compose a new *document* using the Personnel Information *form,* type **Ted Farrell** in the Full Name *field,* and then enter some other *data* and save the whole thing in the database as a new document that will be listed in the All Employees by Name *view.* Then you can go out and plant a turnip.

Finding a New Notes Database

Your boss — communicating with you through Notes e-mail, of course — tells you to start using a particular Notes database to respond to customer inquiries. Although you've heard other people in the department talking about this database, you've never used it before. What do you do?

Get the specifics. As an employee, you aren't expected to know about the existence of every database in use in the organization or where each one is located. Don't expect to find the database in question on your hard disk; databases are usually placed on a server somewhere so everyone can use them. After all, databases aren't *yours;* they're *ours.*

Ask your boss or a coworker for both the database's name *and* the server's name before you try to find it. Knowing its filename may be helpful, too; often several databases have similar names — Customer Tracking, Customer Data, Customer Leads. Knowing the filename guarantees that you are accessing the right database.

Whenever you need to open a database that you haven't used before, just follow these steps:

1. **Choose File⇨Database⇨Open.**

   Selecting this command gives you the dialog box displayed in Figure 9-1.

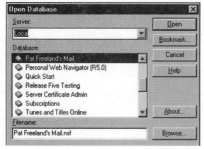

Figure 9-1:
The Open
Database
dialog box.

2. **Look in the text box under the word *Server*.**

   In Figure 9-1, this text box says Local. If you're using a Mac, that space says Notes Data Folder instead of Local. The Local (or Notes Data Folder) server is the one you want if the database you're seeking is on your own hard disk.

3. **If you're looking for a database that isn't on your hard disk, click the down arrow across from the word in the Server text box.**

   You now see the names of one, a few, or lots of Notes servers, depending on how your administrator has set up Notes at your company. If you don't see the name of the server you're after, use the scroll bar to move down the list.

If you're looking for a database on your own computer but are having trouble locating it, use the Browse button to search the various nooks, crannies, and directories on your hard disk to find it. Remember that you will be seeing the filename — the name used to store it on disk — not the name the database designer gave it for display in Notes.

4. Select the server you want by clicking its name.

The Database list changes according to the server you choose.

When you click the name of a server in the Server list box, a list of the databases on that server appears in the Database list box. Double-click the database you want or highlight it and click the Open button. If you aren't sure which of several databases with similar titles you want, check the file name in the Filename text box.

5. Under Database, select the database you want by double-clicking its name or by highlighting it and clicking the Open button.

If you aren't sure which of several databases with similar titles you want, check the file name in the Filename text box.

If your company has other Notes servers in different groups, their names won't appear in the Open Database dialog box. If you're trying to find a server that's not on your list, try typing the server's name in the Server text box and clicking Open. If that doesn't work, contact your administrator.

I hear you knocking, but . . . (certification problems)

As you might imagine, your administrator has all kinds of tricks to determine which people get to use which servers. If you ever double-click a server name in the Open Database dialog box and get an error message that says either `Your ID has not been certified to access the server` or `You are not authorized to use the server`, it probably means your administrator has to do something to allow you to use that server. You can't do anything to correct this problem, so send your administrator an e-mail to ask for access. Be sure to cc: your boss so that your administrator knows that you're not kidding around here.

To be able to use a server, both your user ID and the server's user ID must have a common certificate. Giving out these certificates is one of the many jobs your administrator does all day. So, if Notes ever tells you that you don't have the right certificate to use a particular server, contact your administrator, who should be able to correct the problem. For more information about certificates, see Chapter 14.

Sometimes, for all sorts of reasons, database designers flip a switch in a database so that the database won't appear in the Database list. In this case, you have no way of seeing the name on your computer, so you have to ask a living, breathing person for the filename. Then you can type that filename in the Filename text box to open that database.

Servers, servers, everywhere

You're on a quest to find a Notes database and you know it's on a server. But which server? Most companies have more than one. Your company may have one server with databases belonging to the marketing department, another with databases for sales, and so on. You get the idea. Some companies have hundreds of Notes servers, some have a few, and some have only one server (for now).

When you're trying to find a new Notes database, knowing where to start looking can be tough. If your boss didn't tell you which server to use, be adventurous: Just start looking on the various servers until you find the database in question. And, hey, you just might come across some *other* Notes databases that interest you.

The server names you see in the Open Database dialog box are based on the whim of your administrator. The names may be functional (and grown-up), such as Marketing or Sales. Or they might be more imaginative, such as Sleepy, Bashful, Doc, or Grumpy (bet you can't name all seven). When push comes to shove, though, you should ask someone which server you're supposed to use. Searching for a particular database can make you feel as though you're looking for hay in a needle stack.

Fumbling in folders

Just as you have folders (subdirectories) on your hard disk to help you organize your files, your administrator may set up folders on the server to help organize the databases. If your server has folders, they appear at the bottom of the list of database titles, as the directories named doc, domino, and gtrhome do in Figure 9-2. An additional hint that something is a folder rather than a database is that its icon is a folder.

Figure 9-2:
At the
bottom of
the list of
databases,
you may find
folders
containing
more
databases.

To see a list of the databases in a particular folder, double-click its name. You can use the item on the list that looks like an up arrow with two periods to return to the parent folder on the server.

Bookmark or Open, which is right?

When you've located the correct server and database in the Open Database dialog box, you have two choices:

- ✔ Open the database right away.
- ✔ Bookmark the database so that you can open it easily later.

If you want to open the database now, click Open (or double-click its title, which has the same effect). Notes does four things:

- ✔ First, it adds that database to the list of bookmarked databases in your Databases folder so you can open it in future Notes sessions without having to go through these steps again.
- ✔ Second, it adds the database to your workspace (which is also in the Databases folder), giving you another way to open the database in future sessions.
- ✔ Third, it closes the Open Database dialog box.
- ✔ Finally, it opens the database you chose.

If, instead, you want to bookmark the database and open it later, click the Bookmark button. When you do, you see the dialog box in Figure 9-3. Use this dialog box to determine where the icon for the new database appears:

Figure 9-3:
In this
dialog box,
you
determine
where the
icon for
the new
database
appears.

✔ By default, the new database is listed in the Databases folder. To designate a different folder, choose a folder in the Add To list box.

✔ If you would like a new folder for your new icon, click New Folder and
type a name for the new folder in the Name text box of the dialog box
that appears. Click OK and the database is added to the workspace and
to your new folder.

Notice what *didn't* happen? The database did not open. It's not supposed to.
Why? You are still looking at the Open Database dialog box. You have a
chance to open or bookmark more databases. The Bookmark button is useful
if you need to collect a few databases and you want to get them all in the
same trip to the Open Database dialog box. Opening each database individually and then returning to the dialog box to open another one can be quite
time consuming and cuts into the things for which you were really hired —
having meetings and doing power lunches. (Or is it *doing* meetings and
having power lunches?)

After you've bookmarked all the databases you need, choose Cancel. Yes,
Cancel. Despite what you might be thinking, Cancel will not undo all your
hard work, it just closes the dialog box.

Whichever method you choose, opening the database or bookmarking, the
next time you want to get into this database, you won't have to go searching
for it in the Open Database dialog box. You'll be able to just double-click the
database's icon from your desktop or bookmark folder.

In a word-processing program, you simply open a document and start reading. Before you open a document in Notes, however, you must open the
database in which that document is contained.

If you add a database to a list and later don't want it there, right-click (we
should say click the secondary mouse button to be politically correct) the
name of the database you want to remove from the list. From the menu that
appears, click Remove from Bookmarks. A confirm prompt appears, asking
whether you really want to remove the database from your bookmarks. Click

Yes and the offending item is gone from the list. You can always add it back if you need to. To remove a database from the workspace, click it once and press the Delete key. Answer Yes and the icon is gone.

About About . . .

The list of database titles on a server can be long, confusing, and not always helpful. If you want to open the company's sales database and you see listed such names as Sales Regions, Sales Forecasts, and Sales Accounts, it might be difficult to know which one to choose. The database's so-called About document (more specifically called About this Database) might give a clue as to what the database contains and what it is used for. So, click About, and if the database creator wrote an About document, you can see whether the highlighted database is the one you want. If there is no About document, you get a message saying `Special database object cannot be located`. Oh well, it never hurts to try.

The Database Door Creaks Open

What's inside a database? That depends.

If you're opening a database for the first time ever, you see what the database designer decides first-time users should see. It might be the About document, a graphic Navigator with places to click to move to important areas of the database, a view that lists some of the more important documents in the database, or a single document the designer thinks you need to see first.

Most often, the first thing you see is the About document, written by the database designer or by the person who commanded the designer to create the database. Of course, some database designers are more conscientious than others, so some About documents are more instructive than others. In fact, a lazy database designer might not create an About document, so don't be surprised if you occasionally see a blank screen when you open a new database. If that happens, just press Esc to dismiss the blank About document, and chances are you will be in the database.

Out of sight, out of mind: Finding the About document later

After you use a database for a few months, you'll probably forget all about the About document. After all, you saw it only once — the first day you used the database. Because the About document could have lots of useful information, you may want to refer to it in the future, especially if you dismissed it quickly the first time you saw it. Don't worry, the About document is always close at hand. Just choose Help⊃About This Database, and — bingo — there it is.

After carefully reading and dismissing the About document screen, you see one of the views in the database. The view you see might be just one of several tables of contents of the database, but it's the view that the designer of the database decided you should see first.

A database might have several views, and many views don't contain all the documents in a database. Under Folders and Views, in the upper-left pane of the screen, you see a list of other folders and views you can use. (We unveil the mysteries of folders and views in Chapter 10.)

Unless the person who designed your database decided otherwise, each time you open a database (after the first time, that is), you see the view or folder you were using the last time you were in that database. Notes is pretty good about remembering what you were doing the last time you were there, even if you aren't.

Opening a Database on the Internet or Intranet

Opening a database on the Web is a bit easier than opening a database in Notes. Crank up your favorite browser, type the URL for the database, and you see first time and every time what the designer wants you to see when you open the database. Your browser forgets what you were doing the last time you visited this database, so you start at the initial screen every time and navigate from there.

That first screen is either a list of views or a map of the database, or it's an opening page with places to click to dig further into the database, create documents, or get more information before you move on.

When You Need Help

Sometimes you try to do something and get caught halfway through the procedure, unsure of the next step. Or maybe you're trying to figure out how to do something new. Look to any of these places for a helping hand:

- ✔ The built-in Help feature in Notes
- ✔ The Using document, which is in every database
- ✔ Your Notes manual
- ✔ This book
- ✔ Your friends

Notes, help!

Notes has a help system that you can use in two ways: You can ask for help about the particular activity you're stuck with, or you can peruse the entire Notes Help database.

Using context-sensitive help

Press F1 anytime, anywhere, for help with what you are currently doing.

Good news: Like most software these days, context-sensitive help is always just a keystroke away in Notes. Whenever you get stuck, you can always press F1 (or the help key on a Mac), and Notes will do its best to show you a help screen that's related to whatever you're doing at the time. As always, you press Esc to close the Help document.

Bad news: The context-sensitive help in Notes will not give you database-specific help. That's because the help that comes with the program deals only with how to use the Notes program, not any particular database. The developers who make Notes are smart, but they have no way of knowing what kind of databases will be created by the thousands of worldwide database designers. When you have a question about the particulars of an application you're using, you have to get to the database's own help screen. Getting database-specific help is covered later in this chapter, under "Turning to a database's Using document."

Reading the Help database

Got a few minutes before your next meeting? All the screens you see when you press F1 come from a Notes database called, appropriately enough, Notes Help. You can rifle through the documents in the Help database the way you read any other database. They have lots of information that you may never even think to ask about with the F1 key.

To use Notes help, use the menu and choose Help.

Turning to a database's Using document

Every database has a *Using document,* which is similar to the About document described previously in this chapter. Like the About document, the Using document (if there is one) is created by the person who designed the database and is intended to help you figure out how to use the database. To see a database's Using document, you have to open the database in question and then choose Help⇨Using This Database.

Some application developers (but not the good ones) are lazy, so don't be surprised if you occasionally see a dialog box that says `No help is available for this database` when you try to see a database's Using document. If this happens to you, call the database designers with your questions. When these folks get sick of answering the same questions over and over again, they might decide to create an overdue Using document.

Dusting off your Notes manuals

Of course, we can't ignore the Notes manuals, which contain everything you ever wanted to know about Notes. Come to think of it, they probably contain *more* than you ever wanted to know about Notes. If you didn't receive a set of Notes manuals when you got the program, give a call to your administrator.

When all else fails, read the manual.

Using this book

Despite the title of the book, we think you were positively brilliant for buying this book. We hope you'll use it as a reference all through your career with Notes. Our intent was to organize the information in such a way that you can find what you need quickly.

You should tell your friends, your coworkers, and your boss about this book. Shouldn't everyone in your company have a copy? *Lotus Notes R5 For Dummies* makes a great gift, too. Imagine the squeals of delight when your children see their own copies decoratively wrapped next to their birthday cakes. Maybe you should buy a couple of extra copies, just to be safe.

Calling on your friends

Given the fact that Notes is *group*ware, it's safe to say that a whole group of people are using Notes at your company, and any one of them (or at least the friendly ones) can be a great resource for help and tips. Don't discount their importance! You can call them, e-mail them, or ask them questions in the cafeteria line.

Many companies even have a special Notes database just so people can ask each other how to use Notes. If your company doesn't have such a database, maybe you should suggest that your administrator create one. If you tell your administrator that such a database would keep you from calling the help desk as often, we bet that the database will appear within the hour!

Chapter 10

Using Databases

*W*hen you open a database, you get your first glimpse of the contents of the database itself. (Check out Chapter 9 for more information about opening databases and About documents.) Depending on what the designer decided you should see when you first open the database, you might wonder "Where do I go from here?" This chapter gives you an idea of what you might see and tells you how to change the appearance of the screen and how to burrow even deeper into the database.

A database designer might set up a database for your first view in one of several ways, so don't be surprised if what you see looks different from what the paragraph you are reading says you might see. That's why we use the words *might see* rather than *will see*. Each database can be designed differently, so read the whole chapter before you start to think we've really lost our marbles. Also, the way a database looks on the Web will probably be different from the way it looks in Notes, and this chapter is about how a database looks *in Notes*.

I Was Just Thinking of View

Every database has at least one view, and most databases have several. A database view does three things:

- ✔ It *summarizes* the documents in the database.
- ✔ It *sorts* the documents in the database.
- ✔ It *selects* at least some documents in the database for display.

Figure 10-1 shows a view in a database that lists various requests. This view is showing (or *selecting*) requests for training only. Requests for supplies or service are not included in this view. This view sorts the documents by the course category and then by the name of the specific course the person is requesting. This view also summarizes the documents by showing additional information (requester's name and the date and location of the course). It's a safe bet that each of the documents selected here has more information than this particular view displays in its columns; the designer of the view decided that this selected information best summarized each document.

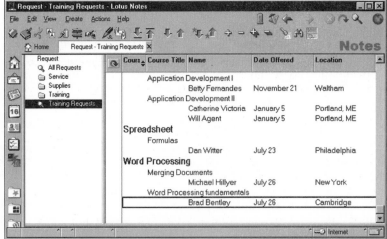

Figure 10-1:
This view shows only training requests in a request database.

What's in a view, anyway?

Each line (row) in a view represents an individual document, and each column represents information contained in that particular document. (We discuss the nitty-gritty details of documents and fields in Chapter 9.) Some views might show alternate lines in a different color, as in Figure 10-1, because the database designer took pity on the users of the view and realized it's difficult to see what data is on what line.

Each column in a view displays the value of a particular field in the document. For example, in Figure 10-1, the first column displays the type of course employees want to take, the second column lists the specific course title, the third column has the name of the person requesting the course, and so on.

Often, the database designer makes it possible for users to change the width of a column. Click and drag the right-hand border of a column head to the left to narrow the column or to the right to widen it.

When the stars come out

In many databases, Notes tracks which documents you have read and which ones you haven't. This distinction is particularly helpful in a discussion database, where you don't want to waste time on the documents you've already read. You can *usually* tell that a document is new (or at least that you haven't read it) because it's a different color from the rest of the documents. A document that you haven't read before *always* has a little star next to it, in the leftmost column of the view.

Usually, unread documents are red. But don't be surprised if they're some other color. The database designer gets to decide what color they are.

Response documents are documents composed by users to, you guessed it, respond to another document in a database. Most databases, like the one shown in Figure 10-2, display response documents indented under the document they are responding to.

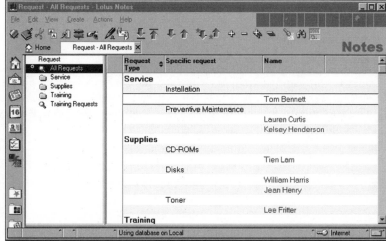

Figure 10-2: The documents are sorted and categorized in this view.

A Sort of Category

Views are great for sorting documents. With the help of the sort feature, you can list documents in a given database in whatever order you choose: by the course type, by the employee name, or by sales results, for example. Some views enable you not only to sort but also to *categorize*.

When a view *sorts* its documents, it lists them in alphabetical or numerical order according to what they have in a particular field, and it shows what each document has in that field even if it's the same as what the document above it has. On the other hand, when a view *categorizes* its documents, it still sorts the documents, but it lists a particular field value only once, followed by all the documents that have the same value in that field.

Confused? It's easier to see than it is to read. Take a look at Figure 10-2, in which you can see all requests entered in the database. Of the three requests for Service, one is for Installation and two are for Preventive Maintenance. In this view, all service requests are listed together, as are specific types of service. If it weren't for categories, the word *Service* and the specific requests would appear in every row. That's one for the Department of Redundancy Department.

Put on your glasses or squint and then look carefully at the heading of the first column in Figure 10-2. See the little double arrowhead? When you see one or two arrowheads, it means that the thoughtful database designer has given you the ability to re-sort the column. In other words, if the column is arranged in ascending alphabetical order, for example, clicking anywhere in that column heading changes the sort order from ascending *(A to Z)* to descending *(Z to A)*.

One of the reasons that views have categories is to make the view a little neater and easier to look at. You can further neaten a view by *collapsing* and *expanding* categories.

In Figure 10-2, the entire view is expanded. In Figure 10-3, the Service category is completely expanded, the Supplies category is completely collapsed, and the Training category is expanded, but its subcategories are collapsed. The documents are still there, and they'll appear like magic when you expand a category.

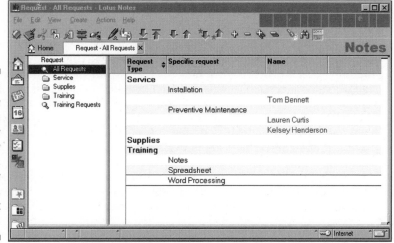

Figure 10-3:
This view
has one
category
completely
collapsed,
one partially
collapsed,
and one not
collapsed.

Okay, how do you do it? It's easy, but it depends on what you want to expand or collapse.

Here are the ways to expand or collapse *a single category:*

- ✔ Highlight the category in question and choose View➪Expand/Collapse. Then choose either Expand Selected Level, Expand Selected & Children, or Collapse Selected Level. (If you have visions of little flat children running around your neighborhood, you missed the point about Expand Selected & Children. It means expand the current category and its sub-categories.)

- ✔ It's even easier to press + (the plus key) to expand a selected section or - (the minus key) to collapse a selected section.

- ✔ Best yet, rather than trying to remember all that, just double-click the category you want to expand or collapse, or highlight the category and press Enter.

Here are the ways to expand or collapse *the whole view:*

- ✔ Choose View➪Expand All or View➪Collapse All.

- ✔ Press Shift + + (that's Shift and the plus sign) to expand the whole view or Shift + - (Shift and the minus sign) to collapse the whole view.

Using Folders as Holders

No doubt about it, views are great, and you won't hear us criticizing them. But they do have a disadvantage. You, the user, can't decide what should be in a view. Oh sure, if you know how to create a view selection formula, you can use it to determine what is and isn't included. But what if you want to store a bunch of documents of your own choosing together in one place? What if, for example, you want to put together all the documents that need your immediate attention or documents on a vague subject (such as industry trends) that might be hard to put in a formula in a view?

The answer to this penetrating question is . . . folders. Like views, *folders* can display some of the contents of a database. In the upper-left corner of the screen in Figure 10-4 is a list of folders and views under the name of the database, Request. For those who like a challenge, can you tell which are views and which are folders? (Hint: The symbol next to the names of folders and views are a folder and a magnifying glass, respectively.)

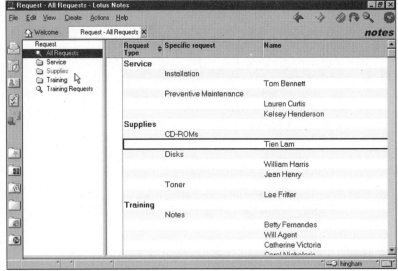

Figure 10-4:
This navigation pane lists folders and views.

The designer of the database might have created one or more folders for you to put stuff in. A folder, despite its name, can be used for anything you like. Chapter 14 shows you how to create and modify your own folders.

Keep the following important facts in mind as you use folders:

✔ You put documents in a folder by clicking and dragging a document from a view or a folder into a folder. You might also find a button somewhere on-screen that enables you to assign the selected document(s) to a folder.

✔ Putting a document in a folder does not create a new copy of the document; it just lists the document in a new place.

✔ You can remove one or more selected documents from a folder by choosing Actions⇨Remove from Folder. You might also have a button somewhere that allows you to remove a document from a folder.

✔ Removing a document using the preceding method does not delete it from the database. It simply removes it from the folder.

✔ Don't press the Delete key to delete a document from a folder. Pressing Delete removes it from the database permanently.

✔ There is no selection formula for a folder; what is in the folder is determined by you, the user.

✔ Folders, like views, have columns. Each column shows the contents of various fields in the documents. If you add a document to a folder, and that document doesn't contain any of the fields listed in the folder's columns, there won't be any data to display in the column, so you won't see the document listed there. The document will be represented by a blank line.

Odds are, you sometimes want to see the documents in a database listed in a different way. In other words, if you want to switch to a different view or folder, click its name. Give Notes a second or two, and the new choice opens.

So, What Can You Do with Documents?

Among the things you can do with documents in a view are

✔ Select them

✔ Read them

✔ Forward them

✔ Add them to a folder

✔ Print them

✔ Delete them

In this section, we give you tips on how to do all these things.

Selecting documents

You can do all kinds of things with documents — print them, delete them, forward them as e-mails — but first you need to select them.

How to select them one at a time

In a word processing program, if you want to make a word bold, you first select the word and then use some command to make the word bold. This concept applies also to selecting documents in a view. If a view has a few documents and you want to do something to one of them — print it, delete it, or recategorize it — you have to select it first.

By now, you've probably noticed that a box surrounds a single document in a view or a folder. It's called the *selection bar,* and you use it to highlight an individual document. The document in that box is thereby *selected.*

But what if I want more than one?

Funny you should ask. Suppose you want to print five documents in a view. Sure, you use the selection bar to select them, but how do you tell Notes that you want more than one? The easiest way to select multiple documents is to select the first document in question and then press the spacebar. When you do so, the document gets checked off in the far-left column of the view, as shown in Figure 10-5. If there are no check marks, the highlighted document is selected; if there are check marks, the documents with check marks are selected.

Figure 10-5: When you select a document, it gets a check mark next to it in the marker column.

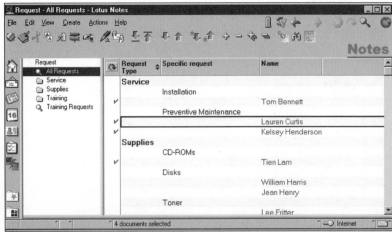

If you need to select a few documents, highlight each one and press the spacebar. If the documents you want are one after the other, it's a little easier to hold down Shift while you press the up- or down-arrow keys to move the selection bar over the documents. Notes checks them off as the highlight bar passes over them.

Better yet, if you use a mouse, you can select a bunch of documents all at once by clicking and dragging them over to the left column where you saw the check marks appear.

Finally, you can deselect a document that you mistakenly selected (oops!) by using any of the methods that you used to select it in the first place. In other words, if you have already checked off the document, selecting it again unchecks it.

Reading documents

If you have the preview pane visible, you can read a document simply by highlighting its line in the view pane. If you see only a tiny sliver of the document in the preview pane, increase the size of the preview pane by clicking and dragging its border. (For more on panes, see Chapter 3.)

Or, if you want the document to fill the screen, open the document by pressing Enter. If you have a mouse, you can just double-click to open the document for reading. You can then press Esc to close the document and return to the view.

Forwarding a bunch of documents

Every now and then, you want someone else to see a document you're reading. You can call them and tell them to open the Sales Database on the Marketing Server, use the Hot Prospects View, and check out the doc with the title, "This Guy Has a Million Dollars to Spend." But why not save the call and a lot of time and just send the document to that person? Highlight one document or select several documents, and then choose Actions⇨Forward. Enter the name of everyone who should see the documents and then send the memo. The selected documents become the body of the memo.

Adding documents to a folder

In the section, "Using Folders as Holders," we describe the process for adding documents to a folder. Be sure that the documents you add to a folder are visible in that folder. If the documents don't contain fields listed in the columns, the documents won't appear to be listed in the folder. There will be a blank line acting as a placeholder for the document that has no fields to display in the columns. Double-clicking the blank line will open the document.

Printing from a view

When you have a view or a folder (as opposed to a document) open, and you choose File⇨Print, you get the dialog box shown in Figure 10-6.

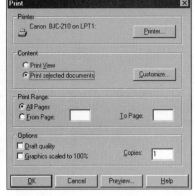

Figure 10-6:
The File
Print dialog
box appears
when you
choose to
print while a
view or a
folder is
visible.

This dialog box has a lot of stuff in it — and you might have even *more* options because what you see depends on the kind of printer you have.

The most important options in the dialog box are the ones in the Content area: Print View and Print Selected Documents. Use these options to specify whether you want to print the view as it appears on-screen or print the actual documents you have.

Use the other options to determine which pages to print, how many copies to print, and the quality of the print job. Click the Customize button to tell Notes how to separate the documents (new page, no separation, line), whether Notes should reset the page numbers for each document it prints, and whether to print using another form. It may be a good idea to click the Preview button to see on-screen what the printed page will look like. Check out Chapter 5 for more information about printing.

Deleting documents

To delete documents, select the document (or documents) that you want to get rid of and press Delete. The documents don't actually disappear, but each document gets marked with a little recycling bin, as shown in Figure 10-7.

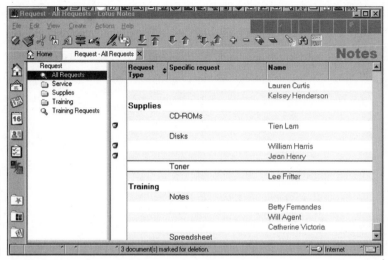

Figure 10-7:
Documents
selected for
deletion.

To actually dispose of the marked document, do one of the following:

✔ Press F9

✔ Choose View➪Refresh

✔ Close the database

If you try to take any of the preceding actions, Notes makes you confirm that you want to delete documents with a Yes/No dialog box. That's good, because you can choose No if you goofed.

If you've marked a document to be deleted (but haven't taken any steps to finalize the deletion) and you decide that you don't want to delete it after all, select the document and press Delete again. The trash can disappears. You can stop worrying, because that document's not going anywhere.

Of course, you can't necessarily delete a document just because you know how to use the Delete key. In fact, in most databases, you can delete a document only if you are the person who composed it in the first place. That means you can't delete anyone else's documents, and you don't have to worry about anyone else deleting your documents, either.

Chapter 11

Siftin' through the Docs in the Database

· ·

· ·

*T*he heart of any Notes database is the documents that are in it. (If you're familiar with a program such as Paradox or Lotus Access, documents are like records.) A *document* is all the information about a particular, well, a particular whatever. Here are some examples:

✔ If the database you're using is a purchase-tracking system, you might have one document for each customer and one document for each order the customer has placed.

✔ In your e-mail database, each document is a message.

✔ If you're using a discussion database, each separate comment on the topic at hand is a document.

✔ In a database full of pages from the Web, each page is a document.

We should also say right up front that we intend this chapter to be more of a reference than anything else, so you may not want (or need) to read it all in one sitting. Just turn to this chapter as questions arise.

A Document with All the Fixin's

When you open a document, you might see all kinds of things: words, pictures, icons, tables, buttons. If you want to be the resident Notes expert, read the following sections to find out what all these things are about.

Static text

No, static text doesn't have anything to do with rubbing your feet on a rug in the winter time. *Static text* just refers to words that are a permanent part of certain forms. Such text is called *static* because you can't change it.

The person who created the forms in the databases you use no doubt included some static text. Static text can be the title of the form, field names, or maybe some instructions about how to use the form. Take a look at Figure 11-1 to see some examples of static text. In this form, the static text is in bold and the fields filled in by the user are plain text. Of course, in the forms you use, the static text might not be bolded.

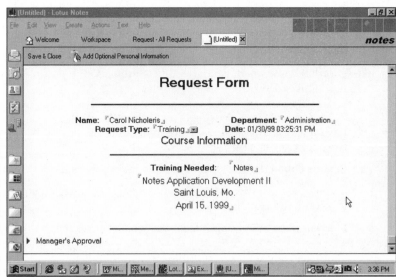

Figure 11-1:
Static text
helps you
figure out
what to do
with the
parts of a
document.

Fields

Fields are where the action is in a document. They contain the information that matters, the information that you can add and change when you're composing or editing a document. Fields come in a number of different flavors (not quite 31). Here are some of the types of fields you're likely to encounter:

- ✔ Text
- ✔ Keyword
- ✔ Rich text
- ✔ Date
- ✔ Numbers
- ✔ Names

If you have a Ph.D. in Notes, you probably know about other fancy fields and speak official fieldname-ese. As for the rest of us, these six field names will do just fine.

 When you're filling out a new document, you might not be able to tell the data types of the various fields. In other words, it's hard to tell, just by looking, whether a field is a date field or a number field or even a text field. Just use common sense; if the field's name is something like Quantity or Price, it's a safe bet that Notes expects you to enter a number. If the field is Address, you can bet it's a text field.

Put away your calculator: Editable versus computed fields

In most cases, when you compose a new document, the fields are empty, and your job is to type the new name, address, and so on. However, you might occasionally encounter a computed field. A *computed field* is a field for which the program automatically calculates the contents.

For example, suppose you're using a database that tracks customer orders, and it has three number fields: a Quantity field, a Price field, and an Extended Cost field. The database manager

has set up this Extended Cost field as a computed field so that, when you enter a value in the Quantity field and then enter a value in the Price field, Notes automatically multiplies the two and puts the answer in the Extended Cost field.

Computed fields are often *noneditable,* which means you can't make any changes to them. But in most cases, such as the preceding example, if your computer is automatically calculating the Extended Cost field, why would you want to change it?

Text fields

A text field is just what it sounds like. A *text field* can contain any combination of characters: letters of the alphabet, digits, punctuation, you name it. A text field might contain a customer's name, your colleague's street address, or a description of property for sale.

A text field can contain a maximum of about 7,000 characters. That's more than most people ever need to put in a text field, so don't worry about running out of space!

You might encounter a special area in a document, called a *section,* that can hide certain information in a document. On-screen, a section appears as a boldface title (sometimes a name) with a triangle to the left of it. To see the information hidden in a *collapsed* section, you must click the little triangle next to the section title. Sometimes, despite clicking the little triangle next to a section's title, you just can't get into it. In this case, the section you're trying to view is probably *protected.* You can't get into this section, but you can double-click the section title to see who *can* get in.

Keyword fields

Another special kind of text field is the keyword field. A *keyword field* is just a text field in which the possible entries have been set by the person who created the database. That's good news, because it means that (A) you don't have to type a keyword field's contents because you get to choose from a list of possible values, and (B) you don't have to worry about making a mistake in the field. Figure 11-2 shows an example of the types of keyword fields you are likely to encounter:

✔ **Dialog list:** The *dialog list field* looks an awful lot like a regular text field, but you can tell it's a dialog list field by the little arrow to the right of the field. When you click that little arrow (or press Enter in the field), you get a list of the possible values.

If the database designer chose to allow it, you may be able to choose more than one item or to enter an item not in the list. To tell whether you can choose more than one item, click one and then click another. If the first selection is unchecked, you are stuck with one. If you are allowed to add new items, you see a text box below the list. You may also be allowed to enter values that aren't in the list.

Combo box field   Check box field

Figure 11-2:
Keyword
fields save
you time
because
you can
choose a
value.

> Course Information
>
> Training Needed: ☒ Notes
>   ☐ Spreadsheet
>   ☐ Word Processing
>
> Bill To [▼] Department
>   Admin
>   Sales
> Course Desired: Marketing e Date: [February ▲▼]
>   IT
>
> Course Location: ○ San Francisco
>   ● Boston
>   ○ Austin

List box field

Radio button field

If you're using a dialog list field, you can press the spacebar to cycle
through available options. (Using the spacebar is a little faster than
using the dialog box.) You can also type the first letter of any of the
options to choose it, which is even faster.

✔ **Radio buttons:** In a *radio button field,* you can choose only one of the
options in the list. You select the value you want by clicking it or using
the arrow keys to highlight the option you want and then pressing the
spacebar to select it. You're stuck with the choices the designer gives
you. In Figure 11-2 the Course Location field is a radio button field.

✔ **Check boxes:** In a *check box field,* you can make more than one selection. Click as many of the values as you want, or highlight them with the
arrow keys and then use the spacebar to select them. In Figure 11-2,
Training Needed is a check box field.

✔ **List box:** Only one choice from the list is visible in a *list box field.* The
box containing the item allows the user to scroll up and down the list by
two small scroll arrows at the right side of the box. The designer can
allow you to choose more than one item. The Date field in Figure 11-2 is
a list box containing months.

✔ **Combo box:** The *combo box field* is a bit like the dialog list, but it's an empty box rather than field markers, and it comes with a down arrow at the right side of the field, outside of the field. The user clicks the arrow, the list appears, and the user makes the desired choice or choices. In this type of keyword field, the designer might decide to let you add items not in the list, but you can choose only one. The Bill To field in Figure 11-2 is a combo box.

Rich text fields

Rich text fields are what separate Notes from all the rest of the database programs in the world. *Rich text fields* are like regular text fields in that they often contain plain words and numbers. So, what's so rich about them, you ask? Well, in a rich text field (unlike a regular text field) you can use the Text menu to make words bold or italicized or a larger font. Just try that in a program such as dBASE or Paradox — or in a regular Notes text field, for that matter. It's also only in rich text fields that you can create the magic of embedded objects, file attachments, and pictures.

How do you tell the difference between a rich text field and a regular text field? You probably can't, or at least you can't by just looking at it. When you're creating a document, text fields don't *look* any different from rich text fields. But there is a subtle trick to determine whether a field is a regular text or rich text field. Put your cursor in the field in question and look at the status bar (at the bottom of the screen, if you forgot). If you see the font name, font size, and paragraph style there, it means it's a rich text field.

You can use the status bar to change the font, font size, and paragraph style in only a rich text field. So the status bar displays the font and font size only when you are in a rich text field.

It's default of de field

The person who created your database might save you some time (and typing) by including *default* values in some fields.

Suppose that most of your customers are from Maine (Ayeh). If you're lucky, someone has set up a default so that every time you compose a new Customer Profile, the State field already says Maine. You can change the State field if

you want to — after all, not *all* your customers are from Bangor — but think of all the typing you *don't* have to do for the people who are in Maine. Think of default values as suggestions.

Many Notes databases have default values in fields that hold things like area codes, state names, and author names. That's good, because these defaults can save you time and typing.

What's even more intriguing (well, moderately intriguing, anyway) is that a rich text field can also contain information from other programs. Using the powers of *object linking and embedding,* you can use a rich text field to store the contents of a Lotus 1-2-3 spreadsheet or perhaps a Microsoft Word document right in the middle of your Notes document. (See Chapter 17 if you want to read more on this topic.)

Often, a Notes document is a compound document. A *compound document* is a document that includes several objects. For example, you might put a document in a database to show your colleagues the progress you've made on a project you've been working on. In the body of the message, you include a Lotus 1-2-3 spreadsheet, a Freelance chart, and an audio recording of the new jingle. That's a compound document. Notes can include all that stuff in one rich text field.

Rich text fields can also contain attachments. You use attachments to include a computer file in a Notes document. In the old days, you would do your expenses in Lotus 1-2-3, print the spreadsheet, and then give the piece of paper to your boss for approval. Now, because you're using Notes, you can actually *attach* the spreadsheet to an e-mail message and get it to your boss electronically. We're one step closer to the paperless office! (But then we'll have to make paper planes out of old floppies.)

Any rich text field can hold many, many megabytes of information — you can send someone an e-mail and include in it a Lotus 1-2-3 worksheet, *and* a Microsoft Word document, *and* a copy of your CONFIG.SYS, *and* a scanned picture of your new baby.

Date fields

Date fields hold (you guessed it!) dates. You might be surprised to find out that you can also enter times in a date field. If you're using a database that tracks customer calls, for example, you might need to enter a date and a time.

The format you use to enter a date or a time depends on the way your computer was set up. If, upon trying to save a document, you get the error message Unable to interpret time or date, you probably used dashes when you should have you used slashes. Or maybe you used slashes when you should have used dashes! Try one way or the other to see which your computer accepts.

In case you should be wondering, Lotus assures us that Notes and Domino are completely Y2K compatible. That means you can use Notes and Domino into the next century, while ATMs swallow your card, your computerized watch runs backwards, and your credit card company tells you that you have owed them big bucks for 100 years and now owe two million dollars interest.

Number fields

Number fields hold numbers, pure and simple. Don't try to enter any non-number characters — such as slashes, dashes, letters, or smiley faces — in a number field. It's also not necessary to enter characters such as currency symbols — Notes strips them out if the database designer didn't want them there, and will add them there if the designer tells Notes the contents of the field should look like money.

Name Fields

Name fields are special because they hold a person's name for some kind of security reason. For example, most Notes documents have a computed field that automatically records the name of the person who composed the document. This feature allows people who read the document to know who wrote it, and it reminds Notes itself who should be able to edit the document later. (In many databases, you can edit a document only if you composed it yourself.)

You might occasionally encounter *editable name fields*. A database might have a field in which you must enter the name of the person who should receive your purchase requisition, for example. If you do someday find your cursor in an editable name field, just type the person's name as it would appear on his or her business card.

Buttons

In addition to static text, fields, and sections, you can count on running across *buttons* during your adventures with Notes. Buttons help you do things quickly. You've probably already used the buttons on the action bar while you were in your mail database. Well, you might also encounter such buttons right on the forms in some databases, like the one in Figure 11-3 that enables you to save and close the document.

If you see a button and you want to use it, click it. (That's pretty easy, right?) You can also use the arrows to select it and then press the spacebar to "push" the button.

Of course, what happens when you click a button depends on what the database designer has programmed that button to do.

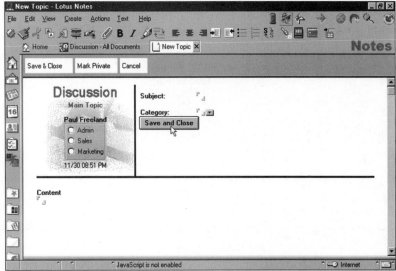

Figure 11-3:
Click a
button once
to use it.

Hotspots

A *hotspot* is a special part of a document that does something when you click it, just like a button. Clicking on a hotspot might display some tidbit of information or open a different document in a different database. To use a hotspot, click it, or select it with the arrow keys and press the spacebar.

Pop-ups

The most common kind of hotspot you'll encounter is called a *pop-up.* Pop-ups usually appear as text enclosed in a green box that you can click to display a reminder, a hint, or more information about a particular word or sentence. Press and hold down the mouse button anywhere in the green box to see the pop-up. (In Chapter 12, we explain how to create your own pop-up.) Figure 11-4 shows a hotspot that says "Need Help Ordering."

Some pop-ups are intended not to show you information but rather to take you somewhere. In Figure 11-4 the text `Link to our Complete Tunes List` is blue in real life, and takes anyone who clicks it to a list of all the tunes the company is selling.

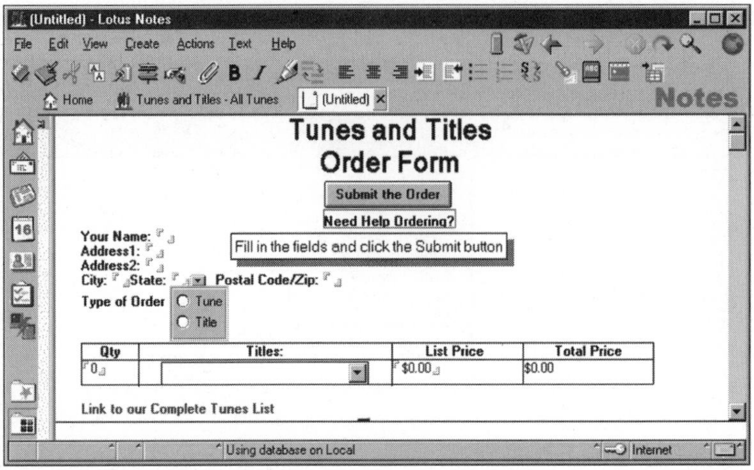

Figure 11-4:
When you
click and
hold on the
word(s)
inside the
hotspot box,
the pop-up
message
appears.

Another kind of pop-up doesn't show you anything and doesn't take you anywhere, either. This kind of pop-up usually has a green box around it (unless the designer chooses not to show the box) and it works very much like a button. When you click it, something happens. What exactly happens depends on a little computer program that somebody writes to work with the pop-up. A smart designer makes sure the text tells you what's going to happen using something clever like "Save and Close."

Links

A *link* is just a quick cross-reference to some other Notes data. It's represented by a small rectangular icon in the document. In Figure 11-5, the creator of the document suggesting a new product wants the readers to see another document he wrote, a view containing other similar documents, and a database containing related data. Rather than pasting all that stuff in the current document, and rather than typing complex instructions about opening and finding the information, he created a link to each.

To see the linked information, you simply click the link. When you're finished, press Esc to return to the document you were reading in the first place. Skip to Chapter 12 if you want to create your own links.

Objects

As you're reading a document, you might notice that it contains an *embedded object* (which is usually just called an *object*). More specifically, the document contains data from some other program; it might be a Lotus 1-2-3 worksheet, a few pages from a Microsoft Word document, or a QuickTime movie. Figure 11-6 shows a document that has one of these embedded objects.

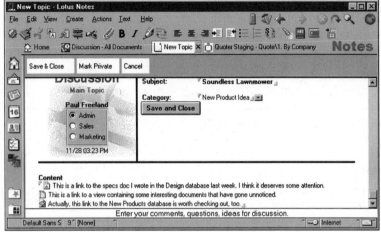

Figure 11-5:
Clicking a link opens other Notes data quickly.

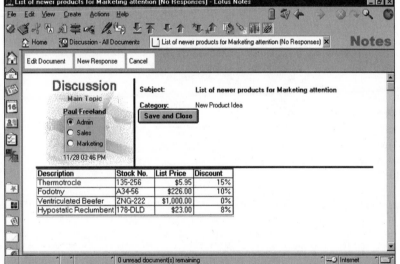

Figure 11-6:
The object in this Notes document is an embedded Lotus 1-2-3 spreadsheet.

Objects are useful for a couple of reasons:

✔ First, Notes displays the object in its original format. In other words, if someone has included an Excel spreadsheet in an e-mail, it looks like an Excel spreadsheet.

✔ Second, through the wonders of object linking and embedding (also known as OLE), when you double-click the object itself, Notes starts the program that created the original object and lets you review it (and maybe edit it) there. And, when you finish your edits, you can save the object back into the Notes database, not on your computer. That way, other people can read (and, if you want them to, edit) your work. Sound awesome? Check out Chapter 17 for more on embedding objects.

You must have the originating program installed on your computer to activate and edit an embedded object. In other words, you can't double-click a Lotus 1-2-3 spreadsheet to open it if you don't have Lotus 1-2-3 installed on your computer. If you don't have the original program, you'll be able to only look at the object; you won't be able to edit it.

Icons

Another way to include data from other programs in Notes documents is to use an *attachment*. If you're reading a Notes document and stumble upon an icon like the one in Figure 11-7, you've found an attachment.

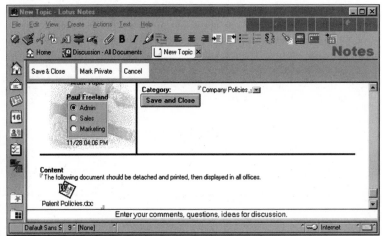

Figure 11-7:
This icon represents an attached file.

Double-click the icon to open the Attachment infobox, where you can decide to view, launch, or detach and save an attached file. Chapter 7 covers attached files in your mail database. Chapter 17 covers attached files in general.

Join the Party — Bring Your Own Document!

You've read a bunch of documents in a Notes database, and now you want to jump into the fray and make your own contribution — you're going to add your own new document.

You have to open the database in which you want to compose a new document before you start messing with the Create menu. More often than not, you'll already have a database open when you decide to create a new document — just make sure that you do, and that it's the database in which you want to create your document.

Using the Create menu

When you choose Create, Notes gives you a list of the documents you can create in that database, as shown in Figure 11-8.

Figure 11-8:
Use the Create menu to compose new documents in a database.

It just stands to reason that the list of documents you can compose from the Create menu varies from one database to the next. In your mail database, you can compose a memo or a reply; in a different database, you can compose different kinds of documents. We can't give you examples of their names, because the names of the documents depend on the databases you use.

Just finding the Create menu doesn't mean that you can actually compose documents in a given database. Some databases allow you to only read documents — not to compose your own. (Don't take it personally.)

Getting your inheritance from the right document

Does it matter which document is open when you compose a new one? The answer to that question is a definite maybe. Many databases have documents that rely on a feature called inheritance. *Inheritance* is a way for Notes to pass information from a document that's already in the database to the new one you're about to compose.

Suppose you have an Orders database. In it, you can compose two types of documents: a Customer Profile and a Customer Order. The database is already set up so that, when you compose a new Customer Order, Notes automatically fills in the name of the customer and other information about them. Notes accomplishes this feat by inheriting the values from the address fields of the Profile document that you selected when you composed your new order. If you don't have the right profile open (or highlighted in the view pane) before you try to compose a new order, you'll get the wrong address in your order.

The moral of this story is: You must have the right document open when you compose a new document if you're using a database that relies on inheritance to compute some fields.

If you're not sure whether you're allowed to compose documents, open the database in question and look in the status bar. If you see a little picture of eyeglasses, you can forget about the Compose menu — you have only *Reader* access to that database and consequently can only read the documents that other people have composed.

Call your administrator if you want to add documents to a database in which you have only Reader access.

Moving around in your new document

Moving around in a document is easy. As you enter values in your new document, press Tab to move from one field to the next. You can also use the arrow keys and the mouse to get from one field to the next.

You can't use Tab to move from a rich text field to the next field. You have to use the arrow keys or the mouse instead. If you press Tab in a rich text field, you move to the next tab stop in the field.

Saving your new document

When you've finished filling out the fields in your new document, press Esc. In the dialog box that appears, choose Yes to save your document in the database.

It's also a good idea to save the document often as you're composing it, in case you goof, the power fails, or your computer crashes. You can save a document anytime by choosing File⇨Save or by clicking the Save SmartIcon.

Abandoning your new document

What if you started composing a new document and now you've changed your mind and don't want to save it? Just press Esc and choose No from the Save dialog box. Presto — it's gone!

Playing by the rules

The person who created the database might have set some rules for the fields: Perhaps you can't leave certain fields empty, or perhaps a rule ensures that you enter one of the approved two-character state abbreviations. When you save a document, Notes validates what you have entered in the various fields against the rules (if any) that the database designer has set up.

Don't be surprised if you get a dialog box (like the one in Figure 11-9) when you try to save a document. This dialog box tells you what rule you've broken and insists that it's not going to let you save the document until you correct the problem. No big deal; click OK, correct your mistake, and then try to save the document again.

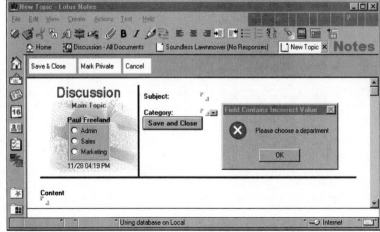

Figure 11-9: Some databases have rules that you have to satisfy before you can save a document.

A Document Catches Your Eye

Besides reading documents and entering new ones, you can also print a document, edit it, delete it, mail it, or put it in a Personal folder.

Print it

To print the document that you have open, click the Print SmartIcon or choose File➪Print. You get the File Print dialog box, as shown in Figure 11-10. You can decide which printer to use, how many copies to print, which pages you want to print, whether to print in draft quality (a faster but uglier choice), and whether to print graphics at 100 percent of their size, even if you changed their shape or size in the document. You might also want to preview the document before you print it. After you have checked out the appearance and made up your mind about the choices, click OK. And out it comes!

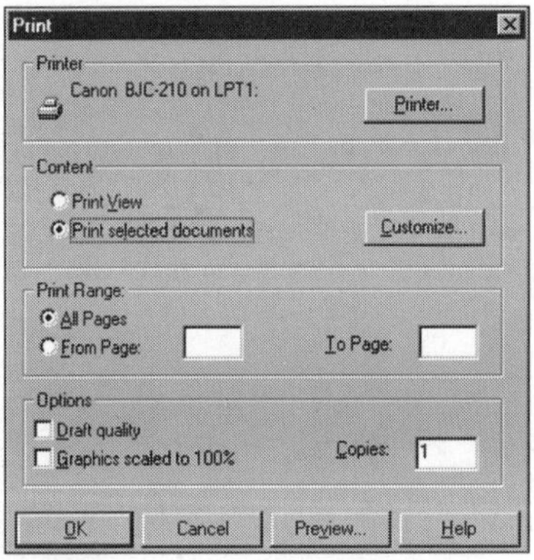

Figure 11-10:
Use the
File Print
dialog box
to print your
masterpiece.

Edit it, maybe

If you want to edit a document, you must first either open it or at least highlight it in the view pane. Then click the Edit SmartIcon or choose Actions➪ Edit Document. Assuming that you are, in fact, allowed to edit the document, Notes puts you in *edit mode,* and you can change any field values. When you've finished making your changes, save the document just as if you were saving it for the first time. (Press Esc and then choose Yes.)

If you already have a document open, you can double-click it (anywhere) to get into edit mode.

Being able to read a document doesn't mean that you can also edit it. In fact, most databases allow you to edit a document only if you are the document's original author. (You wouldn't want somebody else to edit your document and take all the credit for your great ideas, would you?) If Notes won't let you edit a document, it's probably because you aren't the person who composed the document in the first place.

Delete it, maybe

Press Delete to delete the document you have open or highlighted in the view pane. If you have a document open when you press Delete, Notes closes the document you were reading, marks it as deleted, and then takes you to the next document in the database. Notes won't actually delete the document until you update the view (by pressing F9) or exit the database, so you have a chance to change your mind and not delete the document if you decide you've made a mistake. Refer to Chapter 5 to find out more about deleting and undeleting documents.

In most databases, after you compose a document, you (and you alone) control its destiny. You're the only person who can edit it and delete it. (That's good — otherwise, your rivals would be deleting your documents all day long. And that would make you look bad.)

Hey Bob, check this out!

You can turn any Notes document you see into an e-mail message — anytime, anywhere. If you're reading a document and decide that you want to forward it to your friend, choose Actions⇨Forward. Notes takes the document and makes it the body of a new e-mail message that you can send to your associates. You address the e-mail as you would any other message and send it off. Refer to Chapter 5 if you need help using Notes e-mail.

Put it in a Personal folder

Some databases are set up with Personal folders. *Personal folders* let you collect the documents in a database that interest you and gather them all in one place — which makes them easy to find later.

A good example of when you might want to use a Personal folder is in the Lotus Notes Help database. This database is chock-full of documents explaining every possible thing you could ever want to know about Lotus Notes. In other words, it has way, way more information than you need! Suppose you spend an hour in the Help database, trying to find out how to use the status bar. You don't want to waste an hour the *next time* you want to check help on this topic, so you decide to put the document in your Personal folder in the Help database. That way, when you need to read the status bar help again, you can go right to your own Personal folder in the Help database.

Only you can see the contents of your Personal folder. Also, folders names have little folders next to them, but views have magnifying glasses. You can't drag a document to a view.

You can drag the document you want to put in your Personal folder from the view pane into that little folder in the navigation pane. You know when you can let go of the mouse, because the mouse pointer changes into a little cross.

If you're reading a document, choose Actions➪Move to Folder to put that document in a folder.

To see the documents stored in your Personal folder, click the folder icon in the navigation pane.

When Things Get Sensitive

We didn't exactly save the best for last in this chapter. We're not saying that the following two features are bad; it's just that you'll hardly ever use them, if you ever use them at all. In fact, you should read the rest of this chapter only if you absolutely have to — only if you've been told that you'll be *encrypting* fields and hiding documents.

Using encryption to make fields private

Notes has a feature called *field encryption* that is an extremely secure way to make certain field values private. And we mean private! If a field has been encrypted, and you aren't one of the people allowed to see the field's contents, you can do *nothing* to spy on the field.

Okay, so why would you ever use encryption? Suppose your company has a database that tracks information about employees. It has fields such as

Employee Name, Office Location, Phone Number, and Yearly Salary. The whole company uses the database as a kind of corporate directory; people use it to look up other employee names and phone numbers and shoe sizes and other data of interest to the public.

Would you want your colleagues to be able to see how much money you make? Your managers want the whole company to use the database, but they want to make the salary field protected, so that only you, your boss, and the Human Resources department can see the salary field. (A high salary such as yours would breed all kinds of discontent and resentment if everyone could see it.)

When a field has been encrypted, you need a special *key* to see the field's contents. If you read a document that contains an encrypted field, and you have not been given the key to the field, you can't see the contents of the field. Notes stores these keys in your user ID.

If you're going to be dealing with encryption and encryption keys, we recommend that you spend some time in Chapter 14.

Hiding a document

When you compose a document, you can decide that you want only certain people to be able to read the document. By creating a *Read Access List* before you save a new document, you can be specific and particular about the people who will be able to see your document. People who use the database but are not listed in your document's Read Access List will never even know that the document is in the database!

Just before you save a document that you want to make private, choose File➪Document Properties, and then select the infobox tab with the key on it. By default, All readers and above is selected, meaning that anyone with access to the database will be able to see the document you're creating. Right off the bat, you have to uncheck that box. Then you can click the names of the people whom you trust to read the document.

If you want to include a person whose name is not in the list, click the upper Names button — the one next to the list of names of people who can read this document (with Notes' version of a silhouette) — to choose other names from the directory.

Figure 11-11 shows a Document infobox that guarantees that only Doris Day, Dennis Day, and members of the group named Admin Group are able to read this document.

Figure 11-11:
Use the
Document
infobox to
add a
Read
Access
List to a
document.

After identifying the names of the people who can read the document, save it as you save any other document.

If you add a Read Access List to a document, don't forget to include your name in the list; otherwise, even *you* won't be able to see the document!

Part IV
Making Notes Suit You!

The 5th Wave   By Rich Tennant

"I don't care if you do have a coalition of kids from 19 countries backing you up; I'm still not buying you an ISDN line."

In this part . . .

Reading and sending mail and even puttering around in a database are pretty much standard Notes fare. Part IV shows you how to become a power user of Notes by customizing it to your specifications.

Up to this point in the book, all the chapters show you how to use Notes the way it fell out of the box and ended up on your computer. From this point on, we show you how to take command. Reading this part of the book will make you feel as though you've stared the beast down and mastered it. No more intimidation, no more feeling like the program is running you. *You're* in charge here, after all!

Chapter 12

Jazzing Up Your Text

• •

In This Chapter

▶ Selecting text

▶ Changing the appearance of existing text

▶ Formatting text as you type it

▶ Creating non-keyboard characters

▶ Changing margins and setting tabs

▶ Setting pagination

▶ Setting alignment and spacing

▶ Using paragraph styles

▶ Commenting with the Permanent Pen

• •

*W*hen you send a memo or create a document, don't you want people to notice it? Of course you do. Otherwise, you wouldn't have written it. If one sentence or phrase is more important than other text, why not change it in some way so that it stands out?

Sure, you *could* make the text pink and huge (and this chapter can show you how), but perhaps something a bit more subtle will do the trick.

Changing Characters

All truly great documents are composed of individual characters; in fact, *all* documents are composed of individual characters. This section deals with changing those characters, one at a time or in groups such as words, sentences, or paragraphs. You can determine the appearance of a bunch of characters before you even type them, or you can pour out your thoughts onto the screen and then go back and make the changes when you finish typing.

You might want to make all kinds of changes to your text, and that's fine with Notes as long as you play by one rule: The text has to be in a rich text field.

You can find out whether a field is a rich text field by placing your cursor in it and then looking at the status bar. If the font name and font size are visible in the status bar, you're in a rich text field. It's as simple as that. *You* can't make the field a rich text field; the database designer did that back in the bat cave in the dark of night.

You're it!

Many times, after you type something, you later decide to go back and change it. Before you can change its appearance, however, you have to let Notes know what it is you want to change. The act of selecting the text you want to change is called, well, *selecting*. What you can do to the text comes later; right now we'll just talk about selecting it.

Three terms you may as well get straight right now are I-beam, cursor, and insertion point:

- The *I-beam* is the vertical line that moves around the screen as you move the mouse. Notes calls this line an I-beam because it looks like an I-beam used in building construction — a vertical line with little horizontal lines at the top and bottom.
- *Cursor* and *insertion point* are two names for the same thing: the thick vertical line that blinks at the place where something you type will appear.

The mouse pointer is always visible on-screen, often in the shape of an I-beam, but if you use the mouse to scroll up or down, the cursor may scroll off the screen. Don't fear. Press any cursor-movement key (such as an arrow key, PgUp, or PgDn), type something, or press the spacebar, and the screen display changes to show you where the insertion point is.

The easiest way to select text is to click and drag across it with the mouse. When text has a dark box around it, that means it's selected. The dark box is called *reverse video* (light letters on a dark background, rather than vice versa). Using the keyboard, you can select text by moving the cursor to the beginning or the end of the text, holding down Shift, and pressing a directional arrow to move over the characters you want to select. Press the left- or right-arrow key to stretch the highlighter one character to the left or right. Press the down- or up-arrow key to highlight to the same point in the next or previous line. Pressing Shift while using any cursor-movement key combination moves the cursor and highlights text on the way.

Here are some additional tips about selecting text. They are well worth remembering because they will save you a lot of time. Some are included in the cheat sheet at the front of the book:

✔ Use Ctrl along with Shift and the cursor-movement keys to speed up the process of highlighting. Shift+Ctrl+ ← or → moves the highlight one word at a time. Shift+Ctrl+↓ or ↑ moves the highlight to the beginning or end of the next or previous line, respectively.

✔ Double-click a word to select it.

 ✔ If you want to select all the text in the current field, you're in luck — you can use the menu to choose Edit➪Select All, click the Edit Select All SmartIcon, or just press Ctrl+A.

✔ If you want to select text in more than one field at a time while you're in edit mode, you're out of luck. Regardless of the method you choose to select text, you can select text in only one field at a time.

✔ When you use Edit➪Select All in edit mode, you select everything in the current field. If you use it in read mode, you select the whole document. (In the latter case, the only thing you can do with selected text is copy it to the Clipboard.)

✔ If you want to select two separate chunks of text, you're out of luck. You can select only one bit of text at a time.

✔ If you find that you selected the wrong text, simply select other text to correct the mistake.

✔ If you selected some text but meant to select more, hold down Shift and then click at the farthest end of the additional text or use a cursor-movement key combination. Notes adds to the selected text all text between the currently selected text and the place where you click.

✔ To select a big chunk of text, put the cursor at the beginning of the text you want to select and then use the mouse and scroll bars to scroll until you can see the other end of the text you want to select. Press Shift as you click at the other end of the text. Notes selects all the text in between.

✔ To select all text from the cursor to the beginning of the field, press Shift+Ctrl+Home. To select all text from the cursor to the end of the field, press Shift+Ctrl+End.

✔ Please pay for all selections at the cashier, no returns or refunds, have a nice day, and thank you for shopping with us.

I've made my selection; what now?

After you've selected a bit of text, it's time to change it. You can remove the text, change its appearance, change its location, move or copy it elsewhere, or check its spelling. Not only can you do lots of things with the text, you can usually do each thing in several different ways. Don't get nervous about trying to figure out all the different ways to do things; figure out the method that works best for you and forget the rest.

The Ctrl key on IBM-style keyboards and the (⌘) on Macintosh keyboards work with other keys to streamline the things you do most often. Don't be careless about whacking at these key combinations, for one simple reason — if you choose the wrong one, you might be really sorry. For example, suppose you made lots of changes to some text and then accidentally used Ctrl+T. You would remove all the formats you just applied!

If you do use a key combination by accident, remember a more useful one — Ctrl+Z. That tells Notes to *undo* (reverse) the most recent action.

How about making your formatting life a bit simpler? Sure, you can take a few hours to memorize the various key combinations. Or you can play it smart and use a magic box. Yup, a lot of the things you can do to text — plus more — is included in what's sometimes dubbed a *properties box,* but is officially called the *infobox.*

So, when you want to change something about a paragraph or a word or even just a character, simply select the thing you want to change and then click the Properties SmartIcon. Up springs an infobox appropriate for whatever item you selected. Figure 12-1 shows the infobox for selected text.

Figure 12-1:
The infobox
for text in a
rich text
field.

This dialog box is chock-full of ways to change selected text, including giving it a large font size and coloring it pink. The Text and Paragraph infoboxes, like all infoboxes, have tabbed pages to organize the different types of properties. Here's a brief list of the pages for text and paragraphs (we explain them in detail later in this chapter):

✔ **Font:** Set font style, font size, font attributes (bold, italic, and so on), and text color.

✔ **Alignment:** Set the alignment (left, center, right, full, or none), first line and paragraph indent, spacing (between lines, above, and below the paragraph), and list options (bullets or numbers).

✔ **Pagination:** Set pagination options, left and right margins (the right margin is for printing only; it has no on-screen effect), and tabs (for the whole paragraph).

✔ **Hide When:** Hide the selected paragraph(s) under all sorts of conditions. (Stay tuned if you want to know what these conditions are.)

✔ **Styles:** Assign a style to the currently selected paragraph(s). Of course, you have to create styles before you can apply them. Coming soon to a page near you — an explanation of the use of styles.

At times, not using the Text infobox is faster — for example, when you're setting the font, font size, or style. In these cases, get in the habit of using the status bar. Next time you're hanging around a rich text field, stop by the status bar and click the box containing the name of the current font. In Figure 12-2, you can see the results of clicking the font box in the status bar. The variety of fonts you have available depends on the software and the printer you're using.

Figure 12-2:
Click the
font name in
the status
bar and
here's what
you get.

| Century-WP |
| Century Gothic |
| Century Schoolbook |
| Chalk |
| Charlesworth |
| ChelmsfordBook-WP |
| Comic Sans MS |
| CommercialScript-WP |
| CommonBullets |
| CooperBlack-WP |
| Copperplate Gothic Bold |
| Copperplate Gothic Light |
| CopperPot |
| Cosmic |
| CosmicTwo |
| Cottage |
| Courier |
| Courier-WP |
| Courier New |
| Crescent |
| Cupertino |
| Czar |
| Dauphin |
| DawnCastle |
| Default Monospace |
| Default Sans Serif |

The same fonts, sizes, and paragraph styles are available whether you use the status bar or the infobox. The status bar is just a faster way of making a single selection.

If you select a bunch of text and then look at the status bar, you usually see the name of the font used in that selection. Sometimes, though, you may not see the name of a font. Why not? If the text you select contains two or more fonts, the status bar doesn't show any font name or size. But don't fret — even if the font name or size box is empty, you can still use the status bar to choose one font for the whole selection. Click the box where you normally see a font name, and choose the font you want from the list that appears.

The font styles and sizes you see on the Web are very likely different from those you see in Notes. It's the result of the limitation of the browser, not Notes, so don't go blaming Notes. Browsers can display two fonts, one mono-spaced and one variable width, and font sizes (in points) of 8, 10, 12,14, 18, 24, and big.

Putting it all together

Suppose that you're writing a memo to the department inviting them to the annual company party on Saturday. You type the text first and then you decide to realign and enhance some of the text. Just putting your cursor at the beginning of a word and clicking the bold SmartIcon is not enough. Selecting the text and then choosing bold is the only way to enhance text *after* you've typed it.

After you get the hang of enhancing text, you can make your memos more interesting and professional. Figure 12-3 shows an invitation before formatting. With just a few keystrokes to change the font, font size, and style, you get Figure 12-4.

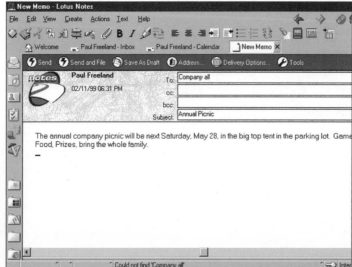

Figure 12-3:
Yawn. No personality to this memo.

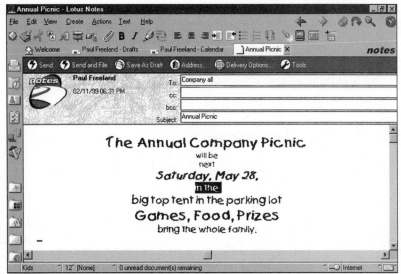

Figure 12-4:
That's a bit more like it. It is a party, after all.

You can improve the appearance of a memo with a new font, italics, and centered lines using only a few keystrokes.

If it's a good idea to do a little interior decorating on your party memos, it's even more important to be sure that you plan just as carefully the documents that you create in the line of work. Choosing the right words is only half the battle: The other half is making a document look good.

A little enhancing goes a long way. If too many words in a document are boldface, they don't seem so important anymore. If you plaster lots of different fonts and different font colors and sizes around the page, your document might look more like a circus poster than an official announcement.

It's hard to be bold when you don't exist

Here are some of the more frequently asked questions about enhancing text:

Q: How can you select text you haven't even typed yet?

A: You can't.

Q: Can't you decide to enhance text before you type it?

A: Yes.

Q: What do you do to enhance text you haven't typed yet?

A: The keystrokes and icons described earlier work for text you are about to type as well as for text you typed yesterday. If you are typing a sentence and know that the next few words should be bold, click the Bold SmartIcon (or use one of the other techniques for bolding), type the text, and then click the Bold SmartIcon to turn bold off and finish typing. If you want to center the next line you're about to type, click the Center SmartIcon and type. Voilà! (Or is it viola?)

If your keyboard doesn't have 600 keys

Our world is shrinking fast. Maybe that's why so many people are trying to lose weight. You can be in New York for lunch and France for dinner. Of course, all that eating won't do much for your weight in this shrinking world, but that's beside the point. The point, in case your mind is wandering, is that we are increasingly called upon to use words and symbols in our writing that come from other languages. You ignore the subtle differences between English and non-English alphabets at your peril.

Ignoring the fact that 0 and Ø are two different characters can bring offense, squelch a deal, or even precipitate a food fight. Referring to the Bürgermeister (the mayor) as the Burgermeister (the man in charge of the burgers at a cookout?) is not the way to ingratiate yourself to His Eminency.

You may be wondering how you're going to type a *U* with an umlaut, when you don't have such a key on your keyboard. Typing **u"** instead is pretty hokey. Notes, recognizing that you might need to type some non-English characters, has a large number of extra characters not available on your keyboard (or in stores). The LMBCS (Lotus Multi-Byte Character Set) includes all characters available in Notes.

The LMBCS includes characters available on the keyboard as well as non-keyboard characters — characters unique to foreign languages and such characters as © for copyright or £ for pound sterling. To see the list of LMBCS characters and the way to create them, check the documentation or use the Help feature (use the index and choose LMBCS). The way to type one of these character sets depends on whether you are using a Macintosh or an IBM-style keyboard. If you're using Macintosh, you may not be able to see the character on-screen. You have to print to see the character.

Mac users should use Keycaps for information on how to create nonkeyboard characters.

As an example of the way to create a character, here are the keystroke sequences used to type Ø. On a Macintosh keyboard, press Option+Shift+O. On the IBM-style keyboard, press Alt+F1, then O, and then / (the slash mark). To find the Alt+F1 sequence (also called the *compose sequence*) for a particular character, look in Help or in the documentation. If you can't find the character you're after there, you need to use the LMBCS character code. Press Alt+F1 twice, then 0 (that's a zero), then - (a hyphen), and then the LMBCS number for the character (such as 157 for the Ø). If the LMBCS code has only two digits, 33 for example, use 033. (This is almost as bad as dialing a long-distance number with your credit card, isn't it?)

After you create the character, you can copy and paste it if you need it again. Using the Copy⇨Paste command is faster than using the LMBCS or composing key sequences

Paragraphs with Character

Armed with the skills necessary to change bits of text here and there, we turn our attention to paragraphs. After all, sometimes you want an entire paragraph to have a unique appearance so that it stands out from the others around it.

Here are a few things you ought to keep in mind as you work with paragraphs:

- ✔ You can select an entire paragraph and change the appearance of all its characters in the same way that you changed individual characters, words, or groups of words in the preceding section.

- ✔ Summoning the infobox enables you to make changes to the format of the paragraph (other than the appearance of its text).

- ✔ You can apply paragraph formats only to text in rich text fields.

- ✔ You can change the characteristics of one paragraph at a time simply by putting the cursor in that paragraph. You don't have to select the entire paragraph.

- ✔ If you need to change several paragraphs, you must select them all.

- ✔ If you need to change all the paragraphs in the field, choose Edit⇨ Select All.

- ✔ If you change one paragraph, only that paragraph contains the changes. For example, if you set tabs in one paragraph, only that paragraph has those unique tabs.

- ✔ If you haven't typed anything yet, use the infobox to set the characteristics you want all paragraphs to have, and then start typing. All paragraphs will have those characteristics until you use the menu to set some new characteristics.

All margins great and small

Use the Pagination tabbed page of the Text infobox to change a paragraph's left or right margins. (The margins at the top and bottom of the page have nothing to do with paragraphs, so they don't appear here. Rather, they're in the File⇨Page Setup menu, covered later in this chapter.) To keep your confusion coefficient high, Notes offers you the chance to set your margins in absolute terms (measured in inches) or relative terms (percentage of the width of the page). So, if you choose a relative margin of 12, which is 12 percent of the width of whatever you are printing to, the margin will be about 1 inch on an 8 ½-inch sheet of paper, and teeny if you are printing on a postage stamp. As you can see in Figure 12-5, you can adjust the left and right margins:

Alignment
Pagination
Hide When
Font
Styles

Figure 12-5:
On one
convient
tabbed
page, you
can set
margins,
tabs, and
pagination
options.

✔ **Left Margin:** The default is 1 inch, if you're using imperial measurements, or 2.54 cm, if you're using metric measurements. (You can switch from one to the other by choosing File➪Tools➪User Preferences, clicking International, and choosing Imperial or Metric.) If you want the first line to be indented differently, switch to the Alignment (second) tabbed page and choose whatever first line option suits your fancy.

✔ **Right Margin:** The right margin is the distance from the *left* edge of the paper to the right edge of the paragraph. That's the left edge of the paper. Paying attention? For a 2-inch right margin on a sheet of paper 8.5 inches wide, the right margin should be 6.5 inches. The default is 1 inch.

Notes doesn't show text on-screen the same way it shows text when printing, so you can't always see how the document will look on the page. To get some idea of where the page breaks are, however, choose View➪Show➪Page Breaks.

Keeping tabs on your paragraph

Back at the factory, paragraphs automatically have their own tabs set at every half inch. This may be fine for you, in which case you don't have to set any tabs at all. But if you're not happy with the preset tabs, you can use the Pagination page of the Text infobox to set new ones.

In the Tabs box, choose Evenly spaced and choose a distance between tabs, such as .75 inch. Or you can choose Individually set and then type the location of each tab, as we did in Figure 12-5. Just type the distance (measured from the left edge of the paper) for all the tabs you need. For that extra touch of variety, you could even enter some tabs in inches and others in centimeters. If you're using inches, you don't have to type any symbol; if you want centimeters, just type **cm** after the number. You can't use yards, miles, quarts, or kilometers, though. Here are a few things to remember:

✔ Four types of tabs are available: Left, Center, Right, and Decimal. The last type aligns a column of numbers so that their decimal points are lined up.

✔ The little example box shows you how to set the different tabs, but you are given a bum steer: The example box shows the setting as 4D (the number comes first), but it's D4 for a decimal tab at the 4-inch mark.

✔ Between each separate tab setting, put a semicolon, not a comma. Notes complains if you use commas.

✔ Tabs work only in rich text fields (RTF). That's why when you press Tab in an RTF, you move not to a new field but rather to the next tab stop.

You may find it easier to use the on-screen ruler to set margins and tabs. If you're rubbing your eyes trying to find a ruler on-screen, try using View➪Ruler. A ruler like the one in Figure 12-6 appears at the top of your screen.

Figure 12-6:
The ruler is a convenient and fun way to set margins and tabs. (Well, convenient anyway.)

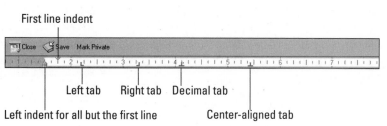

Click in the ruler where you want a tab, and an *L* appears. To get rid of an unwanted tab, click it to remove it. The *L* means the tab is a left tab. To change it to another type of tab, right-click the tab, and choose the type. (You can also choose to delete the tab if you goofed.)

You can add a tab in another way that's especially handy if you don't want the default left tab. Simply right-click in the ruler where you want a new tab, and then select the one you want from the list that appears.

One paragraph, indivisible

When Notes calculates that the bottom of a page is at hand, it inserts a page break automatically so that the printer will start a new page there. The place it chooses may not always be where you had in mind; you may prefer to have a paragraph stay together, even if it means a bit of white space at the bottom of the page. To protect a paragraph from being split, click the Margins page of the Text infobox (refer to Figure 12-5). Then choose one of the following:

- Choose Page Break before Paragraph if you definitely want the current paragraph to start a new page. This is useful when you want to start a new section on a new page.

- Choose Keep Paragraph on One Page to prevent Notes from breaking up a paragraph somewhere in the middle. Notes will either keep the paragraph on the current page or shove the whole thing to the next page.

- Choose Keep Paragraph with Next Paragraph to be sure that a paragraph is always on the same page as the paragraph following it.

The incredible disappearing paragraph

The time may come when you need to hide a paragraph. Why? Well, here are a few reasons:

- You want to save some space by hiding a paragraph when a document is being previewed.

- You want text to be visible only when people are editing a document, not when they are reading it, because the text contains editing instructions.

- You want to hide it from certain readers.

- You have a button that executes a command in a document, and you want to hide it when you print the document so some poor chump doesn't try pushing the button on the paper.

You have nine choices for hiding a paragraph — all listed in the Hide When page of the Text infobox, as shown in Figure 12-7. You can tell Notes to hide a selected paragraph in any of the following ways:

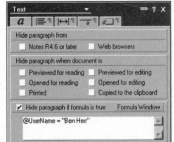

Figure 12-7:
The selected paragraph will not be visible on Ben Herr's screen.

- ✔ **Notes Release 4.6 or Later:** If the item doesn't apply to those users who are seeing the document in Notes, hide it from them. Why Release 4.6? Some new features were added with Release 4.6, and so occasionally separate information may need to be hidden or displayed for users of different versions.

- ✔ **Web Browsers:** If the item or text doesn't work for or apply to folks visiting from the Web, it makes sense to hide it from them. Best to avoid confusion.

- ✔ **Previewed for Reading:** A document highlighted in a view is visible in the preview pane (if you make the preview pane visible), but the paragraph set with this attribute is not visible. Saves valuable screen real estate when space is limited.

- ✔ **Opened for Reading:** The paragraph is visible only when you're in edit mode. It is also hidden for printing.

- ✔ **Printed:** As the word implies, when you print a document, paragraphs with the Hide While Printing attribute do not print. This is useful for suppressing the printing of paragraphs that you want to be visible only on-screen. You might use this option also when the paragraph contains graphics that slow down the print job.

- ✔ **Previewed for Editing:** A paragraph set with this attribute is not visible if the document is in edit mode in the preview pane.

- ✔ **Opened for Editing:** The paragraph is visible when the reader is not in edit mode, but it disappears whenever someone tries to edit the document. This is a way to protect a paragraph from being changed by people who have the ability to edit documents. Be careful — after making this choice, you may never be able to edit the paragraph again.

- ✔ **Copied to the Clipboard:** If you try to copy a paragraph with this attribute while you're in edit mode, you find that you have nothing to paste.

- ✔ **Hide Paragraph If Formula Is True:** In Figure 12-7, we wrote a formula in the formula window and checked Hide paragraph when formula is true. As the name implies, Notes looks at the formula and, if its condition is met, hides the paragraph. If the user is Ben Herr, he won't see this paragraph under any circumstances.

The preceding hide-when choices work for the *entire paragraph,* not for individually selected text. In fact, many text options work on only the entire paragraph — specifically, spacing, list options (bullets and numbering), margins, tabs, hide-when options, pagination, alignments, and styles.

We'll let you in on a way to get around being unable to edit a paragraph — you can use this trick if you goof and choose Hide Paragraph When Document Is: Opened for Editing, or if you want to get around someone else's use of this feature. While you're *not* in edit mode, highlight the paragraph that is hidden when you are editing, copy it to the Clipboard, and then get into edit mode and paste the paragraph into the document. This pasted paragraph will not have the hidden attribute, so you can edit it. Of course, when you're no longer in edit mode, the paragraph will appear twice, unless you choose to hide the paragraph when the document is opened or previewed for reading.

Get in align

Alignment refers to the arrangement of text in each line, relative to the margins. You have five choices in the Alignment tab of the Text infobox:

- ✔ **Left:** The text lines up with the left margin and has a ragged-right edge.

- ✔ **Center:** Want to guess what this does? If you guessed that it centers the text on each line and gives lines ragged-right and ragged-left edges, add ten points to your score and advance three spaces.

- ✔ **Right:** The text lines up with the right margin and has a ragged-left edge.

- ✔ **Full:** The text stretches from margin to margin so that the paragraph has no ragged edges. Full won't work if you type a really short line or if you press Enter at the end of a line.

- ✔ **None:** Text starts at the left margin and goes to the right forever. It doesn't wrap. Often, when you import documents from other programs, you may be shocked to see that lines stretch off the screen. You have to scroll to the right until you reach the end of the paragraph and then scroll back to the left to see the next paragraph. Change the alignment to Left or Full to correct the problem.

Give me some space

Feeling cramped, squeezed, closed in? Do your memos seem to have too much stuff and not enough open space? Then you need to space out. Use the Alignment page of the Text infobox to s-p-r-e-a-d your paragraph(s) out over more space or to show more white space. You have three choices under each of the three types of spacing. You can use 1, 1½, or 2 to determine the distance in each of these ways:

- ✔ **Interline:** between lines of the paragraph

- ✔ **Above:** between the current paragraph and the one above it

- ✔ **Below:** between the current paragraph and the one below it

Choosing all three can be a heck of a mess; you may wind up with too much spacing. Practice a bit so that your screen isn't mostly white space with a line or a paragraph appearing once in a while like an oasis in a desert of white sand. If you make a selection you're not happy with, don't forget the Undo feature.

Don't press Enter at the end of every line in a paragraph to achieve double spacing. Take our word for it, this is never a good idea. If you don't use the spacing choices, you'll wind up with gaps all through your document when you print or change the size of the window.

Puttin' on the style

You have to make the coffee, you have to put paper in the copier, and now you have to jump all around your documents applying the same formatting, one paragraph at a time. It's enough to raise your hackles.

Calm your hackles. You may still have to make the coffee, but you don't have to go through all those keystrokes again and again to format paragraphs scattered around your document. Imagine that you wrote a report with lots of sections, and each section had its own title. You want the titles to be centered and boldface, to have one line of space after them, and to have a larger font with blue text. All you have to do is format one title, turn that format into a _style,_ and then use that style for all the other titles, thus saving you lots of time and getting you home for dinner.

Applying styles also guarantees that you are consistent. After formatting 15 titles, you're bound to get bored and careless, and you may forget to add boldface along with all the other formats to a title. Using styles guarantees that the same characteristics are applied to every paragraph you select.

After you've written a title, centered it, colored it blue, boldfaced it, added the spacing, and changed the font, keep the cursor in the title, activate the Text infobox, click the Styles tab (the last tab), and then click the Create Style option. Figure 12-8 shows the Text infobox with the Style page visible, and — for the same low, low price — the Create Style dialog box that appears when you choose to create a new style.

Figure 12-8:
These two
dialog
boxes,
working
hand-in-
hand, allow
you to
create
styles.

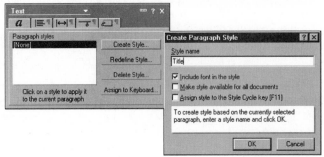

You name your new style in, wonder of wonders, the Style Name text box. You can then choose to Include the Font in the Style, Make Style Available for All Documents in the Database, and Include This Style in Cycle Key [F11] — which means that, when someone highlights a paragraph and presses F11, the paragraph shows each available style in succession. Click OK to get out of the dialog box and finish with the current style.

After you create your styles, you can apply them to the current paragraph (the one where the cursor is) or to all selected paragraphs. Press F11 to cycle through all the styles you've created and stop when you find the one you want. Or you can apply one of the styles by clicking the style box (immediately to the right of the font size box) in the status bar. Click a style name and Notes automatically applies that style to the paragraph where your cursor is or in which at least part of the text is selected.

Permanent Pen — Does It Stain?

Not to worry, the Permanent Pen has nothing to do with ink that won't wash out. It has everything to do with editing, though. Have you ever read a document and wanted to add some comments of your own scattered throughout the paragraphs? Every time you do, you have to specify a new font or color or something so that readers can tell your brilliant comments from the drivel you're commenting on.

The Notes Permanent Pen does just that — it allows you to specify a different appearance to whatever you type. All you have to do is designate the different font as the Permanent Pen — we show you how in a moment — and then, whenever you want to edit a document, you activate the Permanent Pen and enter your comments.

Figure 12-9 shows a discussion document with a few pointed interjections written in Permanent Pen by someone in charge.

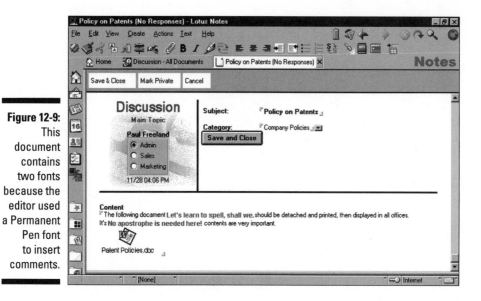

Figure 12-9:
This
document
contains
two fonts
because the
editor used
a Permanent
Pen font
to insert
comments.

To designate a Permanent Pen font, you don't need to type anything. Activate the Text infobox, choose a font, font size, color, and enhancement (such as bold or italics); then choose Text⇨Permanent Pen⇨Set Permanent Pen. Fini.

Now open a document to which you have editor access, get into edit mode, and find something you want to comment on. Click the Permanent Pen SmartIcon or choose Text⇨Permanent Pen⇨Use Permanent Pen and start writing. To turn off the Permanent Pen font, click the Permanent Pen SmartIcon (or choose Text⇨Permanent Pen⇨Use Permanent Pen) again.

Chapter 13

Doctoring Your Documents

· ·

In This Chapter

▶ Inserting page breaks

▶ Creating tables

▶ Modifying tables — adding and deleting rows and columns

▶ Adding headers and footers

▶ Changing the page setup

▶ Searching and spelling

· ·

*I*f you took tips from Chapter 12, your characters have character, your sentences make sense, and your paragraphs have punch. Now, what about whole pages and entire documents? This chapter takes you from concentrating on the individual characters to having a global view, seeing the big picture, and making your single- or multi-page document a complete, professional, and well-crafted entity of which you can be proud.

As you're making nifty adjustments to individual pages and sweeping modifications to the whole document, you might not see a single change on your screen. Is it time to lose your temper? No! Individual pages are what you see when you print. You don't see separate pages on the screen unless you choose View➪Show➪Page Breaks. You don't see headers or footers, either. The only way to see what a page will really look like when it's printed is to print it or to preview it.

Break It Up!

Notes is a very smart program; it even knows when text is at the bottom of a page. When you print a document, it automatically puts a *page break* in the proper place. That way, you don't print text off the page and into thin air.

There may come a time when you need to put a page break where Notes wouldn't. For example, if a paragraph starts a new section and you want it to appear on a new page (even if the previous page isn't full), you can insert a page break. You can insert a page break in one of two ways:

- From the keyboard (press Ctrl+Shift+L)
- From the menu (choose Create➪Page Break)

If you want to see the page break, select View➪Show➪Page Breaks. The break appears as a solid line across the screen. To remove a page break that you don't want anymore, place the cursor on the first character after the page break and press Backspace. If you delete a page break and it appears right back again, maybe one line before or after the place where it used to be, you're trying to remove a break that Notes put there all by itself because the text is at the end of the page. That's a page break you're going to have to live with. Check out the pagination options covered in Chapter 12.

Putting Your Cards in a Table

If you're having dinner, a table is something you keep your elbows off. When you're using Notes, a table is something that makes it a whole lot easier for you to keep rows and columns of information lined up without having to set a million tabs.

A *table* is a spreadsheet you can place in your document, with rows and columns of *cells* into which you type information. One of the advantages of using a table instead of tabs is that tabs normally allow text to wrap back to the beginning of the next line, whereas tables keep text aligned in columns.

Here comes a surprise — you can put a table in only a rich text field.

Building the table

Suppose, for the sake of argument, that you need to send a message that includes a schedule. The schedule itself would be a great candidate for a table — it involves small bits of data and needs to be in tabular format.

 When you get to the place in the message where you are ready to place the schedule, choose Create➪Table or click the Create Table SmartIcon. Figure 13-1 shows you the Create Table dialog box. You get to decide in advance how many rows and how many columns you want in your table. You can also choose the type of table. There are four types:

- ✔ **Standard:** All rows and columns are visible all the time.

- ✔ **Tabbed:** Only one row is visible at a time, and each row is represented by a clickable tab.

- ✔ **Timed:** A new row appears alone every two seconds. (Yes, you can change the interval for users who aren't speed readers.)

- ✔ **Programmatic:** The table is based on a field in the document.

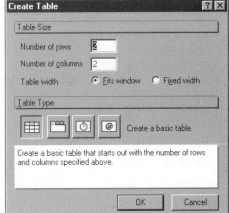

Figure 13-1:
The Create Table dialog box, preparing for a 2-row, 2-column table.

If planning isn't your forte, don't panic; you can always change your mind later using the Table infobox, and you can add and delete rows and columns.

Figure 13-2 shows a table with a course schedule. A schedule is just one example of a good reason to use a table; if you try hard, you can think of lots of other examples. When you add a new table, Notes automatically fits it to your screen and makes each column the same width. You can change the column widths, too.

After you add a table to your document, and whenever you put the cursor in your table, Notes is smart enough to change the menus (did you notice?). When your cursor is in a table, you'll notice a new menu command called, appropriately enough, Table. It's right after Text and right before Window. You can use this menu choice to do things such as change the table's properties and add, insert, or delete rows and columns.

By default, new tables are set to Fit to Window, which means the table size and column widths change, depending on the size of the window the reader is using to read the document. Two other choices are available in addition to fitting your table to the size of the window.

Choosing Fixed causes the table (and its columns) to be the same width, no matter how big or small you make the document window.

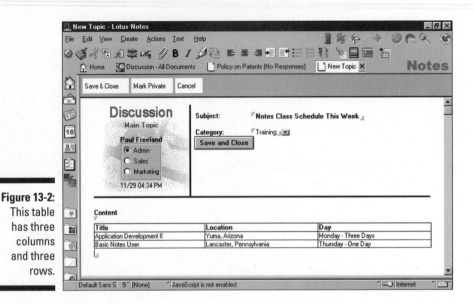

Figure 13-2:
This table
has three
columns
and three
rows.

Figure 13-3 shows two tables. The first is set to Fit to Window, so it's been adjusted to the rather small window size. The other table is not set to Fit to Window, so it stays the same size, even though the window is too small to display all of it.

Figure 13-3:
You can
decide
whether a
table's size
should
change
when you
make a
document
window
smaller.

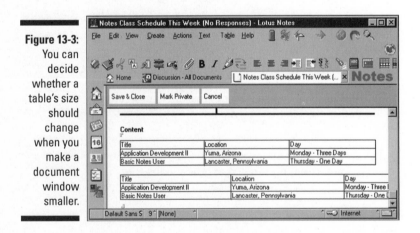

The third choice for setting up your table is Same as Window, which means that the document will appear with the table fitting exactly between the sides of the window.

Setting the table

After you build the table, you may decide to change its appearance or the way it behaves. When you do, the time has come to call to the screen the Table infobox. The pages of the Table infobox contain many options to transform a plain table into one that will really catch your readers' eyes.

If you want to make your new table the same size no matter what, make sure that the cursor is in the table and choose Table⇨Table Properties (or click the Table Properties SmartIcon). Make sure the first tabbed page is visible, and then click Fixed Width. Figure 13-4 shows the Table infobox open with the Layout page exposed.

Figure 13-4:
Use the infobox to format a table.

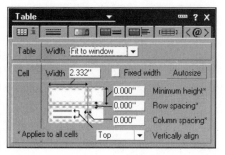

You can also use this dialog box to set the space between rows, the space between columns, the table's left margin, and a particular column's width. It's often best to accept the defaults simply because Notes sets the table attributes for best appearance. If you want to take control of any or all of the table's dimensions, use the first tabbed page of the Table infobox. You can set the width of individual columns, but the minimum height (which changes if you add more lines of text in a cell), the row spacing, and the column spacing (which spaces the text in adjacent cells) are settings that affect the whole table. If you set the minimum cell height fairly large, you can use Vertically Align to put text in the cells at the top, in the middle, or at the bottom of the cells. The minimum height of the cells in Figure 13-5 is set at 2 inches, and the text is aligned in the center of the cell.

Figure 13-5:
These cells are 2 inches high, and the text is center aligned.

Title	Location	Day

The one setting you will most often want to change is the width of different columns. You have three options for changing the column width. The first option is to use the ruler (explained in the section "Changing column widths the easy way," later in this chapter).

The second and third options involve the Table infobox. The more difficult way to set the column width is to enter the dimension in the Width box. Express your desires in inches (or in centimeters by adding *cm* after the number).

The other way to set column width is to click the Autosize button, which tells Notes to make the column as wide as the widest cell entry in that column. Clicking the Fixed Width box means that no matter how much you resize the window, no matter how much you squeeze the table, the column you selected when you checked Fixed Width will stubbornly keep its width.

Cell borders are not people who live in jail, but are the lines that surround each cell. If you use the same dialog box (choose Table⇨Table Properties) and click the Cell Borders tab, you can change the appearance of the borders. Figure 13-6 shows the dialog box. You can change the following:

- **Border Style:** The three styles apply to all cells.

- **Border Color:** The many colors apply to all cells.

- **Border Thickness:** The thickness ranges from none to a thickness of 10. The numbers don't stand for inches or anything that need concern us. You can change the individual borders of individual cells or of all selected cells.

Figure 13-6:
Use the Cell Borders page of the Table infobox to outline cells in the table.

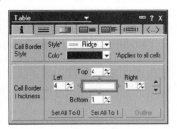

Use the Table/Cell Colors tab of the Table infobox (Figure 13-7) to change cell colors. This tabbed page offers a lot of choices, and if we took pictures of every choice and described every possible combination of choices, this book would be very big. Instead, here's an overview. We recommend that you create a table and experiment to find all the nuances of coloring the cells.

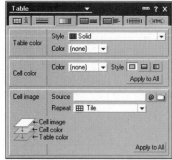

Figure 13-7:
Use the
Table/Cell
Colors page
of the Table
infobox for
background
colors.

Here are a few of the myriad changes you can make:

- **Table Color:** Color groups of cells — all cells, certain border cells, or alternate rows or columns. You need to choose two colors.

- **Cell Color:** Color the selected cells with a solid color or with two colors fading into each other vertically or horizontally.

- **Cell Image:** Add wallpaper to the cell or cells, then use it once or repeat it throughout the cells.

In Figure 13-8, you see the Table Borders tabbed page and the settings in that page that we used to set the table border in the figure.

Don't confuse table borders with cell borders. Table borders are the halo around (outside) the entire table.

Figure 13-8:
Provide a
halo for your
table with
the Table
Borders
page.

In Table Borders page, the settings include but are not limited to the following:

✔ **Border Style:** Not too surprisingly, this option allows you to choose the type of border. Choose from more than eight (that means nine) options, including dotted, solid, double (the one we chose), and the ever popular none. Just to the right of the Border Style option is the place to set the table border color. It's a pity you can't see the beautiful shade we chose in Figure 13-8.

✔ **Border Effects:** This option is simple — it adds a drop shadow to the right and the bottom of the table so that the table looks like it's floating a bit above the page. The wider you set the width, the higher the table appears to be floating. Set it wide enough and your readers will have to get a ladder to see what's in the table. *Note:* You can set the width by typing a number as well as by clicking the little up or down arrows.

✔ **Thickness:** There are three settings in the bottom section of the Table Borders page. You can set Inside, Outside, and Thickness. Changing the Inside number determines the distance from the table to the border. Outside determines the distance from the border to whatever stuff is above, below, to the right, or to the left of the table. Thickness determines the thickness of the border. For each of these options, you can set each measurement separately by changing just Left, Right, Top, or Bottom. To save time, you can click the larger arrowheads to the right of the little table and change the entire border at once.

The Table Margins page, which you can see in Figure 13-9, is where you make the settings that tell the table how to fit in with whatever surrounds it and still fit into the page. First come the margins, left and right. You can set table margins the same way you set margins for any line of text. For more information, check the section in Chapter 12 on setting margins.

Figure 13-9:
Use the
Table
Margins
page to
determine
how the
table gets
along
with its
neighbors.

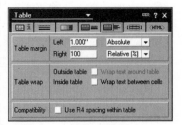

The next setting on the Margins page is for wrapping text around the table. The first option, Outside Table — Wrap Text around Table, is available only if you set the table to Fixed Width on the first tabbed page of the Table infobox. By selecting the Wrap Text around Table option, you make it possible to type text beside the table. You can't just type text and expect it to start wrapping, though. You need to place the cursor beside the table to be able to enter text there. When text is even with the bottom of the table, it begins to wrap around it.

The other wrap setting has to do with what happens *inside* cells. Pay attention here or you might get hurt. When you select Inside Table — Wrap Text between Cells, a new box appears in which you enter a number representing the maximum height you want for the row. When you type enough stuff to cause the cell to reach that height, the new text spills into the cell to the right.

When you click this selection, all *existing* text in the cell to the right is moved into the current cell, so that the cell to the right is empty and ready to receive the extra text you might type. If you click this selection, you may have a lot of arranging to do unless the cells to the right are already empty.

The last choice, Use R4 Spacing within Table, uses the slightly larger cell and spacing settings from Release 4 of Notes.

Changing the display of rows

A normal, run-of-the-mill table consists of rows and columns, with all the data visible all the time. Now Notes has changed all that. You can display one row at a time, either letting users decide which row they want to see or displaying a new row every few seconds. How? Use the Table Rows page in the Table infobox, which is shown in Figure 13-10. Right above it is the table we are working with, which consists of a small list of classes to be offered, their locations, and their cost.

Note that we started with a plain table consisting of related data placed in rows, but with one big exception. If you plan to let users choose the row they want to see, make sure that the upper-left cell contains the title for the data in row one, the next cell to the right in the first row contains the title for the data in the second row, and so on. That's the way we did it in Figure 13-10. If you plan to use the automatic display of one row at a time, make sure that all related data is in the same row.

As soon as you click Show Only One Row at a Time, the table changes to a single row and defaults to a tabbed table, with a tab for each cell at the top above the single displayed row. Click a tab to display the corresponding single row.

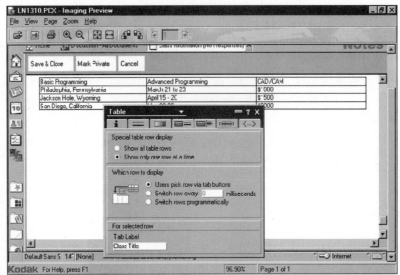

Figure 13-10:
Change the
way your
table is
displayed in
the Table
Rows page.

The Which Row to Display area is visible only if you click Show Only One Row at a Time. In this box, you can choose one of three options. The first, Users Pick Row via Tab Buttons, does exactly what the words say, no false advertising here. The second choice, Switch Row Every xx Milliseconds, conducts a sort of automatic slide show. You set the interval, measured in thousandths of a second, for the display of a row. After that interval, the next row appears automatically. The third choice is not one we can discuss here, because you need to tinker with the design of the form to make it work. Database designers do not allow their users to mess around with the inner workings of their databases.

When you click the Show Only One Row at a Time option, a new text box appears at the bottom of the Table infobox that allows you to enter some text. That text appears to the left of the table tabs.

If you choose to have the table switch rows automatically, remember that not all of your users are speed readers, and many will eventually get tired of the table constantly changing. Notes lets you control the slide show. First, you can change the interval. The default speed is 2 seconds (2,000 milliseconds is 2 seconds). If you have a lot of data in each row, you probably want to leave the rows on the screen long enough for the readers to get the message. Otherwise, they may feel like TV viewers who are seeing one of those commercials in which every picture is on screen for so little time that they can't figure out what they've seen.If you choose to switch rows automatically, you have two more choices in the area that appears, which is labeled Transition when Switching Rows. You can see the choices in Figure 13-11.

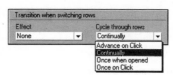

Figure 13-11:
Use these
lists to
decide how
the new
rows will
appear on
the screen.

You won't see the changing rows while you are in edit mode. You need to save the document, and then open it in read mode to see the rows magically change before your very eyes.

We can't take a picture of a changing slide show to put in a book, so the best we can do is suggest that you choose each of the Effects, open the document in read mode, and then see how each row unfolds. *Note:* The only choice under Effects is None unless you put an image (wallpaper) color in the cells. Any other choice will bring a reminder to the screen that a color or image is needed.

To prevent the rows from cycling forever, use one of the four Cycle through Rows options.

- ✔ Continually is the default; the rows cycle forever.

- ✔ Advance on Click means that every time a user clicks the table, a new row appears. Users won't know that the table will change when they click unless you tell them. A bit of text near the table telling them to click the table to see other data would be a good idea, don't you think.

- ✔ Another Cycle option is Once when Opened, which means (in case it isn't obvious) that every time someone opens the document containing the table, the rows will cycle once and then stop on the last row.

- ✔ Once on Click allows the user to click the table, cycle automatically through all the rows, and then stop on the last row. Don't forget that you can change the interval for displaying the rows.

The last page of the Table infobox concerns the use of HTML and JavaScript and is beyond the scope of this book. For information on HTML, check out *HTML For Dummies,* 2nd Edition, by Ed Tittle. And for more information on

JavaScript, check out *JavaScript For Dummies,* 2nd Edition, by Emily A. Vander Veer. (Both books are published by IDG Books Worldwide, Inc.)

Entering data

When you've made all the decisions and set all the settings, feel free to dismiss the dialog box, put the cursor in a cell, and start typing. When you're finished with one cell, move to the cell to the right by pressing Tab, move to the cell to the left by pressing Shift+Tab, move to the cell below by pressing the ↓ key, or move to the cell above by pressing the ↑ key. Of course, you can click a cell to move to any cell in the table.

All you have to do to change the height of a cell is type. If you have too much text to fit on one line in the cell or if you press Enter, the height of the cell increases to accommodate the additional text. The whole row becomes as tall as the cell with the most text in that row. If you want to change the width of a column, however, you have to mess with the menu, the ruler, or an icon. Read the section "Changing column widths the easy way," later in this chapter, for more information.

Open table, insert row

You are finished with the table and are about to send it when — "Eeek!" — you cry in frustration and disbelief. You forgot to include a column for the Instructor's name. Is it tragic? Sad? Are you out of luck? Is it difficult to add a column? Nope! You can add a new column or row as quickly as you can choose Table⇨Insert Column (or Table⇨Insert Row, depending on the circumstances).

Be sure that your cursor is in the column where you would like the new blank column to be (the column where your cursor is located is pushed to the right). If you want to insert a row, put your cursor in the row where you want the new row to appear (the row where your cursor is located is pushed down). In other words, when you insert a column, the new column appears in the column where you have the cursor, and all other columns move to the right to make room for the new one. When you insert a row, all other rows in the table move *down* to make room. Use Table⇨Insert Special to insert or append multiple rows or columns.

No more row four

What if you don't need a row anymore? Time to smear white correction fluid on the screen? Wait a minute, this is the computer age. There has to be a better way of getting rid of a row or a column.

If you want to delete an existing row, be sure to start by placing the cursor in the row you want to delete. That sounds like a simple enough suggestion, but if you aren't on your toes, you'll wind up deleting the wrong row. Choose Table➪Delete Selected Row(s) or, perhaps, Table➪Delete Selected Column(s). When you do, you'll get a warning that the action can't be undone. It's a one-way street.

If you have the cursor in the wrong row or column, or if you choose to delete a row when you meant to delete a column, you could end up in big trouble! So *be careful.* Because an ounce of prevention is worth two in the bush, here's a piece of advice. Save the document first, and then do your deleting. If you goof, you can close the document — without saving it — and reopen it. Now try again, and please be more careful this time!

More than one cell at a time

You may have noticed that many of the instructions in these past few pages began with some pithy instruction such as "make sure that you're in the right cell" or "click the cell whose border you want to change and then. . . ." So, the burning question is: What if you want to make some kind of change to *more than one* cell (or row or column) at a time? Can you do it? Is it possible? Could it be? You bet, and it's easy.

To make changes to more than one cell, just use your mouse to click and drag from the first cell to the last cell you want to change. After you've highlighted a bunch of cells (by pressing the left mouse button and holding it down while you highlight the cells), you can make any kind of change you want to those cells; a new font, italics, or even a new cell border are only a menu choice away.

Always make sure that you have selected the correct cell (or cells) in a table before you try to make a change to the table.

Changing column widths the easy way

Way back in Figure 13-4, we showed you how to change a column's width by using the Table Properties dialog box. That's great if you know exactly how wide you need a column to be or if you want to autosize the column. But what if you want to eyeball it? In other words, you're not sure of the exact column width, but it's obvious by looking that the column in question is too wide (or too narrow), and you want to make it smaller (or bigger), and you want to do it now (not later).

First, make sure that the cursor is in the column whose width you want to change. Then choose View⎓Ruler. In Figure 13-12, the ruler contains square symbols for the left and right margins of the column (that's column, not cell) and the familiar houses indicating the text indents for the cell (that's cell, not column).

You set the width for the whole column in the ruler, but you have to change the text indents for each cell in the column individually. The moral? Highlight all the cells in the column if you want a consistent text indent.

Finally, grab that little square symbol (shown on the right side of the column in the ruler in Figure 13-12) to change the column's size. Most people find this method easier than using the aforementioned dialog box, but if you would rather use the dialog box to enter a column's width manually, go right ahead. All that clicking and typing, you could break a nail.

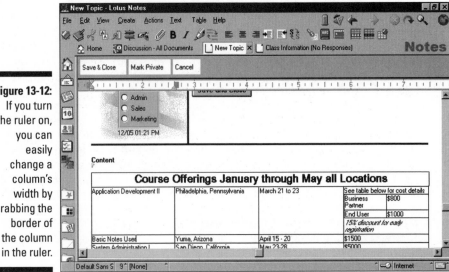

Figure 13-12:
If you turn the ruler on, you can easily change a column's width by grabbing the border of the column in the ruler.

Putting a table in a table

Huh? It's true, you can put a table inside another table. Not only that, but you can also combine several cells into one. In Figure 13-13, we have merged all cells in the top row to make room for a title. In the second row of the table, we inserted a table in the rightmost cell to show the different prices for the Application Development II course.

Deleting a table

Although it's rare, sometimes people want to get rid of an entire table. Getting rid of a table once and for all is a little tricky. You *cannot* select all the cells and then just press Delete. In fact, if you do, you'll end up deleting all the table's contents, but the empty cells will still be there.

Instead, you have to first select the entire table by putting the cursor at the end of the line just before (and outside) the table, and then pressing Shift+↓. Then, and only then, can you press Delete to get rid of the whole thing.

Figure 13-13:
This table has merged cells and a nested table.

Course Offerings January through May all Locations			
Application Development II	Philadelphia, Pennsylvania	March 21 to 23	See table below for cost details
			Business Partner $800
			End User $1000
			15% discount for early registration
Basic Notes User	Yuma, Arizona	April 15 - 20	$1500
System Administration I	San Diego, California	May 23-28	$5000

To merge cells, highlight the cells you want to merge, and then choose Table➪Merge Cells from the menu. If you merged some cells and want to split them back to the way they were, use Table➪Split Cells. You cannot split a single cell unless it was first merged, and you cannot merge a single cell, period.

To add a table to a table, first click the cell where you want to insert a table, and then choose Create➪Table. Make the usual decisions about the number of columns and rows, and then click OK. Enter data and impress your users with your table prowess.

Trying to Get a Header the Situation

Imagine this heartbreaking situation. You print a 50-page monster report. A breeze blows through the open window just as the last page comes out of the printer, and your document blows all over the place. You pick up the pages and try to put them in order. You have a tough time because the pages aren't numbered. Sad, isn't it? What's a body to do? Next time, create a header and put page numbers in it; that's what.

One doc, one header

Page numbers appear in headers or footers, which are bits of text at the top *(header)* or bottom *(footer)* of each printed page. You can choose to put other information in a header or footer, too, if you want. If a document is urgent or contains the kind of information spies and bad guys could use against the company, put that information in the header. If every page says "URGENT!" or "Don't Show This to Bad Guys," the reader is likely to get the message, even if one page is separated from the others.

To create headers and footers, choose File⇨Document Properties, and click the tab that has the cute little printer. When you do, you see the infobox featured so prominently in Figure 13-14. If you want to enter the text that's destined to appear at the top of each page, click the Header button. You don't have to be Einstein to figure out that you have to click the Footer button to enter text for the bottom of every page.

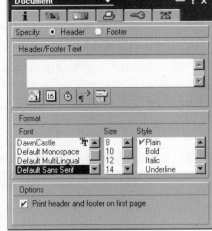

Figure 13-14:
Use the
Printer page
of the
Document
infobox to
create a
header or a
footer.

Remember, you won't see headers or footers on-screen because they appear only on the printed page.

"What can the Notes user put in a header or footer?" you ask. Glad you asked:

✔ **Text:** Type anything you want. If you want the header (or footer) to be several separate lines of information, such as an address, press Enter at the end of the first line, the second line, and so on.

✔ **Page number:** Click the Page Number button to automatically insert a page number in the header or footer. You can even get fancy and type **Page** and then click the Page SmartIcon. The header or footer looks like this: Page &P. The &P turns into the proper page number when you print, so on page 5 you'll see Page 5. Now, if the document gets blown around, putting it in order will be much easier. Of course, you can close that drafty window and avoid the problem altogether.

✓ **Date:** Click the Date button to automatically insert the date in a header or a footer. Printing the time or date in a header or footer is handy if the reader needs to tell which is the most recent printout among a lot of printed copies of the same memo.

✓ **Time:** Click the Time button, and the header or footer shows the current time (according to the computer's clock) each and every time you print your document. Notes prints the time in this format: 03:48:42PM.

✓ **Tab:** When you click the Tab button, Notes moves the next part of the header over to the right, just as if you pressed the Tab key when typing a document. Clicking Tab allows you to make more complete headers and footers with, for example, the date in the lower-left corner of the page, the time in the middle of the bottom of the page, and the page number in the lower-right corner of the page.

✓ **Window title:** When you click the last button, Notes puts the title of whatever document you're working on in the header (or footer) for all to see.

You can use the Font, Size, and Style lists to determine how the Header or Footer looks — but you can't mix and match. All text in a header is the same font, the same size, and the same style. How boring!

So, to wrap it all up, imagine that you're working in the Daily Schedule document and you enter this in the Header box:

```
           This is a Header|Page &P|&W
```

When you print the document, something like this appears at the top of page 6:

```
This is a Header          Page 6 Daily Schedule
```

Headers and footers appear on every page except the first page unless you click the Print Header and Footer on First Page option.

A chicken in every pot and a header for every doc

Creating a header or a footer in the aforementioned manner is just fine and dandy, but doing so affects only *the current document.* Note the dramatic use of italics to show you that, when you open a document and create a header, that header applies only to the document you are editing at the moment.

You may, instead, prefer to create a header or a footer for any document that is printed in a particular database. Although the preceding sentence doesn't contain any eye-catching italics, it is important to note that you can create one header or footer for every document that you print in the current database. Documents printed from other databases won't have a header unless you create one for that database, too.

 How to accomplish this technological feat? Click the Properties SmartIcon, and then be sure to choose Database from the Properties for list. Next, click the little tab with the picture of the printer, and you're in business! You enter the text and other items just the same way you would for a document header or footer (as we discuss in the previous few pages).

 The dialog box you use when you're working with a document's header looks remarkably like the dialog box you use when working with a database's header, so be careful and pay special attention to the Properties for list.

Set 'em Up, Boys

Setting up any printed page is an art. So put on your beret and choose File➪Page Setup to see the dialog box shown in Figure 13-15.

Figure 13-15:
The Page
Setup dialog
box.

You'll use this dialog box most often (if you use it at all) to adjust the margins by entering numbers in the appropriate fields. As we discuss in Chapter 12, you can set margins for individual paragraphs; use the Extra left and Extra right fields when you need to add even more space to your paragraph margins.

 If you've included page numbers in a header or a footer, tell Notes to start with a page number other than 1 by using the Start Page Numbers at field. You may find this option useful if you are printing a report from, say, Microsoft Word and you want to include a few pages from a Notes database. You print pages one through five in Word, and then print pages six through eleven in Notes. Use the Start Page Numbers at field to make your reader think that all the printed pages came from the same place.

If you intend to send your printed pages to a printing service to be reproduced, you could make the job easier for the staff of the printing service by using the Cropping features. On the other hand, if you're like most people and don't often send material to a professional printing company, you probably won't use the Cropping features.

Click the Paper button to tell Notes which paper tray in your printer to use for the first page when printing and then which tray to use for all the rest of the pages. Obviously, if you don't have one of those fancy printers with more than one paper tray, you won't spend too much time with this feature! But if you do have a fancy printer (lucky you!), this is a nice way to have the first page print on that fancy company letterhead.

Search and Rescue

Everybody makes mistakes. Remember: To err is human, to forgive is divine, and to make the same mistake again is inevitable. So, in the spirit of mistake-making, suppose that you type a long memo and then find that some of the text you typed is wrong. Of course, you made the mistake over and over again. You might, for example, have referred to Sue when she prefers to be called Susan.

The time has come to find all the Sues in the document and change them to Susans. Select Edit➪Find/Replace or press Ctrl+F. Watch for the dialog box that's pictured in Figure 13-16, which we have already tailored to our specifications.

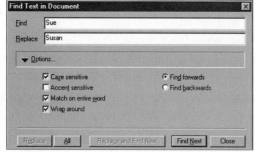

Figure 13-16:
The Find
and Replace
dialog box.

Searching for text to rescue your document takes a bit of planning if it's to work correctly. Notice, for example, these choices we made in Figure 13-17:

    ✔ We chose Match on Entire Word so that Notes doesn't go around changing *suede* into *Susande*.

✔ We would have chosen Accent Sensitive if we were searching for a word that contains a diacritical mark such as an accent, a circumflex, a cedilla, a freckle, or a mole. When you choose Accent Sensitive, Find and Replace looks specifically for that mark and ignores any occurrences of the word without it.

✔ We also chose Case Sensitive so that, if the document includes the word *sue* (the legal action), Notes won't replace that with Susan's name.

To be sure that you find all occurrences of a word you want to replace, it's best to put the cursor at the beginning of a document before you start beating the bushes for that special word.

After you've made all your decisions and typed the text you want to find and the text you want to use as a replacement, it's time to start the process. You can choose one of the following:

✔ **Find Forwards:** Begin at the cursor and go forward through the document to the first or next occurrence of the search text, but don't do any replacing.

✔ **Find Backwards:** Search from the cursor back to the beginning, but don't do any replacing.

After you decide which direction to search, choose:

✔ **Replace:** Find the first occurrence of the search text. Click Replace to replace that text but not find the next occurrence.

✔ **All:** Do the job quickly by replacing every occurrence of the search text with the replacement text without checking each time.

Use this choice carefully because strange and unpredictable things could happen. For instance, look what happens if the word Sue starts a sentence: *Sue us at your peril* becomes *Susan us at your peril.*

✔ **Replace and Find Next:** Allows you to make changes one at a time. It replaces the current instance and finds the next.

✔ **Find Next:** Leaves the current occurrence alone and looks for the next occurrence.

The clever little searcher might find an occurrence of the search text behind the Find and Replace dialog box, which means that you sometimes have to move the dialog box out of the way to see the highlight. Just drag the dialog box out of the way by the scruff of its title bar.

If You're a Bad Spellar

 Even if you're a really good speller, you're bound to make an occasional typographical error sometime in the next few years. You need to be ever vigilant for that eventuality — ready to pounce on an error and correct it before it gets sent to thousands of recipients who will laugh quietly up their sleeves at you for an easily correctable oversight.

In the dialog box in Figure 13-17, you see that the person who knocked out the memo didn't notice that *corporate* was spelled wrong. Then again, maybe he or she didn't know how to spell it. No matter, the spell checker found the mistake.

Figure 13-17:
Notes can
even
correct your
spelling —
just make
sure that its
guess is the
correct one.

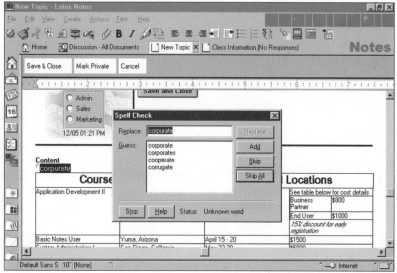

After you save your document (just to be safe), choose Edit⇨Check Spelling or click the Spell Check SmartIcon. Regardless of where you last saw your cursor, the spell checker starts at the beginning of the document. If the spell checker finds a word it doesn't recognize, it highlights the word (sometimes behind the dialog box) and waits for you to take some sort of action. Among the actions you can take are these:

- ✔ Go get a cup of coffee and let the spell checker wait until you're ready.

- ✔ Choose Add to add the word to the Notes dictionary so that Notes will never, ever highlight the word again.

- ✔ Choose Skip if you want to accept the misspelling this time, but you want Notes to continue to watch for it in the rest of the document.

- ✔ Choose Skip All if you want to ignore every occurrence of this word in this document.
- ✔ Choose Stop at the bottom of the dialog box if you are not prepared for the shock of seeing what you spelled rong.

If you just want to spell check a small section of a document, highlight all the text you want to spell check, and then kick off the spell checker.

Use the Add button carefully, because adding a misspelling to the dictionary can be very embarrassing. Forevermore, Notes will ignore that misspelling.

Chapter 14

Notes the Way You Want It

• •

• •

*W*hen you get a new office or desk (or place to stand, if you're a real junior in the company), one of your first official acts is to make your new location seem familiar. Out come the pictures — your family, your significant other, your pet dog, cat, or cobra. You arrange articles in the drawers so they're right where you need them and spread out your personal treasures across the expanse of your desk.

In similar fashion, as you snuggle into using Notes, you may find that you want to change some things about the way the program looks and works. The reasons may be cosmetic, such as changing the color of the background and text of your memos, or functional, such as designating your server, changing the Web page in your headlines, or choosing a password for your user ID. Speaking of pictures, if you're a bit artistic, you could even change the icon for your mail database so it looks like something especially meaningful to you, such as someone you love, your car, or your favorite dessert.

Mail That Has "You" Written All over It

In your company, it's probable that everyone's mail memos look the same. They don't say the same things, of course, but they have the same appearance. You have at your very fingertips the capability to completely change the appearance of every memo you send, so people will notice when your memos arrive at workstations around the world. Not only that, you can change several other aspects of your mail database as well (read on!).

When you create a memo in your mail database, you call to the screen a blank memo form on which you write your message. This form also acts like a lens through which you read the memos that others send you. Think of this Notes form as an electronic version of the blank memo pads some companies give their employees to write memos on. Perhaps your blank paper memo forms have your name or a logo on them and maybe even come in a color other than white. Why not have the same qualities in your Notes memos?

The following are some reasons why you may want to change a memo form:

✔ You want to change the way memos look on your screen as you read or write them.

✔ You want people who receive your memos to see a different memo format than the one they normally see.

✔ You want some fields — for example, the To field — to always have a certain value automatically (a *default* value).

Changing the way memos look on-screen

If we wrote about every detail of redesigning your mail memo form, this book would be twice as thick as it is now and would cost twice as much. Instead, we're going to talk about just the things you're most likely to want to change in the mail memo form. If your curiosity gets the best of you, use the Help feature to find new things to do or to find out how to respond to an unfamiliar dialog box.

To start the process of customizing your mail memos, follow these steps:

1. **Start the Designer Client.**

   Click the Launch Designer Client icon from the set of navigation icons.

2. **If your mail database is not listed in the Navigator (left-hand) pane, use File⇨Database Open and select your mail database.**

   For more information on opening databases see Chapter 9.

3. **In the Navigator pane, be sure that your mail database is expanded so that you see listed under the database name the list of design elements: outlines, framesets, and so on. Click Forms.**

   If you do it right, your screen will look like Figure 14-1.

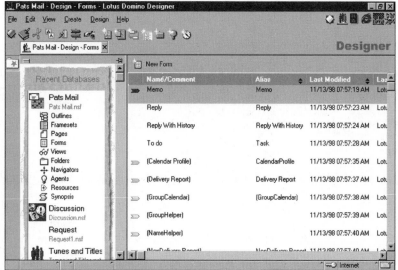

Figure 14-1:
This is the
mail
database
open with
forms high-
lighted
in the
Designer
Client.

4. **Double-click Memo.**

   Dismiss the warning that starts out "If you make changes to this form" because we'll be dealing with its dire warning soon. Don't be daunted by the confusion on your screen. Resizing the panes so you can see more of the form, and then scrolling around the mail memo form will show you there's nothing to fear. See Figure 14-2.

5. **Change the memo form to your satisfaction.**

   Among the quick changes you can make to your form are the following:

   - Change any field titles (static text) such as To, From, or Subject by simply editing them.

   - Change the font, font size, or color of field titles by highlighting the text and using the Text infobox.

   - Change the font, font size, or color of any field itself by high lighting the field definition box and then activating the Field infobox and choosing the changes you want. You could, for example, make one of the fields bold or make it a different font from the rest.

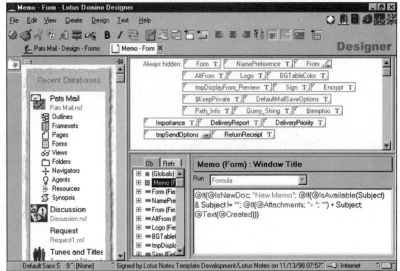

Figure 14-2:
This is the
mail memo
form open in
design
mode.

- Add other text or objects to the form. For example, you could
  place below the body of the memo a sincere, heartfelt, and
  original message like "Have a nice day" to warm the cockles of
  the reader's heart, or you could add the company logo or an
  image of your motorcycle.

6. **When you're finished, press Esc.**

7. **At the prompt, choose Yes, you do want to save the form.**

   From now on, whenever you compose a memo, you will do so on your
   new form.

The words in boxes on your memo form represent the fields themselves. As
you highlight a field, you see its formula in the Programmer pane at the
bottom of the screen. Some fields have no formula associated with them, in
which case that pane is empty. Surprise. Double-click any field to see the
actual field definition in an infobox. Don't forget to close the infobox when
you finish making changes.

Mess with the formula and the more technical aspects of the field at your
own risk — changing field definitions is beyond the scope of this book. When
we say "field definition," we don't mean its appearance; we mean just the
technical stuff such as field data types. If you do start to make some changes
and get panicky, dismiss the infobox by clicking the X in its upper-right
corner and then press Esc and choose No when the prompt asks whether you
want to save the form.

One other change you may want to make to the memo is the background color. Once again, you use the infobox, but you need to select Text at the top of the Properties box. Next, select the Background page and then click the down arrow in the background color box to display the dazzling choice of colors.

If this book were in living color, you could see the rainbow of hues available for your memo form's background in Figure 14-3. To select a color, click the one you like. This dialog box has other options, but they're a bit too advanced for this book.

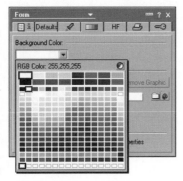

Figure 14-3:
Here is
how you
choose a
background
color for
your mail
memo form.

Keep in mind the colors you plan to use for your fields and static text as you choose a background color. You can create some hard-to-read combinations if you're not careful. Imagine black letters on a brown background. If you change text colors, too, you can even get stuff like yellow letters on a pink background. It might sound springtime fresh and colorful, but the lack of contrast means that no one will be able to read it! As a general rule, keep backgrounds light and letters dark. Light letters on a dark background are much harder to read.

One little point you ought to know: All these changes are visible only at your end — that is, when *you* are looking at memos. So far, you've been changing forms for the first reason listed earlier in this section: to change the way the memos you read and write look on your own screen. That is, when the recipients open their copy of your memo, they see the plain old memo form they're used to seeing, because *their* form is the one used at *their* computer to read all the memos they've received.

Can you do anything to remedy this sorry situation? Yes! Read on.

Changing the way your memos look on everyone else's screen

After you make changes to your memo form, you may want to send those changes along with your memo. Here's how:

1. Open the infobox and select Form.

2. Click the Defaults page.

What you see should look a lot like Figure 14-4.

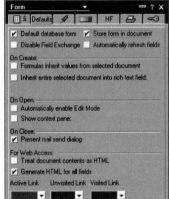

Figure 14-4: The Form infobox Defaults page.

3. Click to select the Store Form in Document option.

Now, when you send a message to other people, Notes uses *your* form to display your message on *their* computers. You pay a price, however, for including a form in a memo when you send it. The memo becomes much bigger, byte-wise, meaning that e-mail databases fill up faster and transmission over networks and modems takes longer. But that's a small price to pay for your work of art, right? Well, perhaps in the interest of being a good citizen, you should select the Store Form in Document option only for special forms, rather than just on a whim. You have to do one more little job to prevent these changes from being reversed by Notes. Click the Design tab and select Prohibit Design Refresh or Replace to Modify.

If you store the form in the document, your form is the one that others see when reading your memos.

Adding fields — a form is born

The third reason for changing memos is to have Notes fill in some fields for you automatically. You can create a form for special occasions that does just that. There's no reason a person as capable as you can't create a form. After all, this is *your* mail database, isn't it?

How about a form to send memos to your inner circle of coworkers and friends? You can base its design on the memo form.

Follow these steps to create a new form that is identical to the memo form:

1. **In the Navigation pane, click Forms.**
2. **In the View pane, highlight the memo form.**
3. **Click the Copy SmartIcon and then click the Paste SmartIcon.**

Eventually, you see a new form, called "Copy of Memo," in the list of forms. This new form is a twin of the original memo form. To modify this new form, double-click its name.

Remember that anytime you want to create a new view, form, or other database element based on an existing one, just copy and paste the one you want right into the same database.

You probably don't send courtesy copies or blind courtesy copies of personal memos, so you may want to delete those field titles and the field definitions. Highlight them and press Delete to remove them.

Although deleting the cc and bcc fields is okay, Notes uses many of the other fields behind the scenes (such as the To and From fields), so your best bet is to avoid deleting any other fields.

If memos written on this form are always going to go to certain friends, you can permanently place their names in the To field. If you are sending a memo to the department, you can put the name of the group in the To field (assuming that the group name has been defined in either the company's or your personal name and address book). To change the To field, highlight it and, in the Programmer pane, type the new names enclosed in quotes and separated by commas (for example, you might type **"John Smith, Sue Brown"**). We recommend that you copy and paste names of people and groups from the name and address book so that you get each name in its entirety and correctly spelled.

Feel free to change the background color using the Form infobox. Also, Copy of Memo is not much of a name, you no doubt agree, so use the infobox Basics page to give your form a new name. How about "Personal Memo"? Also, be sure to use the Defaults page to select the Store Form in Document option so that your memo will look the same on other people's computers as it does on yours.

When you finish designing your form, press Esc and save the new form.

Now you have a new form to use. Choose Create, and there, in the list of things you can compose, is your new form. Won't the crew be impressed! They'll crowd around you in the lunchroom asking how you did that. Mention this book, please. You're well on your way to becoming a true Notes nerd.

The form you just created exists only in your mail database, so it will definitely be necessary to select the Store Form in Document option so that your readers will see your documents with the proper form.

A Folder to Fit Your Needs

Folders are holders for documents. You put selected documents — such as memos from people giving you things to do — in a folder to keep them together in one place. Of course, if you want to sound really corporate, you don't say "To do." No sirree, you say "Action Items." Everyone, regardless of their status in the organization, gets the occasional memo discussing something they have to do. You should create a folder so that all those memos are in one place, rather than scattered around among other memos about meeting for coffee and doing lunch.

What'll it look like?

The first step in creating a folder is to look at all the views, not to see what documents are in them, but to see their design, especially the columns. Choose one you want to use as the design for your folder. Of course, you can modify the design, but if you have a similar design starting out, you can finish your own folder faster so you have more time to do your power lunch. Your choice should be easy; views in a mail database are fairly similar. The difference among views more often has to do with which documents they contain for display rather than their design.

Our suggestion is to base your new folder on the All Documents view. If it contains all documents, it should be capable of displaying any mail database documents you put in it. If it can't, you can always try to get your money back. To create a folder, you do not need to be in the Designer Client as you were when you modified the memo form. The following steps assume that you are in the regular Notes Client:

1. **Choose Create⇨Folder.**

2. **In the first dialog box you see (the one in the lower-left portion of Figure 14-5), type the name of your new folder.**

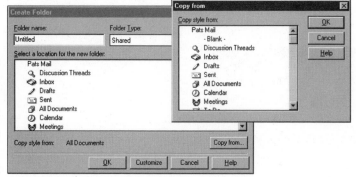

Figure 14-5:
The two dialog boxes used to design the new folder.

We prefer "To Do" — thanks very much.

3. **Click the Copy From button.**

4. **In the second dialog box (shown at the right side of Figure 14-5), designate the All Documents view as the view to Copy Style From, and then click OK.**

5. **In the Select a Location for the New Folder area, click the name of a folder if you want the new folder to be cascaded under an existing view or folder.**

   If you don't choose a folder, the new folder will appear in the list of main folders and views.

   Cascaded means that a green arrowhead appears next to the existing view or folder. Clicking that arrowhead displays the name of your new folder tucked in underneath the name of the view or folder you selected. If you don't make any selection, the folder appears in the list with all the other views and folders as an equal.

6. **Click the Customize button so you can get right to work.**

   On the other hand, don't choose the Customize button now if you plan to use the folder without changes.

Your To Do folder takes its rightful place, and you go into design mode — you may now put on your construction hat.

Do folders have properties?

Yes indeed, every element of a database has its own properties; folders are no exception. Set those properties in the Folder infobox (see Figure 14-6). There's a bit of clicking first: You have to open your mail database in the Designer Client and then open the new folder to get to its infobox.

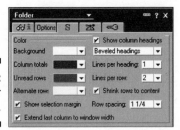

Figure 14-6:
The Folder
infobox.

The following list describes the types of settings you can make and tells which page of the Folder infobox they're on:

- ✔ **Name (Basics page):** If you want to change the name of the folder, this is where you do it.

- ✔ **Style (Basics page):** The style can be either a Standard outline or a Calendar.

- ✔ **Colors (Style page):** Here you can choose from over 200 stunning colors and patterns for the background, rows containing unread documents, and column totals. In addition, you can choose a color for alternate rows of the view. Figure 14-6 shows you what the Style page looks like.

- ✔ **Lines per row (Style page):** This setting is useful if some long-winded person wrote a long name for the task or included a lot of people in the Assigned To list. If you choose more than one line per row, you can also choose to shrink a row to content so that it won't take any more room than it needs to.

When you don't want to make any more changes to your folder in the Folder infobox, just click the box marked X in the upper-right corner. Then press Escape to dismiss the folder, choose to save it, and you're finished.

Icons Customized While-U-Wait

Actually, to customize icons you have to do more than just wait. You have to do the work. Your desktop has a box with an icon for each database you've added. Your e-mail database icon, which looks like everyone else's, is yours to change if you want — here's your chance to strut your stuff, be an individual, leave the pack behind, show off your creative genius . . . and waste a little time.

Start by opening your mail database in the Designer Client. Then, in the Navigation pane, select Other in the list of database design elements, and select Icon in the main pane. A palette appears with the tools and colors you need to create an eye-catching crowd pleaser. Of course, the crowd normally seeing this icon is just one (you), but don't let that dampen your enthusiasm.

Figure 14-7 shows the standard mail database icon with a framed *T* added to give it that warm, personal touch.

Figure 14-7:
The mail
database
icon,
personalized
for someone
whose
name begins
with *T*.

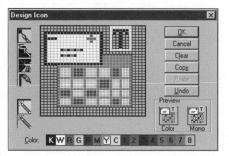

The boxes to the left in Figure 14-7 are *tools,* allowing you to do such things as color whole areas at once, color individual squares (called *pixels*), or draw straight lines with the color you choose. The pencils in the lower left are for drawing and erasing (should you drip a little paint in the wrong place).

If, *sacre bleu,* you've made a series of mistakes and want to start over, click Clear, and the entire palette is emptied of color — you may start again. When you make a simple mistake, click Undo, and it's as though the most recent action never took place.

As you work, you can check the Preview window to see how the icon will look on a color or monochrome monitor. When you're satisfied, click OK and, voilà, your database has a new icon.

To copy another master's work, open another database icon in the Designer Client, select Icon in the main pane, click Copy to move the icon from another database to the Clipboard, and then click Paste to place it into the current palette. Or why not get into PaintBrush, create an original drawing, and then copy and paste it into the icon palette?

Now, to Etch It in Stone

To finalize the creation of your database, you must take one more step. Otherwise, when you open your mail database tomorrow, all your work will be gone.

When you try to enter design mode for design elements in some databases and see a warning saying that your changes may be lost, follow these steps:

1. **In the Navigation pane of your mail database in the Designer Client, click Forms.**

2. **In the main pane, click Personal Memo (or the name of whatever form you have changed).**

   Don't double-click; just select it.

3. **Now activate the infobox by clicking the Infobox (Properties) SmartIcon.**

4. **Select the Design Tabbed page of the Form Properties box.**

5. **Click the Design tab, and select Prohibit Design Refresh or Replace to Modify.**

6. **Close the infobox by clicking the X in its upper-right corner.**

Now you can sleep soundly, fully confident that, when the midnight marauder comes around reversing changes made by the unsuspecting to their mail databases, your changes are safe and permanent.

What am I protecting my document from?

Some databases are associated with a *template,* a special database that provides its design to one or many real databases. Late at night, when nothing is stirring, not even a mouse, the template quietly steals into where good little databases are sleeping and removes any recent design changes, replacing them with its own design.

When you follow the steps in this section to etch your new form or view in stone, you're preventing changes to one database element. If you want to cut the cord that ties the database to its design template forever (be sure that you know what you did and understand what you're doing), activate the infobox for the database, click the Design tab, and deselect Inherit Design from Template. From now on, your changes will be permanent. If some wise, distant designer makes changes to the template, those changes will not be made to your database. Of course, this means you won't be able to take advantage of improvements anyone makes to the template, because you've blocked them from being added to your database.

Certify Me, Quick

When you go out of the country, you usually need a passport. Sometimes you need to have your passport stamped with special permission to visit specific places. Notes uses a kind of passport and visa, too. In Notes, your passport is your *Notes ID,* and the visa is a *certificate.* Your ID says that you are a Notes user, and the certificate tells which organization will allow you to access its server.

Normally, you use Notes in only your own organization. Sometimes, people leave an organization — and not always for the right reasons, if you get our drift. Some of those people may become bad guys. Of course, every organization should keep an eye on comings and goings to be sure that only current members have access to Notes. But, just in case someone slips through the cracks, everyone's certification expires after a few years.

When your certification is about to expire, you need to get recertified; otherwise, on some dark day in the not-too-distant future, you will find that you simply can't access any Notes servers. Ordinarily, you receive a notice from the Notes administrator telling you that your number is up, and you need to get recertified soon.

To see when your certificate expires, choose File⇨Tools⇨User ID and then click Certificates. Highlight each certificate (assuming that you have more than one — most people don't) and information appears telling you when that certificate expires. Figure 14-8 shows what the dialog box looks like.

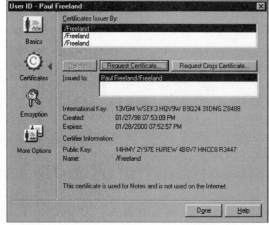

Figure 14-8:
The User ID dialog box shows all sorts of information about your user ID.

There's another reason to get certified — you may need to use databases on a server in another company or in another *domain* (users and servers created with a different certificate) in your company. Because that company or domain uses a different certificate, you won't be allowed to gain access to the server or databases.

The good news is that getting certified is easy. And it's free. And you don't need to get recertified very often (usually only once every few years). And the sun'll come out tomorrow. Here's what you do:

1. **Choose File➪Tools➪User ID.**

2. **Click Certificates, and then choose Request Certificate.**

3. **Choose Request Notes Certificate.**

4. **In the dialog box that appears on your screen (see Figure 14-9), type the name of the person to whom you're sending your request.**

Figure 14-9:
We're in the
process of
requesting
a new
certificate.

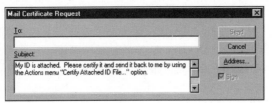

Ask around your organization to find the name of the *certifier,* the person who issues certificates.

5. **Click Send.**

Wait for the certifier to send you a return memo with your certification attached. When this joyous event occurs, open the memo and choose Actions➪Accept Certificate. Type your password in the dialog box that appears, and then click Accept. You're now the proud owner of a certificate.

Honey, Where Are My Encryption Keys?

Cloak and dagger stuff, this encryption. You encrypt information when you want to be absolutely sure that it won't be seen by the wrong eyes or even a wrong whole person. *Encrypting* means scrambling the information in a field. It takes place behind the scenes, and the only teeny little hint that something is encrypted is that sending or opening a document containing an encrypted field takes a little longer.

You may encrypt information in two places: your mail messages and specified fields in other databases. Encryption uses *keys* to scramble and rearrange the data so that it doesn't make any sense during transmission. In the case of mail messages that you want to encrypt, you don't have to do anything about keys. Encrypted mail scrambles only the body field and uses the public and private encryption keys associated with the user ID for each recipient. It's all automatic. See Chapter 6 for more information about encrypting mail memos.

You use the following procedure to encrypt only fields in databases, not your mail memos. Encryption in the mail database is performed automatically when you choose to encrypt a mail message.

If you're using a database that has an encryptable field, you may choose to encrypt the data in that field. In that case, you have to supply legitimate readers of the data with a special encryption key that you create. No key means no reading; the field will appear empty.

You can tell whether a field is encryptable because the *field markers* (the little corners showing the beginning and end of the field) are red in encryptable fields. Red field markers mean that users who can edit a document can choose to encrypt that field.

Suppose that you're entering data in a product planning form in which one field is for super-secret design information. Other data is information everyone in the company might need, such as the product name, what the product does, or why everyone needs one of these gizmos immediately. That information doesn't need to be secret, but the design information does. So you decide to encrypt the field.

Creating your key

First, you have to create the encryption key. Follow these steps:

1. **Choose File⇨Tools⇨User ID, enter your password, and then click the Encryption button.**

2. **Choose New.**

   A dialog box appears, as shown in Figure 14-10.

Figure 14-10:
The way to
create a
new
encryption
key.

3. **Give the new key a name, preferably something you'll associate with its purpose.**

   The Comment field is optional.

4. **Make a selection in the Use area.**

   Choose North American Only if this database will be seen only in North American installations of Notes. If you have offices around the world that may use the database, you should choose International.

Places outside North America have a different way of encrypting information. The United States government requires this distinction. We could tell you why, but then you would have the CIA following *you* around, too.

Attaching your key to a document

After you create the key, you add it to the document you are writing:

1. **Choose Create to start a document.**

   Of course, if you've already started the document you want to encrypt, you can ignore this step.

2. **Choose File⇨Document Properties.**

3. **In the infobox that appears, click the tab with the picture of a key.**

   The Security page appears, as shown in Figure 14-11.

4. **Choose an existing key from one of the two list boxes.**

   Use the Secret Encryption Keys list box to choose a key that you've created, or click the person icon next to Public Encryption Keys and choose the person or people whose public key (in the public name and address book) you want to use to encrypt the message. Only the people you choose will be able to decrypt the field.

Okay, you've added an encryption key to your document, so you can encrypt the field. But who can *decrypt* it? You? Yes, but no one else . . . yet.

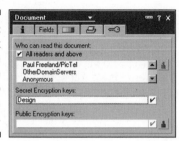

Figure 14-11:
This infobox is where you choose the key to encrypt a field.

Sending your key

You need to send the new key to anyone who needs to see the encrypted field. Choose File➪Tools➪User ID, click the Encryption button, and then select the key you want to send. Click Mail to open the Mail Address Encryption Key dialog box (shown, for your viewing pleasure, in Figure 14-12).

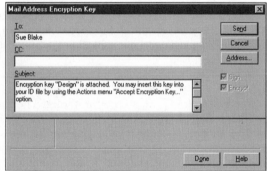

Figure 14-12:
Here we are sending a new encryption key to someone.

Enter the name, names, or group to whom you are sending the key. You can send carbon copies (CC) to people who ought to know you've sent the key, but those folks will not receive the key itself. The Subject line of the memo automatically contains whatever text is in the Subject box, but you can change that text if you want it to say something else. Happy with everything in the dialog box? Fine; choose Send.

One more question from Notes, and the key is on its way. A question box appears, asking "Should recipients be allowed to send this key to other users?" This is your call. If the information is terribly sensitive and you want control over who sees it, choose No. People can ask you to send the key to others if necessary. If you don't want people to bother you by requesting the key all the time, choose Yes.

Using the key

After you send the key, you're finished with your part. But the recipients have a small chore when they receive the key. They need to highlight the memo containing the key. Associated with the memo is an Accept Encryption action button. They click that, choose Accept, and the encryption key is theirs. Now they can read the encrypted field.

Tooling around in Notes

The little Notes engine is throbbing quietly and efficiently somewhere inside your computer: Messages are moving, secrets in encrypted fields are being kept, and you've even succeeded in customizing the look of some of your forms. We still have a few odds and ends to tell you about.

Some IDeas

Your *user ID* is the file that allows you to use Notes. If someone gets hold of your ID, that person can use Notes pretending to be you — sending off messages, reading your mail, and peeking into encrypted fields that only the chosen few are supposed to see.

Where is your ID? Only you know that for sure, but it's probably in several places: in the Notes directory (folder) of your computer, on a floppy disk for backup storage in case something happens to your computer, and if you have a laptop, in the Notes directory there, too. So you may have three separate Notes ID files that some ruthless person could use to his or her advantage. Even somebody with a few ruths might take your ID and use it for dubious purposes.

Anyone with access to your computer has access to your ID. The solution is to protect your ID with a password *right now*. Of course, if you are already required to enter a password, these steps are not necessary. Some organizations, however, don't require the use of passwords. Strange!

If you do need to create a password, choose File⇨Tools⇨User ID and then click the Set Password button on the Basics tab. Figure 14-13 shows the relatively simple dialog box into which you type your password.

Figure 14-13:
Use this
dialog box
to create
a new
password.

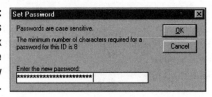

Keep the following facts in mind as you think about what you will use as a password:

✔ You may use a password of any length, although your administrator may have set a minimum length. If there is a minimum length, the dialog box will tell you so, as it does in Figure 14-13.

✔ Notes recommends a minimum of eight characters, simply because it's many times harder to figure out a long password than it is to figure out a short one.

✔ This may be obvious, but be sure that your password is something you can remember. We all have to remember social security numbers, credit card codes, logon names and passwords, gym locker combinations, in-laws' birthdays, and the date of our tetanus booster. Anytime we forget one of these, somebody treats us as though we're wearing a clown suit. If you set a Notes password and forget it, you are out of luck. You'll have to get a new ID and start all over — and all your old encrypted messages will be unreadable.

✔ This, too, may be obvious, but make sure that the password isn't something that someone else will figure out. Using your first name is not the most secure password.

✔ Passwords are case sensitive, so *PASSWORD* is different than *Password,* which is different than *password,* which is different than *pAssword,* which is . . . well, you get the point.

✔ As you type your password, only Xs appear on-screen. This is to protect your password from over-the-shoulder snoopers. Notes takes passwords seriously.

✔ After you create your password, Notes prompts you to type it a second time to be sure that you didn't make a mistake.

If you don't know where your Notes ID file is, use the file find feature in your operating system — the Tools➪Find➪Files or Folders menu item in Windows Explorer, for example. Tell it to find *.id. You need only one Notes ID file on your computer, and it should be in the Notes folder or in the Data directory under the Notes folder. If you are required to log on to a network, the Notes ID file can even be located on the network in your home directory. Delete any extras.

Password-protecting the ID file on your main computer has no effect on your laptop's copy of the ID. The best way to handle this is to password-protect the ID on your main computer, then copy it to a floppy disk, and then copy it from the floppy disk to your laptop. Delete any copies of the ID file that are not password protected, or keep them under lock. (Usually, people say "lock and key," but if the key were around, why bother with the lock?)

Each of your ID files might have different certificates associated with it. If you have an ID on a floppy disk and one on your hard disk, choose File➪Tools➪Switch ID and choose each ID, one at a time. You can see what certificates are associated with an ID file by choosing File➪Tools➪User ID and clicking Certificates. Add a password to the ID with the largest number of certificates and copy that ID to the floppy disk and your other computers. If each ID has different certificates, add the password to each separately.

Always keep copies of e-mail messages that contain encryption keys for you to accept. That way, they are available if you lose the ID file that contained the certificate.

If you leave your computer, you ought to take steps so that any lowlifes bent on no good can't gain access to Notes on your computer. Press F5 or choose File➪Tools➪Lock ID. That command immediately disables your access to Notes until you enter your password again.

There's even a way to get Notes to lock your computer automatically if it notices that you've been away for a while. Of course, Notes doesn't know whether you've physically left the computer, but it does know how long it has been since you used it. After a certain amount of time, Notes starts missing your gentle tapping on the keyboard and disables your access until you enter your password.

To enable this time-out procedure, choose File➪Preferences➪User Preferences, click Basics, and then enter a number of minutes in the Lock ID after xx Minutes of Inactivity option. You can see in Figure 14-14 that we are allowing 15 minutes of inactivity to pass before disabling our personal access.

If the specified time goes by, or if you press F5, a screen prompting you for your password appears the next time you try to access a database or a function that's available only from the server. Type your password, press Enter, and off you go.

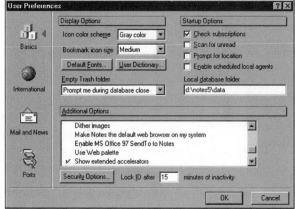

Figure 14-14:
Use this
dialog box
to log out of
Notes
automatically.

If you decide to remove password protection from your ID file, choose
File➪Tools➪User ID and click Basics. Click the Clear Password button, type
your password, and click OK. The password is no more.

Perhaps you just got married and have a new name, or you're in the witness
protection program and need a new name, or the name you've been using in
Notes isn't quite right. You can see a bunch of information about your user ID
by choosing File➪Tools➪User ID and clicking More Options.

But don't try to change your user name by clicking Change Name. If you do,
you won't be able to use Notes anymore. Instead, click Request New Name
and type the name you want to use in the dialog box which appears. When a
mail memo like the one in Figure 14-15 appears, fill in the name of the Notes
administrator. Mail this request and wait for a response. When the response
arrives, open it and choose to accept the certificate.

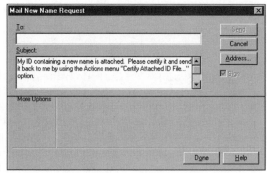

Figure 14-15:
Identity
crisis?
Request a
new name.

Tools that set you up

When you start your car, you fasten your seat belt, adjust the mirror, and set the volume on the radio before heading out into traffic. Likewise, when you start Notes, you may have some adjustments to make. To do so, choose File⇨Preferences⇨Notes Preferences.

The basics

Back in Figure 14-14, we show the Basics part of the Notes Preferences dialog box. The following list includes the most important items you can select in this figure:

- ✔ **Scan for Unread:** Automatically checks for unread memos. If you select Scan for Unread, the next time you start Notes, you get a dialog box telling you how many unread messages or documents you have. Tell Notes which databases you're interested in having it check. After all, you probably don't want to know about all the unread documents in all the databases you may have on your desktop.

- ✔ **Prompt for Location:** Tells Notes to ask you what type of location you're using in each new session. This is useful if you use your computer in different defined locations every time you start Notes.

- ✔ **Empty Trash Folder:** Offers three choices for getting rid of documents you dragged to the trash folder of a database:

  - • Prompt Me during Database Close tells Notes to confirm that you want to empty the trash when you close a Notes session.

  - • Always during Database Close tells Notes to empty the trash automatically when you close a database.

  - • Manually means you must empty the trash yourself.

- ✔ **Startup Launch:** You can choose to open a specific Notes Database, a specific Web Page, or Bookmarks (the default).

- ✔ **User Dictionary:** Allows you to create a dictionary for words you don't want the spell checker to flag. You may want to include your name in the user dictionary — or unusual acronyms you frequently use.

- ✔ **Right Double-Click Closes Window (Advanced options):** A throwback to earlier releases of Notes, when you could always close a window by double-clicking the secondary (usually the right) mouse button. Select this option if you've grown accustomed to the old method and choose not to learn any new tricks this late in your life. Even if you aren't used to the option, it's very handy.

Internationally speaking

Click International (below Basics in the Notes Preferences dialog box) and, among other things, you'll be able to change the collation sequence (the way Notes sorts documents in views), the measurement units from Imperial (gallons, inches, miles, six-packs) to Metric (meters, liters, tweeters), and the dictionary (so that when the spell checker finds errors, it will present the right alternative spellings for your context).

Checking the mail

Click the Mail button (below International in the Notes Preferences dialog box) to designate which mail program you're using: Notes, cc:Mail, or Other VIM (Vendor Independent Mail). If you select and enter a number in Check for New Mail Every xx Minutes, Notes automatically checks for new mail in your mail database. Audible Notification sounds a tune each time you get mail — which will quickly annoy your neighbors. When you have new mail, Visible Notification puts an envelope in your status bar and a message window appears. You may also want to encrypt all outgoing or incoming messages, or add a digital signature to all your memos to verify the memos are really from you and have not been tinkered with in transition.

Choose the Internet Message Format to determine whether HTML or plain text or both will be used for Internet mail. You can also choose to edit your memos using Microsoft Word or Lotus WordPro instead of the Notes editor.

Smartening up the SmartIcons

Choose File➪Preferences➪SmartIcons to change the way you display these handy tools. If it bothers you to have SmartIcons at the top of the screen, or if you just want to experiment with other locations for them, click Position and choose Left, Top, Right, or Bottom.

You may have noticed that Notes doesn't display the Print SmartIcon, so you have to use the menu when you want to print. You can change all that by using SmartIcon Preferences to add the Print SmartIcon to a new set and choose to use that set. Here's how:

1. **Choose File➪Preferences➪SmartIcons.**

2. **Scroll down the Available Icons list on the left side until you see the File Print icon.**

3. **Click and drag the Print icon to the right-hand column.**

   You can click and drag it to the specific place in the column where you want it to be placed.

4. **Click Save Set, and give the new set a name and a file name.**

   In Figure 14-16, we are saving the new set as New List. We named the file new. Notes adds the .smi automatically.

5. **In the top list in the SmartIcons dialog box, select New List.**

Figure 14-16:
The
SmartIcons
dialog box
lets you add
useful new
icons to the
available
set.

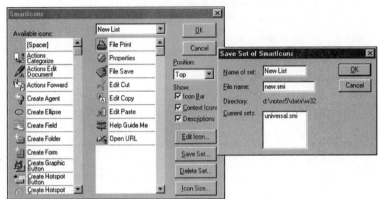

If you lost your glasses, or your contacts are in upside down and you can't make out one SmartIcon from the next, click the Icon Size button and then click Large. Expect the complete set to disappear from the screen when a large set of icons is needed on the screen. You can't have your SmartIcon cake and eat it, too.

The Notes Welcome Page

When you start Notes, you are confronted with the Welcome page, as shown in Figure 14-17. What you see on the Welcome page is determined by a few things. For example, you can change the Welcome Page's layout and con-tents. (Your Administrator has some control over what you see — so that he or she can make sure that you see important announcements and so on.)

In general, though, it's a safe bet that your Welcome page (however it's set up) will be divided into a few sections, known as *frames*. For example, Figure 14-18 shows a sample Welcome page belonging to some guy named Steve Londergan. It has three frames: One contains his inbox, one has his schedule, and the last frame shows a Web page.

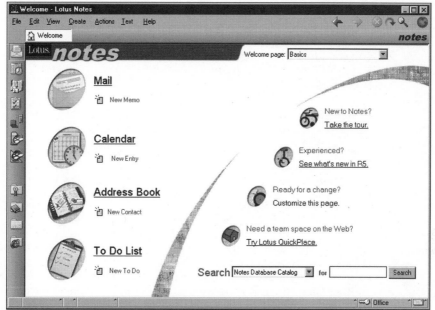

Figure 14-17:
The default
Notes
Welcome
page.

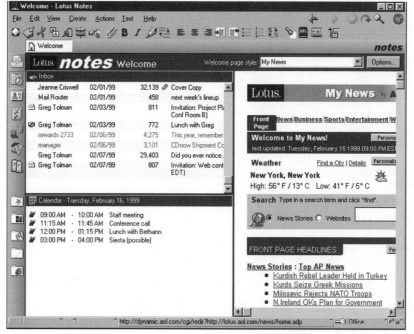

Figure 14-18:
A customized
Welcome
page can
contain
just about
anything —
such as
your
calendar,
or your
inbox, or
even a
Web page.

Changing the Welcome page

It's easy to change the Layout of your Welcome page: Just choose the layout you want from the Welcome Page Style list, as shown in Figure 14-19.

Notes offers the following three styles:

✔ **Basics** is the simplest Welcome page of all; it's the one with all those pictures of kids. This is the default Welcome Page.

✔ **My News** is a little more informative. It contains three pages: one for your inbox, one for your calendar, and one for a special news page from America Online.

✔ **Notes and Domino News** is similar to My News, but it has a Web page from the Lotus Web site instead of from America Online.

If you're happy with the layout and content of one of these Welcome page styles, just choose the one you like, and you're in business. If, on the other hand, you would like to customize it more to your liking — perhaps to add another frame or to change what's in one of the frames — select the style you want, and then click the Options button.

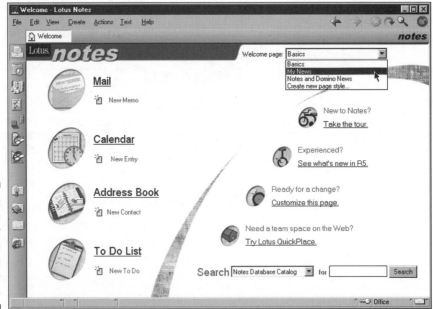

Figure 14-19:
Change the
style of your
Welcome
page using
the drop-
down list.

Customizing the pages

As mentioned, you can customize the Welcome page in a few different ways. You can choose exactly how many frames of information are contained in the page, and you can change the content of each frame.

To modify the layout or content of a Welcome page, first select the Welcome page you want to change from the Welcome Page Style list, and then click the Options button. The screen shown in Figure 14-20 appears.

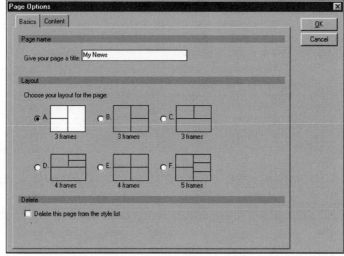

Figure 14-20:
Changing
the
Welcome
page's
layout.

Your first task is to select the presentation style and number of frames that the Welcome page will use. Select one of the six layouts — but remember that the more frames you have, the less information you'll be able to see in each. You can also change the Welcome Page's name by editing the Give Your Page a Title field.

When you are ready to change the content of the Welcome Page's frames, click the Content tab on the Page Options dialog box. The screen changes to that shown in Figure 14-21.

Changing the content of a frame is a simple process:

1. **At the top of the Content page of the Page Options dialog box, click the frame whose content you want to change.**

2. **In the Frame Content list, select what you want as the frame's content.**

   You can choose one of the following as any frame's content:

   - **Basic tasks** shows the Open Mail, Open Calendar, and Open Address Book buttons.

   - **Inbox** shows the inbox folder in your mail database.

   - **Calendar** shows your meetings and appointments.

   - **To do list** shows your tasks.

   - **Web page** shows a Web page. If you choose to display a Web page, you also have to select or enter the page's URL.

   - **Quick links** lets you display a set of links to your favorite places.

   - **Search** presents the Notes search options.

   - **Database Subscriptions** shows you the results of your subscriptions (if any).

3. **When you have finished customizing the page's layout and content, Click the OK button.**

The good news is that it's pretty hard (impossible, actually) to screw this up, so the best approach is to experiment with the various layout and content styles until you find one that you like. You can change from one style to another, anytime you want.

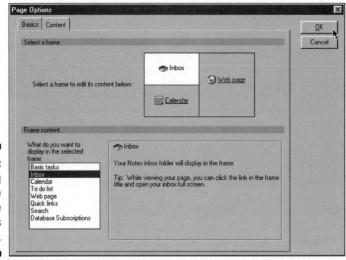

Figure 14-21:
Changing
the
Welcome
page's
content.

Creating a subscription

One of the things you can choose to display on your Welcome page is a subscription. Suppose that every morning, you check a discussion database to see whether anyone has added anything since yesterday. Using a subscription is an easy way to let Notes' fingers do the walking; it will check to see whether new documents have been added, and then (optionally) display them on your headlines. You can subscribe to any Notes database.

To have Notes track a database for you, first open the database, then choose Create⇨

Subscription, and then use the form shown in the figure to tell Notes what you want to track. For example, you can ask Notes to notify you whenever documents have been added to the database, or when documents are added by a particular person, or when documents are added that contain a particular word or phrase. Click the action bar's Save and Close button when you have finished defining the subscription.

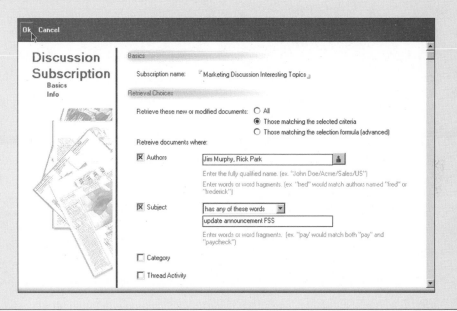

Chapter 15

Looking for *Needle* in a Worldwide Haystack

· ·

· ·

Databases — documents piled up in each one — crowd your servers, and hundreds of millions of documents are tucked in dusty corners of the Internet. Mountains of data are there for the reading. Now you need to find some important piece of information that someone entered somewhere. All you have to do is read every document to find it. Cancel your plans for the weekend because you have a lot of reading to do. Or do you? We live in the age of electronic miracles, so isn't there some way to find a text without having to read every document in every database?

Rest assured we wouldn't raise the question if the answer was bad news. Notes has several ways for you to find information, from quickly searching a single document to full text searching (a slick way to let Notes do the digging) to letting Notes search the net. Take our word for it, no matter how many speed reading courses you take, Notes can find information faster than you could ever hope to.

Starting Small — Searching Documents and Views

Frequently, you may simply want to find some text in the document you're reading. If you're busy and looking at a mammoth document that trails off the bottom of your screen and well into the desk below, reading the whole document to find a small section you need is a waste of time. Quickly and easily, you can tell Notes to find a word or a phrase.

 Click the Edit Find SmartIcon, choose Edit⇨Find/Replace in the menu, or just press Ctrl+F. We discuss Finding and Replacing in Chapter 13; simply finding text is similar. Enter into the text box the word or phrase you want Notes to find for you, click OK, and before you can snap your fingers several times (if it's a long document), Notes highlights the text. To find the next occurrence of the word, it's easiest to press Enter, though you can click Find Next if you're particularly fond of using the mouse. After you've found the specific occurrence of the text you want, click Close or press Escape to clear the Find dialog box from the screen.

It's also easy to find a document in a sorted but not categorized view — type the first few characters of the item you're looking for. A small dialog box appears, showing you what you typed — in case you forgot.

 You don't need to type the whole word you're looking for; just type enough characters to distinguish what you're looking for from other similar words, and then press Enter. Notes jumps to the first document whose first word contains whatever text you typed. To continue your search, leave the current document highlighted and repeat the same procedure to find the next document containing the text.

 You can tell that a view is sorted because the documents in the view are in some sort of order. If it's categorized, documents are clustered under special shorter rows.

If, for some reason, the technique we just described doesn't work, all is not lost. Go back to the beginning of this section and read about how to use Edit⇨Find/Replace. The same search technique finds text in the view.

 Keep these three methods in mind when you're searching for documents:

✔ If you use Edit⇨Find/Replace you can find text in the view, but not inside the documents themselves. We explain how to look inside documents later in this chapter in the section, "A Full-Power Search."

✔ You can use the menu or a SmartIcon, but you can't use Ctrl+F.

> ✔ If you search a view, you find the word in the view even if it isn't the first word in the title of the document. For example, if you're looking for the word *directions,* using Edit⇨Find/Replace finds a document listed in the view as *Follow these directions to install Notes* even though *directions* is not the first word in the title.

A Full-Power Search

By using the Search icon in the navigation bar, you have everything at your fingertips from a view to the world. Where you look, what you look for, how you want the search results displayed, and what specific search conditions you want to use are all contained somewhere in that Search icon. The choices you're able to make, however, are determined by where you look.

The options available to you and the appearance of the search results depend on whether the database you're searching has a full text index (FTI). If the manager of the database didn't create an FTI, you can still search the database, but more elaborate features such as Searching by Form aren't available.

Searching through all the documents in the view

You just got a new job, and you're going to be taking business trips once or twice a month. The first thing you need to do is find out your company's policies for travel — what airline should you use, what hotels can you stay in, and, most important, do *you* get to keep your Frequent Flyer miles? So you open up that trusty Human Resources Policies database, but it must have at least 700 documents in it. How are you going to find all the documents that have the word *travel* in them? We're talking about the whole document now, not just the title or whatever other text is displayed in a view containing the documents you want to rifle through.

The Search icon in the navigation bar comes to the rescue. The Search icon allows a *full text search,* a way for you to find all occurrences of a word (or of a few words) very, very quickly. You can search a huge database in no time at all. Most searches don't take more than two or three seconds. And, when you ask Notes to search for the word *travel,* it finds *all* the documents for you, no matter where (or how many times) the documents contain the word *travel.* Notes calls this a full text search, not because it finds full text (there's no such thing), but because it is full of neat features.

Hide and go seek with the search bar

To do a full text search you need to see the *search bar* to enter the criteria for your search. To display the search bar, click the Search icon in the navigation bar, or choose <u>V</u>iew⇨Search <u>B</u>ar from the menu. In Figure 15-1 we show the search bar.

Figure 15-1:
The search
bar.

| Search for | gold and silver | | Search |

When you perform a search, Notes searches only documents in the current, open view. So you have to be careful to choose the right view, such as an All Documents view, before you start your search. If the view you have open shows documents from only the first half of the year, for example, your search will not look through documents from the second half of the year.

Belly up to the search bar

The search bar contains several important parts. Starting from the left, the blank box is where you type the text you want to search for. Here are the types of things you can enter:

- ✔ **A single word.** For example, type **gold** to find all documents containing the word *gold*.

- ✔ **A phrase in quotes.** For example, type **"gold and silver"** to find documents containing the phrase *gold and silver*.

- ✔ **Words connected by and, without quotes.** For example, type **gold and silver** to find documents with both the word *gold* and the word *silver* in them.

- ✔ **Words connected by or, without quotes.** Type **gold or silver** to find documents that contain either the word *gold* or the word *silver* — maybe both, but at least one of the two.

Get into conditions

Most of the time you'll be happy to simply find documents containing some text. So enter the text you want to find, click Search and wait for the proper documents to appear. But suppose you search for _travel_ in the human resources database and find 150 documents. You still have too much to read. If you can somehow refine your search, you can narrow the number of search results. You might, for example, know that the author of most of the travel policy documents is Dwight Blake in human resources, so you could narrow the search to documents he created that contain _travel_.

Click More, and then click the Author button and type the author's name. That's what we're doing in Figure 15-2. Note that the search window contains the word _contains_.

Figure 15-2:
Specifying documents created by Dwight Blake.

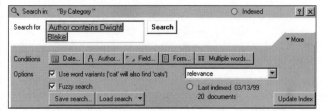

As you click the various buttons and specify conditions, each condition is added to the search window, so that you can find documents, for example, written by Dwight Blake, not written by Dianne Thiel, and containing _travel_. In the search bar, each condition is represented by a condition token, which is a gray box containing the specific condition. To see or modify the condition, double-click its token. To delete the condition, highlight its token and press Delete. Figure 15-3 shows the search window with the text _travel_ and a condition token.

Figure 15-3:
The search window.

But wait, there's more, much more. In fact, there's too much for us to crowd into this chapter. So we suggest you spend a few minutes improving your search skills by clicking around the buttons in the search bar to see all the options available to you. The more important options follow:

✔ **By Date:** A dialog box appears so you can enter a date and tell Notes to find documents newer or older than that date. You can find documents created between two dates, all documents not created between two dates, documents created in the last specified number of days, and on and on.

✔ **By Author:** A new dialog box appears for you to enter the name of someone whose documents you would like to see or don't want to see.

✔ **By Field:** A dialog box appears for you to enter a field name and the data you want that field to contain, or not to contain, in the documents you want to find.

✔ **By Form:** This allows you to look for documents created in a single form. If the view you're searching through has many types of main documents and responses, you may want only a certain type of document. For instance, in the travel policy example, you may want documents created only with the Policy form.

✔ **Multiple Words:** Another way to refine your search is to look for several words, for instance *travel* and *policy* and *employee*. Rather than entering words or phrases you want to find in the text box, you can enter them in the numbered boxes in the Search Builder dialog box. Click Multiple Words, and then enter one word in each numbered space. In Figure 15-4, we specified three words and chose to find them All. Choosing Any is like using the word *or* in the text box between *gold* and *silver;* the resulting search finds all documents containing either of those words. Choosing All finds documents that contain every word in the list.

✔ **Fill Out a Sample Form:** You can fill in specific fields in a specific form. Included among the options in this button is the famous query by form, explained in further detail in the next section because it's so important.

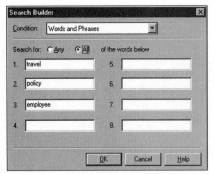

Figure 15-4:
We want
to find all
these words
in the
documents.

Query by form

A way to make your life easier is to do a *query by form*. That means you use one of the forms in the database to tell Notes which words you're looking for and in which fields you want to find them. This method narrows and refines your query substantially.

Say you want to search through a personnel database for a person's name, but that person is the author of many documents in that database. Complicating the problem is the fact that the documents in the view are of many different types (composed with different forms). You're interested only in documents where the person's name is mentioned, not in documents the person wrote, and you want only one type of document. You can use query by form to tell Notes to be sure that the name occurs in the Body field of a particular form. (The name of the field might be different in the form you're using.)

Here's how you make a query by form:

1. **In the search bar, click the More button.**

2. **Click the Form button.**

   The Search Builder dialog box appears.

3. **Click the down arrow at the end of the Condition text box, and select By Form (not "By Form Used").**

   Notes gives you an empty version of the form.

4. **Move the cursor into the field where you want to find the word or phrase, and type the text you want Notes to find in that field.**

   In Figure 15-5, we entered *travel* in the Category field of the Main Topic form. Tired of choosing and clicking? Sorry, one more.

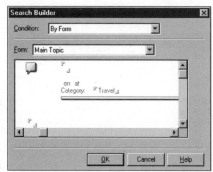

Figure 15-5:
Query by
form.

5. **Click OK to close the dialog box, and then click the Search button in the search bar to find the documents.**

Fuzzy search: The latest toy craze?

Don't go racing off to wait in line at 5:00 A.M. at your local Toyland for Kiddies store to buy a Fuzzy Search for that special child just yet. In fact, don't do it at all. We suspect that special child would be just as happy with a simple toy you didn't have to risk being killed for. But wait, Fuzzy Search isn't a toy anyway, it's a search option.

In the search bar, below the places where you place your order for search conditions, are some search options you may want to choose before you send the search engine purring off into the database on a scavenger hunt. You can see the options in Figure 15-6. You can see them on your screen as well if you click the More button.

Figure 15-6:
The search
bar is
expanded,
and the Sort
Results By
list is visible.

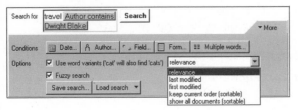

Following are the options available to you when you have a full-text indexed database:

- ✔ **Use Word Variants:** Tells Notes that you want to look for the text you typed, but also the base word with possible prefixes or suffixes — searching for *sneeze,* for example, also finds *sneezed* and *sneezing.* Bless you.

- ✔ **Fuzzy Search:** Tells Notes to use not only the word you typed, but corrected spellings if you misspelled your criterion as well as similar phrases. For instance, searching for *travvel* will find *travel;* searching for *known problems* will return *known serious problems.*

Here are the Sort Results By choices:

- ✔ **Relevance:** The documents are arranged so that the ones with the largest number of examples of your criteria are at the top.

- ✔ **Last Modified or First Modified:** The documents with the earliest date of modification or the latest date of modification head the list that Notes gives you.

> ✓ **Keep current order (sortable):** The documents are kept in the order they were in the view; they aren't sorted by relevance. Only the search results are displayed in the view, and they appear with check marks.
>
> ✓ **Show all documents (sortable):** All documents in the view are shown, but a check mark appears next to documents that satisfy the search results.

On your mark, get set, search!

After you have set your conditions and chosen your options, it's time to start the search itself. That part's easy — just click the Search button. If you have a lot of documents in the view, it may take a few minutes to find them. On the other hand, if you're searching a database with three small documents, the search won't take any time at all. The point? The amount of time a search takes depends on three factors:

> ✓ The size of the documents in the database
>
> ✓ The number of documents in the database
>
> ✓ The complexity of the conditions you set

Seek and ye shall find

When the search is finally finished, Notes changes the view to show the search results in the way you specified in the Show Results By list.

If the database is full-text indexed, Notes lists the documents that match your criteria in order of their weight. No, Notes doesn't measure a document's weight in grams or pounds or even bytes. Rather, in this case, *weight* refers to the degree to which each document satisfies the search criteria. It lists first the documents that have the most occurrences of your criteria and then the documents that have fewer occurrences of the criteria. The vertical bar, called the *marker bar,* in the left side of the view represents the relative frequency of your criteria in each document. The darker the bar, the more occurrences in that particular document.

In the Options drop-down menu, you can choose to sort documents in ways other than by weight. Just be sure you make the decision before the search.

You open a document uncovered by a search in the same way you open any other document: double-click it or highlight it with the cursor keys and press Enter. When you do, Notes shows you the document and highlights the words you asked it to find.

As you read a document retrieved by a full text search, you can jump quickly to the next occurrence of the search word in the current document by pressing Ctrl++ (that's the Ctrl key and the plus sign). You use Ctrl+- (Ctrl and the hyphen key, which represents minus) to jump quickly to the preceding occurrence of the word.

Resetting the stage

When you've read the documents that interest you, click the Reset button to clear the search and return all documents to the view.

If you want to conduct another search, it isn't necessary to click Reset first. Just type a new bunch of text and set your conditions; then click Search and off you go. Typing a new search word makes Notes forget all about the old search, and returns only documents that satisfy the new set of criteria. It's necessary to use the Reset button only when you're completely finished searching.

Surveying Your Domain and Your World

So far, we have confined our text searches to one document, the view you see on-screen, or the documents in the current view. Two much broader searches are possible. One involves your domain, and the other is the world. Your domain is defined as whatever databases you designate plus any files not in Notes databases.

Conducting a domain search

Before you can do a domain search, your administrator must set up the search. Until then, the Domain Search option mentioned in Step 2 in the following list appears dimmed.

To do a domain search — after the administrator has set it up — follow these steps:

1. **Click the arrow to the right of the search icon.**

2. **Choose Domain Search.**

    The title that your administrator used may be something other than Domain Search.

3. **If you want to search the contents of databases, select Documents. If you want to search only the titles of databases, select Databases.**

4. **If you want to include non-Notes documents in your search, click More, and then select File System.**

5. **In the search box, type your query.**

6. **Select Terse or Detailed results, and then select an option in Sorted By.**

   Choosing either Terse or Detailed returns relevance, date last modified, and document title. Choosing Detailed also returns a summary of the content and the URL (if they are available).

7. **Click More.**

8. **Choose the conditions and options to specify the search.**

   These become part of your query, along with the text you type. You can also type certain operators in the query.

9. **Finally, click Search.**

To search the world (as in the World Wide Web), use the Search button to specify your favorite Internet search engine site, and then enter your search criteria as you normally would to search around the virtual world.

How's your Boolean?

It's time we bore into Boolean briefly because the wrong choice can give you the wrong search results. If you look closely at the figure, you see that we chose to connect the two conditions with *and.* That means that the search results have to contain Bemesderfer in the Last Name field. The second condition refines that first condition: It tells the search engine, "Now that you have all the Bemesderfers, take out the documents where the first name is Jackie." What's left are all the Bemesderfers not named Jackie.

What if we used *or* between the two conditions instead of *and?* First, as before, we'd get all the Bemesderfers. But then the second criterion says, "Find all people whose first name is not Jackie." We are not refining anything, so our list will be a combination of everyone whose last name is Bemesderfer and *everyone* whose first name is not Jackie. That could be a big list because lots of us aren't named Jackie.

If you plan on doing a worldwide search frequently from inside Notes, you may want to bookmark that favorite Internet search engine, as follows. First use Notes to activate the Internet search site. Then click and drag the task button for the site (near the top of the Notes window) to the More Bookmarks icon. Keep holding down the left mouse button, and when the More Bookmarks folder opens, drop the task button in the place where you want it to be.

Looking for People

Notes can even find a person for you, without your having to open a bunch of databases, such as the directory. To find some, just click the down arrow next to the Search icon. From the list, choose Find People. In the dialog box that appears, choose the places to Look In, enter some helpful text in the Starts With box, and click Search. The results of your search appear in the Search dialog box. Highlight a line in the results and then click Details if you want to see more. The page in the appropriate registry opens so you can see more about the person. Click Add to Personal Name & Address Book if you want to be able to use the name to address memos in the future.

In Figure 15-7, we clicked the Detailed Search button to refine our search (because we're such refined people). Our criteria were, first, all the people in the location we chose whose last name is Bemesderfer. Second, after clicking Add Condition, we specified that we didn't want the search results to include any people whose first name is Jackie. In other words, anyone named Jackie would not be included, but we will find all the other Bemesderfers in the search location.

Below the Welcome page is yet another way to search. Click the down arrow in the text box next to the word Search, and then select Notes Database Catalog or an Internet search option. Enter some search text in the text box to the right, and then click the Search button.

Figure 15-7:
Looking for a person whose name is Bemesderfer, but not Jackie Bemesderfer.

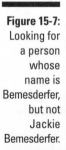

Part V
Worldwide Notes

The 5th Wave — By Rich Tennant

In this part . . .

We can't all stay in our offices, do the daily routine, and be satisfied with our basic groupware features. Some of us just have to zip into the fast lane of life. If you're such a person, you're probably aching to know how to take Notes with you on your business trips, and how to get Notes to interact with other programs.

Okay, hot-shot. You asked for it. This part of the book is devoted to the Notes features of interest to a person like yourself.

Chapter 16

Data In and Data Out

- -

In This Chapter

▶ Copying data to your Notes document with the Clipboard

▶ Copying Notes data to a non-Notes document with the Clipboard

▶ Moving data into Notes by importing

▶ Moving data out of Notes by exporting

▶ Linking data in Notes

▶ Embedding data in Notes

- -

*U*sing Notes has many advantages over your average, run-of-the-mill, do-only-one-thing programs. Unless you're just joining us, you're probably already aware of many of these advantages — for example, that Notes works in Windows, OS/2, Macintosh, and UNIX. In all of these environments, you can take information of all sorts from another application (Microsoft Word, for example) and use it in Notes.

This chapter explains the ways in which you can bring data from other programs into Notes and use Notes data in other programs. The business of getting the information from one application into another varies from the simple to the complex. Here are your choices:

- ✔ Copying to and pasting from the Clipboard
- ✔ Creating attachments
- ✔ Using File⇨Import, and File⇨Export
- ✔ Linking
- ✔ Embedding

Where's the Glue?

Back in the good old days, when you wanted to include a picture, a chunk of text, a graph, or a table of data in something you were typing, you began by pulling the paper out of the typewriter when you finished typing. Then you used scissors to cut out the picture or text or graph or table and found a bottle of glue to paste it into the blank space in the typed copy. This system was not very high tech, could be messy, and made it pretty hard to jam that piece of paper back into the typewriter if you needed to type some more.

But this is the age of bread makers, laser-guided missiles, and (with the advent of the personal computer) cutting and pasting without using scissors or glue. You can use your friendly Clipboard to add objects — such as a graph from 1-2-3 for Windows, a paragraph from Word, or a graphic from Freelance — directly to your Notes documents. Here's how:

1. **Open the program and file that contains the object you want to snag for your Notes document.**

   Technical types call this program the *home program* or the *source application.*

2. **Highlight the desired object and copy it.**

   In most programs, you use the Edit⇨Copy command for this.

3. **Switch to Notes, position the cursor where you want the object, and choose Edit⇨Paste. (Note that you must be in a rich text field.)**

   Unless the object was too big to fit in the Clipboard (for example, if you tried to copy 3,000 cells from a Lotus 1-2-3 worksheet), you see a copy of the original data in the Notes document.

This system is preferable to the scissors-and-glue system because the page with the pasted item doesn't stick to all the other pages. It's also faster and seamless, and it gives you the ability to move the pasted object around or delete it if you change your mind. Besides that, you can edit the pasted object after you've pasted it in Notes.

This copy-and-paste system works fine as long as the source application supports the use of the Clipboard and you're able to open the source application to get at the information you want to copy. But keep in mind that if the data in the source application changes, Notes can't update its copy of the data. After you copy and paste something into Notes, Notes has no way to know what goes on in the source application.

Unlike most of the other techniques in this chapter, you can use the copy-and-paste method to copy data from one Notes document into another. Most other techniques work only with data and files created outside Notes.

Throwing Out Your Paper Clips

What if you can't use the Clipboard? Your next weapon in the arsenal of using non-Notes data is *attaching* files to documents. It doesn't matter whether Notes supports the file format, whether the original application has ever heard of the Clipboard, or what kind of laundry detergent you're using — in a rich text field, you can attach any file to any Notes document.

 Place the cursor where you want a symbol of the attached file to appear and then choose File⇨Attach, or click the File Attach SmartIcon. Figure 16-1 shows the dialog box that appears. Use the Look In box to find the file you're importing, and then select the filename in the list box or enter its name in the File Name box. After you've found the file, click Create and, voilà, the file appears in your Notes document.

Figure 16-1:
Use the
Create
Attach-
ment(s)
dialog box
to attach
a file.

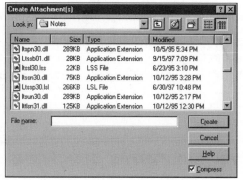

 Notice in Figure 16-1 that you can see lots of fascinating information about the file — its size, the program in which it was created, and its date and time of creation — because we've clicked the Details button, one of the five buttons in the upper-right corner of the Create Attachment(s) dialog box.

 By default, the Compress option in the Create Attachment(s) dialog box is checked. This feature squeezes the file to make it smaller as it attaches it. The attached file might end up only 20 percent of its original size after Notes compresses it, meaning that the memo itself takes up less disk space and requires less time to send. (That's good.) The argument against compressing a file is that the attachment process takes a little longer. Your recipients won't know whether or not you compressed the attachment, because it automatically decompresses when it's detached. So don't worry about someone complaining about receiving a squashed file.

If a memo has an attached file, all the reader sees is a symbol of the file in the memo. If possible, that symbol is an icon of the original program. A WordPro icon, for example, represents a WordPro file. Because you can attach any kind of file, sometimes the icon doesn't match the source application. For example, if you attach a batch file or an executable file (one with the .EXE extension), Notes represents that file with what looks like a piece of paper with the corner folded over.

You can't see or edit the data from an attached file in a Notes document. The purpose of attaching a file is simply to give that file to others, not to use the data in your Notes document.

If you receive a memo or open a document with a file attached, you can choose to view it, launch it, or detach it. Find out more about each of these options in Chapter 7.

Importing and Exporting

Okay, so you want to include some information from another source in your document, but the original application doesn't support the Clipboard, so you can't use copy and paste. And you don't want to attach the file because you want the reader to see the data rather than an icon. Your next option is to import the file from its native format into Notes. By the same token, if you can't copy Notes data to the Clipboard to paste it into the other application, you can export the Notes data.

Importing from non-Notes programs

Imagine that you're composing a Notes document and you need to include a bunch of pages that you've already typed in WordPerfect for DOS. You can't use the Clipboard to include the document because WordPerfect for DOS isn't even a Windows program and doesn't know anything about the Clipboard. If you attach the file, the people who read your document don't see the actual text of the WordPerfect document — all they see is a crummy little icon.

What do you do? You import the WordPerfect file. *Importing* is how you convert a file from WordPerfect right into the Notes document you're composing and right into the rich text field in which you are typing. You can also convert files from many of other programs, such as Lotus 1-2-3 or WordStar.

How do you import something? Like this:

1. **Get your cursor to the spot in the rich text field where you want to insert the file.**

   By the way, don't even think about importing a document into any kind of field other than rich text.

2. **Choose File⇨Import.**

   You see a dialog box like the one in Figure 16-2.

Figure 16-2:
The Import
dialog box.

3. **In the Look In list box, choose the drive and directory where you think that the file is located.**

4. **In the Files of Type list box, select the type of file you're importing.**

5. **Either highlight the filename or type it in the File Name list box, and then click Import.**

   Ta-da. The file appears inside your Notes document.

When you import a file, Notes converts it to regular text, so feel free to liven it up by changing the fonts, making some of the words bold, or whatever.

Choosing File⇨Import to include a foreign (non-Notes) file in a rich text field is your technique of choice if the file's source application either isn't installed on your workstation (maybe someone else gave you the WordPerfect file, but you don't have WordPerfect on your computer) or can't be copied and pasted with the Clipboard.

Although File⇨Import does convert foreign documents, try the Clipboard first when incorporating information from other programs. It's quicker and cleaner.

Here's a list of the types of files you can import into a rich text field:

   ✔ ASCII text file

   ✔ Binary file with text

   ✔ BMP, CGM, GIF, JPEG, PCX, and TIFF 5.0 image files

   ✔ Excel 4.0 and 5.0 files

   ✔ HTML files

✔ Lotus 1-2-3 Worksheet and PIC files

✔ Microsoft ExcelAmi Pro (97) files

✔ Word for Windows 6.0 and Word RTF files

✔ WordPerfect 5.x, 6.0, and 6.1 files

✔ WordPro 96 and 97 files

If you need to import a file that is not on the list, see whether the originating program can save the file in one of the formats that Notes supports. For example, if you need to import a Quattro Pro spreadsheet, you can use Quattro Pro to save the file as a Lotus 1-2-3 worksheet, and then import the converted Lotus 1-2-3 worksheet into Notes.

Exporting: A document leaves home

You probably guessed that, just as you can convert documents from other programs to Notes, you can also convert a Notes document into a file that can be used by a different program. Perhaps you have a Notes document that you want to give to a few colleagues who don't have access to Notes (do they know what they're missing?). You can convert the Notes document to, say, a Microsoft Word document, and then deliver the file to your colleagues through Internet e-mail or on a floppy disk.

In the information age of the '90s, copying a file onto a floppy disk and then walking down the hall to hand-deliver it is euphemistically known as using *sneaker net*.

To convert a Notes file into another format, follow these steps:

1. **Find and open the Notes document that you want to export.**

2. **Choose File⇨Export.**

   This brings you face-to-face with the dialog box shown in Figure 16-3.

Figure 16-3:
The Export
dialog box.

3. Use the Save In box to specify the location of the file you want to export.

4. In the File Name text box, type the name of the file.

5. Use the Save as Type drop-down box to tell Notes what type of file you want it to be.

6. Click Export and you're finished.

   Now you (or your friends) can open the new file in the appropriate program.

Here's the list of file types to which you can export a Notes document:

- ✔ AmiPro file
- ✔ ASCII text file
- ✔ CGM and TIFF 5.0 image files
- ✔ Word for Windows 6.0 and Word RTF files
- ✔ WordPerfect 5.1, 6.0, and 6.1 files

Just as with File⇨Import, use File⇨Export only if you can't use the Clipboard to transfer the Notes document to the other program.

Documents come into view

Another way to bring information into Notes is to import not an individual document but rather lots of documents at the same time. This method would be the appropriate choice if, for example, you have a Lotus 1-2-3 worksheet and you want to import it in such a way that each row in the spreadsheet becomes a separate document in a Notes database. If your worksheet has 4,362 rows worth of information, you get 4,362 new documents in your Notes database.

First steps . . .

First things first: You have to use 1-2-3 to set up the spreadsheet in a very particular fashion. You have to remove all the fancy formatting and blank rows in the worksheet. The following are two specific rules for preparing a spreadsheet to import to Notes:

- ✔ The column headings for the worksheet must be in row 1 of the worksheet, and they must be the same as the field names in the Notes database. This is important, so call the person who created the database if you're not sure what the *exact* field names are in the Notes database. Don't mistake static text next to the field for the actual field name.

✔ The rows of spreadsheet information must begin in row 2 of the worksheet and must be in a solid block. If you include any blank rows in the middle of the spreadsheet, you end up with empty documents in your database.

Your best bet probably is to take the worksheet you intend to import and rearrange it to conform to the aforementioned rules. But be sure to save it with a different name so that you don't replace the original worksheet.

If you need to import any other kind of file, such as a big text file or an Excel worksheet, it's best to convert *that* file into a Lotus 1-2-3 worksheet and then import the Lotus 1-2-3 worksheet into Notes. It should come as no surprise that the easiest type of file to import into (Lotus) Notes is (Lotus) 1-2-3.

Second steps . . .

After you get the worksheet all shipshape, open the database into which you want to import the worksheet and choose File➪Import. Make sure that you have a view on-screen when you choose File➪Import. In other words, just open the database without opening one of the documents or trying to compose a new document. Otherwise, Notes thinks that you want to put the worksheet into just one document.

Use the dialog box shown in Figure 16-4 to indicate the place to find the file (Look In) and the type of file (Files of Type). Then select the file or type the name in the File Name box. In Figure 16-4, we chose a 1-2-3 worksheet.

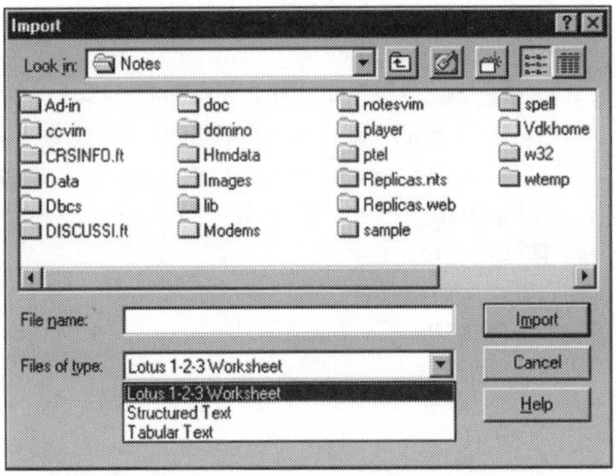

Figure 16-4:
The Import
dialog box.

When you click Import, Notes presents you with yet another dialog box, as you can see in Figure 16-5. Here, you can tell Notes how to import the rows of the spreadsheet. You need to decide whether you want Notes to import all rows or only selected rows as documents and whether you want Notes to include the column heads in the new spreadsheet.

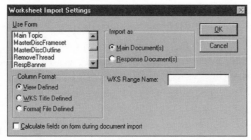

Figure 16-5:
How will the
view be
imported?

You have five questions to answer (roughly clockwise from the upper-left corner of the dialog box):

- ✔ Which form should Notes use to display the new documents?

- ✔ Are the new documents main documents or responses?

- ✔ Which range should be imported from the spreadsheet? You may enter either the cell coordinates (such as **A1 . . D341**) or a range name.

- ✔ How should the fields (columns) be named? Because you followed our advice and were careful to make the spreadsheet column heading match the field name, choose WKS Title Defined.

- ✔ Should Notes calculate field formulas defined on the form for each document as it is created? If that's what you want, click the Calculate Fields on Form during Document Import box. If you're not sure whether you should check this box, consult the person who created the database.

After answering these questions, click OK and you're in business. Notes imports the worksheet and converts each row into a new document for your database.

As with most tasks in computerland, you can import documents in a number of ways. We discuss importing only a Lotus 1-2-3 worksheet because it's the most common type of import and because the other types of view-level imports are complicated. If you're convinced that you need to import a file that's not a 1-2-3 worksheet, we recommend that you seek help from the person who created the database or from your local Notes guru.

Hey, view, make me a spreadsheet

Exporting from a view is even easier than importing into a view. The idea behind a view-level export is that you want to create a spreadsheet based on the columns in a view.

Exporting a view to a spreadsheet is the most common type of view-level export. You can also export a view to any of the following file types:

✔ **A 1-2-3 worksheet,** compatible with any version of Lotus 1-2-3 and also accessible by most other spreadsheet and database programs, such as Excel, dBASE, and Paradox

✔ **A structured text file,** which is an ASCII file that would then be imported into some other program

✔ **A tabular text file,** which is easy to import into other spreadsheet and database programs

To make a new spreadsheet file out of a view, follow these steps:

1. **Open the database in question, and switch to the view that will be the basis of the spreadsheet you are creating.**

When you export a view, Notes exports only the fields that are in the view. If you need to export fields that are *not* in the view, you have to negotiate with the person who designed your database to add a column or two to display the additional fields, or you can create a private view or folder. See Chapter 14 for help on creating a folder in your mail database. You can use the steps in that chapter to create a folder in any database.

2. **If you want to export only some of the documents in the view, use the mouse or spacebar to check off the documents you want to export.**

3. **Choose File⇨Export and watch for the dialog box shown in Figure 16-6.**

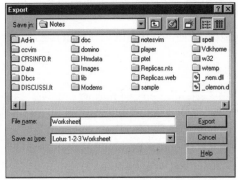

Figure 16-6:
The Export
dialog box.

4. **In the Save In drop-down list, select the drive and directory where you want to save the new file.**

5. **In the Save as Type drop-down list, select the type of file that the resulting export should be.**

6. **In the File Name text box, specify a filename and an extension.**

   You might type ProductList.wk4, for example.

7. **Click Export.**

8. **In the next dialog box, tell Notes whether you want to export all the documents in the view or just those that you selected in Step 2.**

   You also see a check box to Include View Titles. Selecting this option makes each column heading in the worksheet match the database's field names. If you don't choose this option, the spreadsheet won't have any column headings.

9. **Click OK.**

   Notes creates a Lotus 1-2-3 worksheet for you based on the view that's open — and that's all there is to it.

If you intend to export data from a Notes view to a program other than Lotus 1-2-3, you should still export the view to a Lotus 1-2-3 worksheet and then use that other program to further convert the worksheet. Take it from us, using Lotus 1-2-3 is a lot _(a lot)_ easier than using the structured or tabular text formats.

Keeping Links to Home

What if you want to add something from another program to your Notes document, but you want it to retain its identity as data of the original application? You want a have-your-cake-and-eat-it-too way of bringing data into Notes. This data doesn't become native Notes data as it does when you choose any of the File⇨Import options discussed in the preceding section.

A _link_ adds information to your Notes document but keeps an eye on the original data so that, if you or anyone else changes the original, the copy in the Notes document changes, too. You can't use linking in Notes to link two Notes databases. To do that, you use copy and paste or DocLinks.

What makes linking a bit confusing is the terminology; some words used for linking are also used in other Notes contexts. For example, the program in which the original data was created is called the _server._ The program into which the data is placed is called the _client_ (a term sometimes used also for _workstation_). Keep in mind as you read this section that we are not talking about Notes servers and Notes clients, but link servers and clients.

To create a link, follow these steps:

1. **Open the server application and create or open a file containing the data to which you'll be forging a link.**

   If this is a new file, be sure to save it before trying to create the link.

2. **Highlight the data to link and choose Edit⇨Copy.**

3. **Switch to the Notes document and place the cursor where you want to place the data (be sure that it's a rich text field).**

What's a DocLink?

Cufflinks for your favorite doctor? Sausage for physicians? Not in Notes-speak. A *DocLink* is a connection between one document and another.

Suppose that you are sending a memo to an associate about a report in another database. Rather than saying, "Find the document for yourself, you lazy bum," you can put a little icon of the report in your memo. When the lazy bum receives the memo, a mere double-click on the symbol opens the document.

The recipient must have access to the database and the document you are linking in your memo. An error message appears on-screen if someone clicks a DocLink and he or she doesn't have rights to access the document or the database itself or doesn't have access to the server that contains the database that contains the document that lives in the house that Jack built. One of the databases to which others do not have access is your own mail database, so you wouldn't even think of linking to one of your mail messages, right?

To create a DocLink, you first need to open (or highlight in a view or folder) the document *to which you are creating a link* and then choose Edit⇨Copy as Link⇨Document Link. Then switch to the document that you want to contain the DocLink, make sure that you're in a rich text field, and choose Edit⇨Paste.

When your recipients receive the memo, each can double-click the DocLink. The document itself opens before their very eyes. It beats typing the whole report all over again, doesn't it? Just for the record, you need to be in edit mode to add a DocLink to a document, but you don't need to be in edit mode to open a DocLink. And even though the example presented here is a mail memo, you can paste a DocLink into any Notes document in any Notes database.

Here's a tip: When reading a document that has a DocLink in it, choose View⇨Document Link Preview to see a little bit of the linked document (without actually opening it). It's just like previewing a document in your mail database.

4. **Choose Edit⇨Paste Special.**

   The dialog box in Figure 16-7 appears.

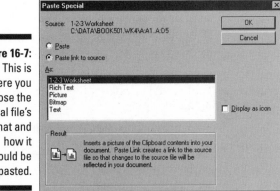

Figure 16-7:
This is where you choose the original file's format and how it should be pasted.

5. **In the As list box, select the format for the data to be linked.**

   You may choose the file's native file format (1-2-3 Worksheet in Figure 16-7), Rich Text (text arrives with all formatting), Picture or Bitmap (usually used for graphic objects), or Text (text arrives without formatting).

6. **Select the Paste Link to Source option.**

7. **Click OK to finish the job.**

   After a few seconds, the data appears in the Notes document. If the original selection contains multiple text formats, you might see an icon rather than the actual text. It's still a real link; Notes just can't display the contents of the link.

By making a link, you create a *compound document,* a document with multiple features, containing non-Notes data that keeps in touch with home. You can't edit the linked data while you're in Notes. To edit the data, you need to double-click the linked data or the icon. Notes opens or switches to the server application and file, where you may edit the data. As you do the editing, the Notes document immediately reflects the changes.

Not only can you edit the data, you can also edit the link itself. In the Notes document, choose Edit⇨External Links. You get the dialog box shown in Figure 16-8.

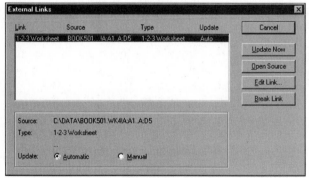

Figure 16-8:
The External Links dialog box.

In the External Links dialog box, you may choose to use any of the following:

- ✔ **Update Now** if the data in the Notes document is not up-to-date with the server document

- ✔ **Open Source** to edit the source document

- ✔ **Edit Link** to use new data or a new file as the original document that is linked into the current Notes document

- ✔ **Break Link** to permanently sever the link between server and client

In the External Links dialog box, you can also change the link from Automatic (for the link to make changes immediately in the client when the server file changes) to Manual (you have to choose Edit⇨External Links and click Update Now to update links). You usually want to choose Manual if editing the server file slows down your computer's performance.

A link requires that you have a saved file *and* the server application available to Notes. Often, the server file itself resides on a network server so that the same file is available to all users. If all users of the Notes document don't have the same directory structure for the server application, Notes can't open the application to allow updating. Also, if the file is moved or renamed, everyone loses the link between the original information and the information in the Notes document. So watch it!

If You Can't Link 'Em — Embed 'Em

To the person reading your document, an embedded object looks and acts almost the same as a linked object. Either one may be an icon or data, depending on the complexity of the data in the server file. The difference between the two is that data embedded in a Notes document uses the file itself, not a link, so changes to the original file are *not* reflected in the embedded file.

Suppose, for example, that you want people to enter expense reports in a spreadsheet format into a Notes document for storage in a Notes database. You could embed a 1-2-3 spreadsheet in a Notes form containing the text and formulas users need to enter data. When users create an expense form in Notes, the embedded spreadsheet kicks into action, and users find themselves in 1-2-3, where they fill in the data. When they save the work in 1-2-3, they return to Notes, where the data is in the Notes document.

To embed information in a Notes document, follow these steps:

1. **Open the original file in its original program.**

2. **Copy the information to the Clipboard.**

3. **Open the Notes document and position the cursor in a rich text field.**

4. **Choose Edit⇨Paste Special.**

5. **Make a choice of format under As.**

6. **Click Paste.**

You can also create a placeholder for an object that you might want to embed later, but that doesn't even exist yet. To accomplish this miracle, choose Create⇨Object, and then select Object in the Create New area, as we did in Figure 16-9. In the Object Type area, select the application that will be the server, and then click OK. Notes starts the program for the type you chose. Then you enter data, which becomes part of the Notes document.

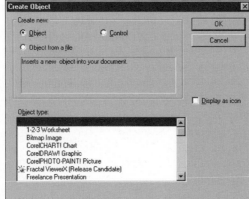

Figure 16-9:
The Create Object dialog box for embedding a new object.

On the other hand, if you want to embed an existing file, click Object from a File, select the file, and then click OK. The resulting dialog box looks like Figure 16-10. Notes embeds the file in the Notes document.

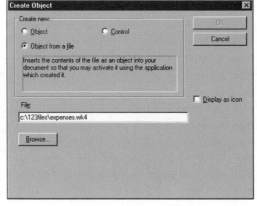

Figure 16-10:
The Create Object dialog box for embedding an existing file.

The third choice, Control, is a way of creating a miniprogram representing the server application that readers can use to open the embedded object. It's a bit complex for us.

Embedding doesn't require that the readers of the Notes document have access to the original file because they have their own copy of the file. However, they must have the *server application* so that they can edit the original data. Double-click the embedded data, and both the server application and the file open. Any changes made to the embedded file on one user's version of a document might not be reflected in other users' copies of the document, depending on whether the documents are replicated to all other users.

Searching for text, covered in Chapter 15, is a valuable tool. Both linking and embedding enable your readers to search for text, as long as you follow two rules:

- ✔ You must link or embed the data as text or rich text.
- ✔ The data must be visible; it can't be represented by an icon.

This business of embedding and linking used to be called OLE and DDE (and still is by people who speak in abbreviations and use pocket protectors). OLE (pronounced Spanish style: *o-lay*) stands for *Object Linking and Embedding;* DDE stands for *Dynamic Data Exchange.* Don't lose any sleep over which one you're using. It doesn't matter. That's something for Notes to worry about behind the scenes.

Chapter 17

Notes for Road Warriors

· ·

In This Chapter

▶ Getting ready to take Notes on a trip

▶ Talking directly to the Domino server

▶ Telling Notes where you are

▶ Replicating your mail

▶ Making your modem manipulate your messages

▶ Saving on your phone bill

▶ Reading selected replication vignettes

· ·

*J*ust because you have to travel away from the office doesn't mean that you can't read your mail, use your databases, and generally stay plugged into what's going on back at the office. In this chapter, we explore what you have to do to use Notes on the road.

Suppose that your company has one Notes server in Boston, one in New York, and one in London. On each of these servers your administrator has placed a copy of a database that your company uses to discuss marketing strategies for the coming year. You need the documents that have been added to the database by your English colleagues to show up in the databases in New York and Boston. And, if someone in New York edits a document, you want the changes to be distributed to Boston and London. And if someone in Boston deletes a document? You want that document to be deleted in both New York and London, too.

Replication is the process that Notes uses to keep the three databases synchronized with one another. Your administrator schedules calls between the servers; the Boston server might call up the New York server at 8 A.M. and then call the English server at 9 A.M. Then it would place another call to New York at 11 A.M., call England again at 1 P.M., and so on, and so on.

That's nice, but why do you care? Because you'll use the same process whenever you need to use Notes away from the office. You have your laptop all set up and ready to go. Grab a cab to the airport, check your bags, and get on the plane. You're trapped in that seat for the next three hours, so why not use the time to catch up on some of your e-mail? By the end of the trip, you have 11 new e-mail messages to send, and you've composed a few documents in the databases that you brought with you, too.

Now fast-forward to your arrival at the hotel. You're all checked in, you've hung your suits in the closet, checked out the treats in the honor bar, and paid off the bellhop. So now how are you going to send that e-mail, post those documents you composed on the plane, and see whether any mail has been sent to you while you were cruising at 35,000 feet? You guessed it, you're going to replicate the databases on your laptop with the Domino server back at the office.

Even if you aren't planning to go on any trips, you should read this chapter anyway. If you need to set up Notes on your computer at home, the steps are almost the same.

Getting Your Computer Ready to Go

Needless to say, you must get prepared for your new-found career as a replicator before you even leave the office; you don't want to be stuck in the hotel room without the proper setup. Here's a checklist of the stuff you have to bring with you:

- Your computer
- Notes
- A modem
- A phone cable to connect the modem to the phone jack
- Your USER.ID file
- Your personal N&A book
- Some databases
- Some phone numbers
- A clean pair of socks and maybe a couple of shirts

There's one issue that you have to clear up before you can connect, and it's related to the kind of dial-in connection you'll have to your Domino server. You can connect in two ways, and you need to know which you'll be using.

The first and most traditional way is known as *Notes Direct Dialup*. In this method, you set up Notes to call your Domino server directly — in other words, your modem calls a modem that is connected to, and answered by, the Domino server.

The second and more modern way of connecting your Notes workstation to a server with your modem is called *Network Dialup.* In this scenario, you set up Notes to dial into the entire network. For example, you would configure your Notes workstation to dial into a special computer on the network that would then connect you through to the Domino server.

Fortunately, the method you'll employ isn't your decision, so you have one less thing to worry about. You need to find out from your Administrator how you'll be dialing in, and then proceed accordingly.

If you will be using Notes Direct Dialup to connect, read this next section called, appropriately enough, "Notes Direct Dialup." If, on the other hand, you're told to use Network Dialup, you should skip this section, and instead read the one called "Connection and Location Documents."

Notes Direct Dialup

This section details the specific things you need to do to get your computer talking, via modem, to your Domino server directly. A modem is a piece of hardware that lets your computer (in the hotel room) and another computer (the Domino server back at the office) talk to one another over the telephone. The long definition is boring and technical, so we'll keep to the basics.

Obligatory plug: The fine folks here at IDG Books Worldwide, Inc. publish a great book that tells you everything you need to know about modems. It's *Modems For Dummies*, 3rd Edition, by Tina Rathbone.

To get Notes ready to use your modem, you have to do two things:

- ✔ Tell Notes that you have a modem
- ✔ Tell Notes what kind of modem you have

Of course, you don't just say, "Notes, I have a modem." What you really have to do is *enable a serial port,* which sounds much worse than it really is.

Enabling your serial port

Think back to when you started Notes for the first time. Did you tell Notes then that you had a modem? If you did, you may not need to read this section — then again, it may be worth a quick breeze-over just to make sure that everything is okay.

To enable a serial port, choose File➪Preferences➪User Preferences, and click the Ports button. You get the User Preferences dialog box, as displayed in Figure 17-1.

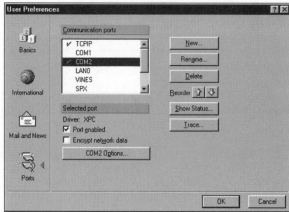

The tough part here is knowing which port your modem is connected to —
unless you use a Macintosh. If you have a Mac, the port name is either
MODEM or PRINTER. The correct answer is probably obvious, unless you
have some compelling reason to plug your modem into your printer port.

If you *don't* use a Mac, the options for Communications Ports are COM1,
COM2, COM3, and so on. Your modem is almost certainly connected to either
COM1 or COM2. If you don't COM ports from crumpets, call your administra-
tor to find out.

After you find out which port to choose, the rest is a piece of cake. Select
the name of the port to which your modem is connected from the
Communication Ports list box, and click the Port Enabled check box.

Taking your computer on a trip

Personal computers are certainly a great deal
smaller than the computers of yesteryear.
(We're resisting the temptation to launch into a
story about how, when we first started in the
computer business, computers were as big
as a refrigerator and took three days to add
up a list of numbers.) If you're lucky, you have
a laptop computer. It's nice and small and

probably even has a color screen. Most laptops
have modems built right in, so that's one less
thing to pack for your trip.

Practice setting up and using Notes from your
laptop *before* you leave for your trip. That way
the administrator can hear you scream (and
come to help) if you can't figure out how to hook
up the @#*^#$ modem.

You're almost finished. Hold off on clicking OK until you read the next section, because you have to tell Notes what kind of modem you have.

Configuring your modem

While you're in the User Preferences dialog box, check out the COM*n* (the *n*
means that the button will match whichever port you've enabled) Options
button. When you click this button, Notes presents you with the dialog box
shown in Figure 17-2.

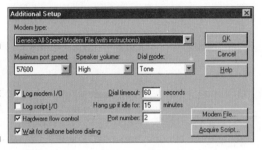

Figure 17-2:
Telling
Notes about
your
modem.

The dialog box has a bunch of options, but you have to worry about only two
things. Okay, maybe three things:

✔ The first thing you need to do is select the brand of modem you own
from the list. This is important, because different modems work differently, and Notes needs to know exactly which you have.

If your modem doesn't appear in the list, choose Auto Configure (it's
near the bottom of the list). And if that doesn't work out, try one of the
Hayes modems, because many modems can pretend that they are Hayes
modems. If all else fails, call your administrator and ask which you
should choose.

The list of modems actually represents a bunch of *modem command
files.* When you install Notes, you automatically get one of these command files for just about every modem under the sun. (They're really
just ASCII files with the .MDM extension.) If you're short on disk space,
you can delete the command files that you don't need from your Notes
data directory. If your modem isn't listed, and the Auto Configure option
doesn't work either, call your administrator and ask for a special modem
command file for your modem.

✔ The next thing you need to worry about is the Maximum Port Speed list
box. All you have to do is click the speed of your modem. Don't get your
hopes up; if you have only a 28.8 Kbps modem, selecting 56.6 from the
Maximum Port Speed list is *not* going to make it work any faster. (Nice
try, though.)

TECHNICAL STUFF

A few words about modems

Modems are rated by their speed. Your modem might be called 56.6 Kbps (if you're lucky) or 14.4 Kbps (if you're not so lucky). The *Kbps* stands for kilobits per second, and it represents how fast your computer can send information over the phone. A 14.4 Kbps (sometimes they say "baud" instead of "Kbps," which means the same thing) modem sends 14,400 bits per second, which is pretty slow. A 28.8 Kbps modem is twice as fast, and a 56.6 Kbps (which actually stands for 56,600 bits per second) is about the fastest modem that's commercially available right now.

You don't even have to know what a *bit* is to realize that the faster you can send them, the better! The moral to this story is: No matter how fast your modem is, it's *a lot* slower than your network.

The speed of your modem is especially important when you're dialing in to the server to replicate. The faster the modem, the faster you can replicate. And the shorter the phone call, the smaller the phone bill. (That's really important if you're calling from a hotel room, because many hotels add a *huge* surcharge to outgoing calls. A 25-minute call to the home office can end up costing a lot of money.)

Most people find that a 14.4 Kbps modem is too slow to be practical to use with Notes. A modem that's 28.8 Kbps is pretty good. A modem that can go 56.6 Kbps is *really* fast and about the best you can have.

Of course, it takes two to tango. If the modem on your laptop is 56.6, but the modem on the server you call back at the office is only 28.8, your modem is going to be forced to slow down to 28.8 to talk to the server.

✔ The last thing you *might* want to worry about is the Speaker Volume, where you can choose Off, Low, Medium, or High. When you make a call from your computer to a Notes server, you briefly hear some high-pitched whistles and squeals and pops and squeaks as the two modems figure out how fast they can talk to one another (the server's 28.8 Kbps modem might have to slow down to talk to your crummy 14.4 modem). You can decide to turn off the volume, but then you won't be able to listen in to the beginning of their conversation. You may just want to listen in sometimes — especially if you're having trouble connecting — so that you can hear what's going on. On the other hand, if your modem works A-okay, you may decide to turn the speaker off so that you don't have to hear all that noise.

After selecting your modem's name from the list, setting the speed at which it communicates, and (perhaps) setting the volume, click OK twice.

After you have configured your modem, the next step is to create some connection and location documents to take advantage of it.

Connection and Location Documents

Do you know the old joke about the three most important things in real estate? Location, location, location. And the same is true when you take your computer away from the office — Notes needs to know about your *location*. For example, when you're at the office and connected to the network, mail you send is delivered immediately. But if you're working at home, Notes should hold mail messages until you call in with your modem. If you're in a hotel room, Notes needs to hold your mail and also remember to dial 9 to get an outside line. If you're dialing in to the network directly or connecting through the Internet, Notes needs to know that, too.

Notes keeps all these details straight with the *location documents* in your personal N&A book. You use these location documents to tell Notes what the rules are for mail delivery, dialing the phone, and whether or not you have a replication schedule.

If you've been using Notes at the office, you've probably already used your personal name and address book to compose a few group documents so that you can easily send mail to your friends. (Refer to Chapter 8, if you haven't and you want to.) Your personal N&A book is an important thing to take with you when you're using Notes from afar, because in it you store the phone numbers and other configuration information for the servers to which you'll be connecting.

Notes comes ready-made with seven location documents. When you're preparing to take your computer away from the office, peruse these documents to make sure that they have the rules you want.

Finding location documents

To view your location documents, choose File➪Mobile➪Locations. Notes shows you the five default location documents, as you can see in Figure 17-3.

Each of these connection documents helps you connect to your Domino server in a different manner, and contains the information that Notes needs, such as your Domino server's TCP/IP name and address, or name and phone number. Table 17-1 explains when you would use each.

Table 17-1	The Location Documents
Location Name	*Use This Location Document When You . . .*
Home (Network Dialup)	Intend to connect to your Domino servers by dialing in to your company's network
Home (Notes Direct Dialup)	Intend to dial your Domino servers directly from home
Island (Disconnected)	Temporarily have no way to connect to your company's Domino servers
Office (Network)	Are at the office and when you can connect to your company's Domino servers directly, through the network
Travel (Notes Direct Dialup)	Intend to dial your Domino servers directly from your home

The only real differences between the Home and Travel locations are that the Travel locations typically dial 9 to reach an outside line and can be set also to use a long-distance calling charge card.

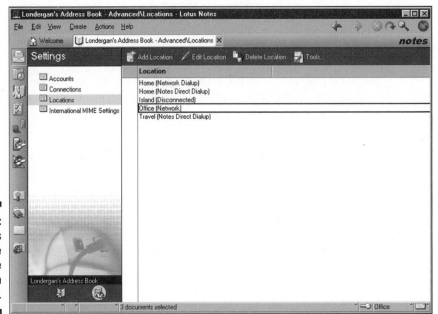

Figure 17-3:
Notes
has five
ready-made
location
documents.

Choosing your location

If you need to tell Notes how you are connected and where you are, choose File⇨Mobile⇨Choose Current Location, and then select the appropriate location document from the Choose Location dialog box, which is shown in Figure 17-4.

Figure 17-4:
Choosing
your
location.

After you click OK, Notes knows the area code, how to access an outside line, and whether your mail should be delivered immediately or held, awaiting your phone call to the server back at the office.

Every time you use your computer, be sure to choose the appropriate location document. In the lower-right corner of the status bar, Notes tells you which location document it's using.

Editing location documents

When you need to edit one of the location documents, first choose File⇨ Mobile⇨Locations; select the document and then click the action bar's Edit Location button. As you can see in Figure 17-5, a location document has lots of fields and lots of tabs. Fortunately, you need to worry about only a few of them, and most of the answers you'll supply will come straight from the mouth of your administrator.

The first field in the Location document form sets the tone for the rest of the location document. In other words, as you change what's in the Location Type field, the other fields and tabs on the Location document form change. For example, if you set the Location Type field to Network Dialup, Notes will ask you about your network user name and password. But if you set the Location Type field to Notes Direct Dialup, Notes will want to know the Domino server's phone number. Table 17-2 explains the most important fields.

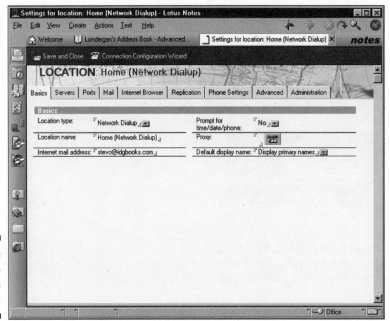

Figure 17-5:
A sample
location
document.

Table 17-2	Fields in a Location Document Form	
Tab	*Field Name*	*What It Does*
Basics	Location Type	This field determines whether you connect by calling a modem connected to your Domino server or to your company's network.
	Location Name	The name you'll choose in the future when you want to select this location document.
Servers	Home/Mail Server	The name of the Domino server that contains your mail database.
Ports	TCPIP or COM*n*	The port that this location document can use to connect to the Domino server. TCPIP is for the network, and COM*whatever* is for your modem.

Tab	Field Name	What It Does
Mail	Mail File Location	Determines whether your mail file is *Local* (on your computer) or *On Server*, which means it's on the Domino server. Typically, when you're using any kind of Dialin location document, you use a local copy of your mail. When you're using the Office location document, you use the on-server copy of your mail.
	Mail File	The name of your mail database.
	Transfer Outgoing Mail If	When you're using one of the Dialin location documents, this field determines how much outgoing mail has to pile up on your computer before it will connect to the Domino server to deliver it. If you set this field to 1, every message you send is delivered immediately.
Replication	Schedule	Setting this field to Enabled means that your computer will regularly and automatically connect to your Domino server to send and receive mail, and to replicate any other databases you have.
	Replicate Between, Repeat Every, and Days of Week	Determines the frequency with which your workstation communicates with the Domino server — only if you set the Schedule field to Enabled.
Phone Settings	Prefix for outside line	What number, if any, your computer has to dial to get an outside line.
	Calling Card Access Number	What number, if any, your computer should dial to connect to your long-distance service provider.

Tab	Field Name	What It Does
	Calling Card Number	What number, if any, your computer should dial for your long-distance account number.

Okay, so you've looked at each field in the Location document form, and you ask yourself: "Self, where do I put the phone number?" When you are working with a Notes Direct Dialup or Network Dialup Location document, it stands to reason that you have to put in a phone number — for either your Domino server's modem or the modem connected to your company's network.

 That's where the action bar's Connection Configuration Wizard comes in. When you click this button, Notes will ask you for either the Domino server's phone number (in the case of a Notes Direct Dialup connection) or the name of the Phonebook entry (in the case of a Network Dialup connection).

 When you've finished editing a location document, click the action bar's Save and Close button.

Taking a Copy of the Database with You

You usually want to make a copy of a database to bring along on your trip. Disk space permitting, you can bring any database you want with you; at the very least, you need a copy of your mail database.

To make a copy of a database that you'll be replicating, open the database and choose File⇔Replication⇔New Replica. Use the dialog box shown in Figure 17-6 to tell Notes the filename for the new database — you can usually accept the default. In fact, you can probably just click OK without worrying about any of those other fancy options in the New Replica dialog box.

Figure 17-6: Choose File⇔ Replication ⇔New Replica to make a copy of a database to take on the road.

New Replica "Stephen Londergan"

Server	Local
Title:	Stephen Londergan
File name:	mail\slonderg.nsf

OK   Cancel   Help

Encryption...   Size Limit...   Replication Settings...

Create: ● Immediately   ○ Next scheduled replication
☑ Copy Access Control List
☐ Create full text index for searching

Forget replicating — dial in to a server live

If you have a relatively fast modem — 28.8 Kbps or better — you may not have to replicate at all. (Now they tell us, right?) You can choose File⇨Mobile⇨Call Server to dial in to the server directly. If you do, you can use the server databases in the same way that you do when you're accessing them over the network — it'll just be slower. When you choose File⇨Mobile⇨Call Server, simply select the name of the server you want to call and, in most cases, click Auto Dial. If you plan to dial in to a server in the aforementioned manner, leave your location set to Office so that your mail will be delivered immediately.

If you are making a replica copy of your mail database, make sure that what you enter in the File Name field matches what's in the Mail File field in the mail tab of your location document.

When you click OK, Notes creates a copy of the database on your computer. At first, of course, this database is totally, completely, we're not kidding around here, empty. It has no forms, no views, no documents, no nothin'. The database won't get filled up until you perform your first replication.

Before you replicate for the first time

You won't be surprised to hear that you can screw up replication, and for once we're going to advise against blind optimism. Before you try to replicate a database for the first time, you should make sure that your database's Access Control List is set appropriately. Select your database and choose File⇨Database⇨Access Control. When you do, you get the dialog box shown in Figure 17-7.

Many of the entries in this dialog box won't make any sense, but that's okay. You're checking to make sure that the name of the server with which you'll be replicating is listed, and that its access is set to Manager. If your server isn't listed, click the Add button to rectify that problem.

In most cases, you want to list the server as Manager in the (local) database's Access Control List, but it may not be a bad idea to check with your all-knowing administrator — he or she may have a good reason to list the server differently. The right answer depends very much on the way your administrator has set up Notes at your company, so it can't hurt to ask.

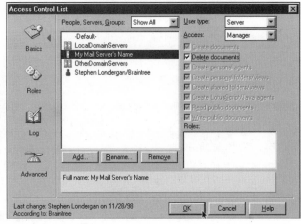

Figure 17-7:
If the
server's
name isn't in
this list,
you'll have
to add it.

Where to replicate for the first time

Time for a short quiz. Please select the one and only correct answer for the following question:

You have a database on your computer that you're going to replicate with a database on a server. This is the first time you've ever replicated the database, and you know that a whole bunch of documents have to get replicated into your copy of the database — several megabytes worth. Do you

- ✔ **Answer 1:** Perform the first replication over the phone from your hotel room, where long-distance phone calls cost about $1.00 per minute? Total time spent to replicate: 2.75 hours. Total cost of this one phone call: $237.50.

- ✔ **Answer 2:** Perform the first replication while you're still at work, over the network, where the process is extremely fast and doesn't cost anything? Total time spent to replicate: 11 minutes. Total cost: $0.00.

We hope you chose Answer 2.

To replicate a database, open the database in question, choose File➪ Replication➪Replicate, and click OK. You can watch the progress by clicking the Replicator bookmark; if you're replicating from home, you should hear the computer placing a telephone call.

Depending on the speed of your modem and how much you have to replicate, it may take a while before Notes finishes. You can go on about your work while you're waiting; Notes replicates in the *background,* which means that you can use other databases and even other programs while you're waiting for Notes to finish.

Well, ten or so pages after you started, you're finally ready to take your computer on the road. The process took so long (both to do and to read about) because you were setting up for the very first time. From here on out, replicating will be a breeze — we promise.

Replication quick reference

In case you need to refer to the steps someday, here's a short-and-sweet list of what you do to prep your computer for a trip:

1. **Choose File⇨Tools⇨User Preferences and select the port to enable your modem.**

2. **Click the COM*n* button in the User Preferences dialog box to tell Notes what kind of modem you have.**

3. **Verify that the location documents in your personal N&A book are set up properly for your area code and outside-line prefix.**

4. **Open the database, and then choose File⇨Replication⇨New Replica to make the first copy of the databases you need to bring with you.**

5. **Open the database, and choose File⇨Database⇨Access Control to make sure that the server's access level is set to Manager.**

6. **Choose File⇨Replication⇨Replicate to refresh your databases.**

We recommend that you do the preceding setup tasks while you're still at work, including replicating the databases for the first time.

Using Your Computer Away from the Office

Sure, most of the time you use Notes while you're at work and plugged into the network. Notes knows that you're connected to the network, so when you dash off an e-mail, Notes knows to whisk it off to the server through that wire snaking out of the back of your computer and into the wall.

But what if you're *not* connected to the network? What if you're working at home or you've taken your computer on a trip and you're in a hotel room? Notes has to know that when you send a mail message, it *shouldn't* try to send it through the network, because you ain't got one. Instead, Notes needs to let the mail messages you compose at home pile up so that it can send the messages later, when you call into the server.

The most important thing to do when you first turn on your computer at home (or in the hotel room) is choose File➪Mobile➪Choose Current Location. This command tells Notes where you are and what it should do with any outgoing messages you create.

When you use the Home and Travel location documents, Notes stores any e-mail messages you create in a special database called Outgoing mail. Don't confuse this database with your mail database; the Outgoing mail database holds messages only until you call the server or return to the office. You *always* read your mail in your mail database — that's the database with the envelope icon.

Sending mail from afar

With two small differences, composing and sending e-mail when you're remote is no different than composing and sending e-mail when you're on the network. Here are those differences:

- **Difference 1:** E-mail is delivered later, when you call into the server. This can take some getting used to. When you're connected to the office network, e-mail is delivered more or less instantaneously. If you're working remotely, though, you won't dispatch messages until you connect to your Domino server.

- **Difference 2:** If you're a fan of the action bar's Address button, you're in for a big letdown. Using the Address button at the office lets you peruse your company's public directory, which is located on your Domino Server. If you click the Address button at home, you can't see the company's public directory; you see only the people and groups in your personal N&A book. (If you want to send an e-mail to folks who aren't in your personal N&A book, you have to type their exact e-mail addresses in your message.)

If you absolutely, positively must have in your personal N&A book all the people in the public directory, contact your administrator.

Composing documents from afar

More good news: As with reading a document, composing a document in a local database isn't any different when you're on the road. Of course, when you compose a document in a database on a Notes server, other people can see it and read it the minute you save it. But if you're composing documents in the bush, those documents won't be accessible by your coworkers back in the office until you replicate your database with the server's database.

Enough Talk! Call That Server and Replicate!

 When you're ready to replicate a database — because you've added some documents to your database, or because you want to see whether any new documents have been added to the database back at the office, or perhaps because you want to dispatch the fifteen e-mail messages you just composed — click the Replicator bookmark, and then click the action bar's Start button.

Notes connects to the server and synchronizes the databases on your computer with the databases on the server. You can see the progress right on the Replicator page.

If you're calling from home or from a hotel room, you may hear the modem clear its throat and dial the server. Then, when Notes finishes replicating, it tells you on the Replicator page what happened during the call. You see exactly how many documents you sent, how many you received, how many databases were replicated, and how many mail messages were sent.

Up to this point in the chapter, we've discussed replicating on demand — in other words, every time you want to replicate, you use the menus to initiate the process. But there's a better way. You can instead schedule calls between your workstation and the server. That way, you don't have to call the workstation manually. Your workstation calls automatically all day long according to a schedule that you define:

1. **Choose File⇨Mobile⇨Locations.**

2. **Click the action bar's Edit Location button.**

3. **Click the Replication tab, which is shown in glorious black and white in Figure 17-8.**

4. **Move the cursor to the Schedule field and press the spacebar to choose Enabled (replacing Disabled).**

5. **Set the Replicate Daily Between field.**

   You can enter either a range of times, such as 8:00 AM – 10:00 PM, or a series of separate times, such as 8:00 AM, 8:30 AM, 1:00 PM, 2:45 PM. A schedule of 8:00 AM – 10:00 PM with a 60-minute repeat interval is common, but you can read the rest of this section to find out all your options.

6. **In the Days of Week field, enter the days of the week when you want to call, separating each with a comma.**

   (Do you get paid overtime for working on the weekend? We hope so.)

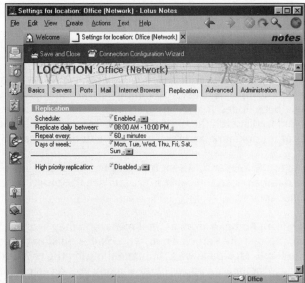

Figure 17-8:
Edit the
replication
settings in
your
location
document to
schedule
regular and
automatic
replication
between
your com-
puter and
the server.

7. **When you're finished filling out your remote connection document, click the action bar's Save and Close button.**

The exact times when Notes calls are determined by both the Replicate Daily Between field and what you enter in the Repeat Every field. The Repeat Every field wants a number of minutes; you enter a number such as 30, 60, 120, or 360.

Suppose that you enter 8:00 AM – 5:00 PM in the Replicate Daily Between field, and 180 in the Repeat Every field. This entry means that you want your workstation to make four calls to the server: the first call at 8:00 A.M., the second call three hours later at 11:00 A.M., the third call three hours after that at 2:00 P.M., and so on until 5:00 PM. If you want to make calls more often, you reduce the Repeat Every field. For example, entering 60 would make ten calls to the server.

If, on the other hand, you enter a series of times in the Replicate Daily Between field, the Repeat Every value tells Notes how long it should keep trying to call back if the scheduled call doesn't work out because of a busy signal or something. If you enter 8:30 AM, 1:00 PM, 2:45 PM in the Replicate Daily Between field and 60 in the Repeat Every field, Notes makes its first call to the server at 8:30 A.M. Assuming that call was successful, it won't call again until 1:00 P.M. If, at 1:00 P.M., the call doesn't go through — maybe the server's phone is busy — Notes keeps trying to call back continuously for one hour. If it still hasn't connected after an hour, Notes gives up on that call and won't try again until the schedule says so. In this case, that would be at 2:45 P.M.

Saving on Phone Bills (Selective Replication)

When you master the basics of replication, you're ready to delve into some of the fancy options available to fine tune exactly what happens when you replicate a database.

Selective replication is a way for you to choose exactly which documents you want to replicate. Suppose that you don't want to replicate all your e-mail when you travel. Rather, you want to replicate messages only from a certain list of people — your boss, your boss's boss, and that guy down the hall who is always sending you jokes. Or perhaps you want to get only the newest and hottest sales leads from your Sales Activity database. In either case, it's selective replication to the rescue.

The benefits of selective replication are obvious: Fewer messages to replicate equals less time on the phone equals smaller phone bills. To write one of these money-saving formulas, follow these steps:

1. **Select the database in question and choose <u>F</u>ile⇨<u>R</u>eplication⇨ <u>S</u>ettings.**

   The dialog box in Figure 17-9 appears.

Figure 17-9: Cut down on replication time and cost by using the Replication Settings dialog box.

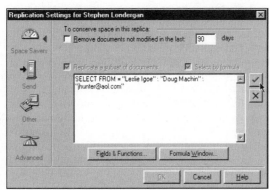

2. **Click the Replicate a Subset of Documents box, and then click the Select by Formula box.**

   Unless you've already modified the formula, the Select by Formula field contains the formula Select @All.

3. **Enter the formula you want in the field, click that little green check mark, and then click the OK button.**

   As usual, you don't have to worry about the rest of the options in the dialog box. If your administrator tells you that you have to mess around with the other settings, your administrator should also tell you exactly what to do.

The formulas used for selective replication can get pretty fancy, but in most cases, they're easy. The basic idea is to type the word *select,* followed by a field name, followed by a comparison operator (usually an equals sign), followed by a value.

In the following example of a selective replication formula, we're asking Notes to replicate documents from only a few people.

```
SELECT FROM = "Leslie Igoe" : "Doug Machin" :
"jhunter@aol.com"
```

The next example formula replicates documents that are both Leads and marked as Hot. (Notice that we now use the word FORM, not FROM.)

```
SELECT FORM = "Lead" & STATUS = "Hot"
```

This example replicates all the documents in the database, except those for the Garden State:

```
SELECT STATE != "New Jersey"
```

As you might expect, it's hard to predict exactly which formula is the right one for you. We *can* tell you that, if you want to replicate only e-mail from certain people, you use a formula very much like the first example, substituting the appropriate names for the ones used above — unless you happen to know Leslie, Doug, and Jeff. If you need a complicated formula to replicate only certain documents from a database, ask the database designer or your administrator for help.

When you've finished entering your formula, click the green checkmark button and then click OK.

If one of your coworkers regularly puts documents in a folder for your attention and you want to replicate only those documents, you don't have to write a formula. (What a relief!) Choose File➪Replication➪Settings and click the Replicate a Subset of Documents box. Then select the folder from the box.

Using the Replicator Workspace Page

You've already seen that the Replicator page is the place to look when you're replicating with a server and want to see what's going on. You can also use the Replicator page to initiate calls, replicate databases, and do a few other things. Figure 17-10 shows the Replicator page.

As you can see in the figure, the Replicator page has a special action bar, chock-full of buttons that are useful when you're living on the road. For example, the Send & Receive Mail button is an easy way to update your mail database.

Use the dialog box shown in Figure 17-11 to fine-tune what happens when a given database replicates. You get the dialog box by clicking the arrow button next to the database that you want to fine-tune.

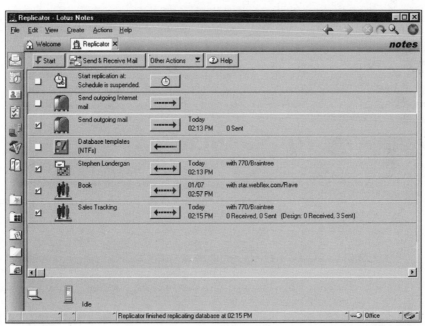

Figure 17-10:
The
Replicator
page.

Figure 17-11:
You can
save time
and space
when you
replicate.

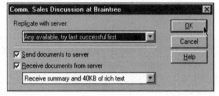

For example, you can make your replication go only one way, so that documents are only received from (but not sent to) the server. Or perhaps you choose to only send documents to the server — this is useful if you have a bunch of updates to post, but you don't have time right now to wait for a full database update. If you click the bottom drop-down box, you can choose Receive Full Documents, Receive Summary and 40K of Rich Text, or Receive Summary Only. The last two options are a great way to save time and space because they enable you to receive partial documents; you don't have to worry about tying up the phone line because someone has sent you a huge attachment or embedded object.

Most people use the Replicator workspace to work remotely; they find it easier than the menus.

Wrapping Up Replication

It's one of the cruel ironies of computer books that pages and pages are spent explaining how to set up your computer for a given task such as replication, and then there's not nearly enough ink about how you use a feature such as replication on a day-to-day basis. So we're going to correct that right here and now.

What if you have already configured your modem port, location, and server-connection documents and have replica copies on your hard disk of the databases you need to take with you on your business trip to, say, San Francisco. Here are a few likely scenarios and how you would use Notes in each.

Our story, Part A, in which our hero shows off her laptop on the airplane and then replicates upon arrival at her hotel room

Your company has a Sales discussion database, and that's one of the databases you've brought with you on your laptop. So, while you're cruising at 35,000 feet (business class, of course), you decide to kill some time by reading the database. You turn on your computer, start Notes, and switch to the Island location profile so that Notes knows you have no way of connecting to your server back at the office while you're in the air.

You open the database and start reading. You see a document you want to respond to, so you use the Create menu to add a document to the database. The document you just added is now saved in the copy of the database that you have with you on the plane, but it's obviously not saved in the copy of the database on your company's Domino server back at the office. Not yet, anyway.

When your plane finally arrives on the *left* coast, you have to do the following:

1. **Get a cab to your hotel.**
2. **Check in at the hotel.**
3. **Plug in and turn on your computer.**
4. **Start Notes.**
5. **Choose File⇨Mobile⇨Choose Current Location to switch to your Travel location settings.**
6. **Connect your laptop's modem to the phone jack.**
7. **Click the Send and Receive Mail button in the Replicator's action bar.**

When your computer finishes replicating with the server back home, two things have happened. First, the document you created and saved while you were up, up in the air is now in the database back at the office. Second, any documents that your colleagues posted in the database at the office are now in your copy of the database on your laptop.

Our story, Part B, in which our hero updates her local copies of other databases from her hotel room

Your coworkers have been not only sending you memos, but also adding, deleting, and editing documents in other databases. To reflect these changes on your local copies of the databases, follow these steps:

1. **Click the Replicator bookmark.**
2. **Select all the databases you want to replicate.**

   All checked databases will replicate, so click to add an X to databases that you want to replicate; click to remove an X from databases you don't want to replicate.
3. **Click Start.**

Our story, Part C, in which our hero heads out to see the sights

You'll be making sales calls in San Francisco for the next few days, so you want your laptop to take care of your replication for you. You want your Sales discussion and e-mail databases automatically kept up-to-date, without the need for you to be there and click the Start button.

Here's what you do:

1. **Choose File⇨Mobile⇨Edit Current Location.**

2. **Switch the Schedule field to Enabled.**

3. **Leave your laptop turned on, connected to the phone line, and with Notes up and running when you leave for the day.**

When you return to your hotel room at the end of the day, you find that both your e-mail database and your copy of the Sales discussion database have loads of new documents and messages — hardly surprising, because your laptop has been calling your server(s) back at the office all day long. As you reply to the e-mail you have received, you do *not* have to worry about calling the server to deliver it. Notes will deliver the messages during its next scheduled phone call back home.

Our story, Part D, in which our hero has returned from San Francisco and prepares her laptop to be used on the network again

You're home. A successful trip — ten new orders, plus treats and gifts for the kids. You plug your laptop back into your docking station, excited at the prospect of using the oh-so-fast network instead of your ever-so-slow modem.

But first, here's what you have to do:

1. **Choose File⇨Mobile⇨Choose Current Location to switch to your Office profile.**

2. **Choose File⇨Replication⇨Replicate (or Actions⇨Replicate with Server from the Replicator Workspace page) one last time.**

   This way, your workstation can synch up any documents you added while you were on the plane flying home.

Part VI
The Part of Tens

In this part . . .

You have ten small toes to wiggle in the sand; ten idle fingers snap at your command. The chapters in this part also contain sets of ten things we thought you would find useful or interesting or perhaps even necessary.

Don't consider these chapters to be frills, icing on the cake, or lace on the shirt-front of life. No, these chapters are the result of hours and hours of list making on the part of the authors, and we like to think that you will be glad we included the information. You'll indulge us, won't you?

Chapter 18

Ten Tricks and Timesavers

● ●

In This Chapter

▶ Closing windows in a flash

▶ Checking for new documents in just one step

▶ Privatizing a document

▶ Keeping a bookmark open

▶ Making music when e-mail arrives or telling Notes to pipe down

▶ Telling Notes to send e-mail replies for you while you're away

▶ Switching to edit mode with lightning speed

▶ Creating your own letterhead

▶ Checking your spelling

▶ Adding names to your personal N&A book

● ●

*I*f you *really* want people to think that you know what you're doing, read this chapter to discover the ten best tricks Notes has up its sleeve.

Close the Window — Faster

Whenever you want to close a document or a view, pressing the Escape key is faster than choosing File⇨Close. If you've been editing or composing the document in the window, don't worry, Notes asks whether you want to save the document before dismissing it from the screen.

You can also double-click the right mouse button to close a window (except on a Macintosh), just as you can in Release 3, but you must enable that feature first. To enable the capability to close a window by double-clicking the right mouse button, choose File⇨Preferences⇨Notes Preferences. In the User Preferences dialog box that appears, click the Basics tab. Under the Advanced options, choose the Right Double-Click Closes Window option.

Press Tab to Check for New Documents

If you're in the workspace (you clicked your Databases folder and selected Workspace), you can press Tab to start checking each database in your workspace for new documents. Pressing Tab in the workspace is really just a shortcut for choosing Edit⇨Unread Marks⇨Scan Preferred.

Make a Document Private

If you're composing a document in a database on a server, you can decide that you want only certain people to see the document. By creating a *Read Access List,* you can specify the people who get to read your contribution. Your fellow users who open the database but whose names are *not* in your Read Access List cannot see your document at all. In fact, they can't even find the document in the view!

To make a document available to only a subset of the people who can use the database, follow these steps:

1. **Press Alt+Enter to activate the infobox for the document you are composing.**

2. **Click the page tab that has a picture of a key.**

3. **Click to remove the check mark from the All Readers and Above option.**

4. **Click the icon at the right (the one that looks like a silhouette).**

5. **From the directory, select those whom you want to be able to read your document.**

Make sure that you include your own name in the Read Access list; otherwise, you won't be able to read the document yourself.

If you know your document will replicate to another Notes server, you must include the name of the server in the list of "people" who can read the document.

Keep the Bookmark Open

When you open a folder on the left side of the screen, a new pane appears listing all the contents of that folder. As soon as you double-click one of the items in the list in that pane, the pane disappears. Usually that's good because you get more screen real estate that way. But sometimes you want the list pane to stay open so that you can open more items. To make the list pane stay on the screen, click the push pin symbol in the upper-right corner of the pane. Now the pane is pinned to your desktop and won't close, and the push pin is replaced by something that looks like a pushed-in pin. Click the pushed-in pin to close the list pane.

Change What You Hear (Or Don't) When You Get E-Mail

If you use Windows, Notes can play a WAV file instead of using the boring old "beep beep beep" sound to tell you when e-mail has been delivered. To tell Notes to play your special tune, add the following line to your NOTES.INI file:

NewMailTune=c:\windows\tada.wav

NOTES.INI is an ASCII file full of configuration information. It's usually located in your Windows folder. You can edit it by using either the Windows Notepad or the SysEdit program.

Substitute your favorite WAV file for tada, and be sure to specify the correct path (the c:\windows part of the file information). To hear this change, your system must include a speaker that can play music. Assuming that you do, prepare for a real symphonic delight!

The bad news is: If you don't use Windows, you can't perform this neat trick. Sorry!

If you are receiving complaints about your noisy computer, the following trick might make you more popular. If you work under, shall we say, *crowded* conditions, and every few minutes someone's computer plays that catchy little tune signifying that new mail has arrived, the office can sound like a nursery full of little kids playing those annoying toy pianos.

To silence the constant "beep beep beep" signal that Notes uses to alert you that new e-mail has been delivered, choose File➪Preferences➪Notes Preferences, and then click the Mail button. After the mail page appears, click to turn off Audible Notification and click to turn on Visual Notification. You can always change your mind later and turn on this option again if you decide that you miss those "beep beep beep" alerts. When you have new mail, a message "You have new mail" appears quietly in your status bar. Sshhhh!

Get into Edit Mode Quickly

You need to be in edit mode to edit a document; just opening the document isn't enough. To get into edit mode, you can use a SmartIcon, possibly an action button if the database designer provided one, or a menu command. But the easiest way to get into edit mode is to double-click the open document. It doesn't matter where you click, as long as it's somewhere in the document. Isn't that easy?

If you don't have the proper access to the database and the document, forget about editing.

Automatically Reply to Incoming Messages while You're on Vacation

If you expect to be out of the office for a while and you won't be checking your mail, you can instruct Notes to send a form letter automatically to the people who send you messages, telling them that you're on vacation, won't be back for a few weeks, will respond to their messages then, and so on.

To get Notes to send automatic e-mail replies, open your mail database, choose Actions⇨Tools⇨Out of Office, and then fill out the form that appears on-screen.

After you return from your vacation, remember to choose the Actions⇨Tools⇨Out of Office again to access the form you need to turn off your automatic replies.

Check out Chapter 8 for more information about this and other advanced mail options.

Change Your Letterhead

Tired of the pictures and graphics at the top of your e-mail messages? Looking for something that is more "you?" You can choose from a long list of alternatives so that your memos match your taste!

To change your letterhead, open your mail database, choose Actions⇨Tools⇨Preferences, and then click the Letterhead tab. Scroll through the list — checking the appearance of each design in the preview window — until you find the special one that best expresses your personality and flair. Highlight your favorite, and then click OK in the action bar. From now on, that picture appears on all your memos.

Automatically Spell Check Your Work

On those occasions when you are rushed and knocking out memos faster than you can think, you may forget to run a quick spell check. Attend to this most important detail as follows: Choose (from a view, not from a document) Actions⇨Tools⇨Preferences and then click in the Automatic Spell Checking box.

Automatically Add People to Your Personal N&A Book

If you receive an e-mail from someone with a particularly nasty and hard-to-remember e-mail address (usually from the Internet), select or open the message and then choose Actions⇨Tools⇨Add Sender to Address Book. Notes automatically adds the person's name to a Person document in your personal N&A book. That way, you don't need to remember the address; Notes remembers it for you. After you use the Actions⇨Tools⇨Add Sender to Address Book command, open the personal N&A book, open the new document, add the person's name to the first and last name fields, and then save the document. The next time you create a memo, just type the person's name and Notes will automatically substitute that person's e-mail address when you save or mail the memo.

Chapter 19

Ten Things You Should Never Do

In This Chapter

▶ The ten worst things you can do when using Notes

▶ The reasons why you should never, ever do them

▶ What to do if you've already blown it

*U*sually, we encourage you to be adventurous, try new things, check out menus you've never used before, and generally live on the edge of life. But, just as the nascent mycologist has to learn to eschew certain dangerous and poisonous mushrooms in favor of the edible ones, you need to know about the ten things in Notes that you should never, ever do.

Don't Change Your Notes Name

Maybe you just changed your name. Maybe you just got married and you're going to start hyphenating your name with your spouse's — from now on, it's "John Deer-Doe." Or maybe you have to change your name because you got a new job at your company — instead of "George Parker/Consulting/Acme," now it's "George Parker/Support/Acme."

You want your name in Notes to change, too, so that the new messages you send and the new documents you compose reflect your new name.

As tempting as it may be, you should never, ever choose File➪Tools➪ User ID➪More Options➪Change Name. If you do (and you won't, because we told you not to, right?), you *will* be able to change your name but, in the process, you'll lose all your certificates.

If you've never even heard of *certificates* before, prepare to find out about them quickly if you change your name. Why? Without a certificate, you can no longer access any of your company's Notes servers.

If you really want to change your Notes name, choose File➪Tools➪ User ID➪More Options➪Request New Name. This way, your administrator can change your name and also make sure that you don't lose your certificates.

If it's too late, because you already did choose File➪Tools➪User ID➪ More Options➪Change Name, your only recourse is to call your administrator. There isn't anything *you* can do to correct the problem.

Don't Delete Your E-Mail Database

You probably have Manager access to your e-mail database. That's good, because you want to be able to customize your mail forms, change the way your folders work, and generally do anything you want to your e-mail database. But Manager access can also be bad, if you're not careful.

As Manager, you can use the File➪Database➪Delete command to completely, totally, irreversibly, forever, we're not kidding here, delete your *entire* mail database. And when we say entire database, we mean it; this command will delete every last e-mail message!

If it's too late because you've already deleted your e-mail database, call your administrator. Be prepared to grovel, and hope that your administrator has a backup copy. Otherwise, the administrator will have to register a new account and generate a new Notes ID — which means you have to start from scratch.

Don't Save or Send a Message Without Spell-Checking It First

As the olde saying goze, yOu onley have one chanse to maik a good furst impresssion — so don't blow it by e-mailing or posting documents that are full of typos. What excuse do you have for sending e-mail with spelling errors when you can always choose Edit➪Check Spelling to correct your errors? Shame on you! Better yet, enable automatic spell checking. Chapter 13 has the details.

Don't Remove Your Password

Passwords are important in Notes for two reasons:

✔ First, you don't want anyone else to read your e-mail, and you don't want the casual passerby to sit down at your desk and compose a few messages (full of four-letter words) under your name, right?

✔ Second, you have an obligation to your company not to let anyone use your USER.ID. If someone from your company's competition gets his or her hands on your USER.ID, that person can act as you — in fact, as far as Notes is concerned, that person *is* you. So that nasty person can read all the company's confidential databases that only you are supposed to be able to access.

So don't even consider removing your USER.ID's password. As long as your USER.ID has a password, even if someone steals your computer, you (and the rest of your company) don't have to worry about the thief getting any unauthorized access.

If it's too late and your (un-password-protected) USER.ID has been compromised, you should contact your administrator *immediately*. If your USER.ID came without a password, you should set one *right now* by choosing File⇨Tools⇨User ID⇨Set Password.

Don't Forget to Press F5 When You Go to Lunch

Did you read the preceding section? The same security concerns apply to an unattended Notes workstation, even when your USER.ID does have a password. So, before you leave your workstation unattended, remember to always press F5. That way, scoundrels trying to use your computer will be prompted for your password and locked out when they can't give it.

Don't Let Temp Files Pile Up

Notes puts temporary files on your hard disk whenever you launch an attached file. That can result in a hard disk full of temporary files. Sometimes, Notes remembers to delete these files when you're finished with them, and sometimes it doesn't. If you find any of these files lying around, you can *always* delete them to recover valuable hard-disk real estate.

Every once in a while — maybe once a month — look in your Windows program directory, your Notes data directory, and your TEMP directory for files whose names begin with a tilde (which looks like this: ~) or whose extensions are TMP. If you find 'em, delete 'em.

Don't Forget to Consult the Manuals

Sure, we know, everyone hates to read computer manuals, but the Notes manuals aren't as bad as some. They're not the most exciting things you'll ever read, but they do contain useful, even vital, information about how to use the program.

So, when you're stumped, consider a perusal of your nearest set of Notes documentation. As they say in the computer business, when all else fails, RTFM. (That stands for Read The Flippin' Manual.) If you need a copy of the manuals, download them free from the `http://notes.net/notesua.nsf` Web site in either Notes database format or Adobe Acrobat reader format (.pdf).

Don't Forget to Save Early and Often

Notes is like any computer program; unexpected power interruptions can be tragic. It's important to get into the habit of saving your work early and often. You can choose File⇨Save, use the Save SmartIcon, or just press Ctrl+S.

Don't Forget to Switch Back to the Proper Location when You Return to the Office

If you use your computer in many different locations — at the office on the network, at home on a modem, or on a plane without any external connection, for instance — you need to choose the current location to have Notes properly manage your outgoing mail and connect with databases.

If you go from the hotel to the office, for example, and forget to choose the proper location in the status bar, you may see a series of prompts on the screen telling you that Notes can't find things, you may wind up storing your mail locally because Notes doesn't know it's okay to send it, or you may not be sending to the server the changes you made to local copies of your databases. When you select the proper location, these tasks and many more are handled behind the scenes by Notes. For more information, go back to Chapter 17 to find out how to be reminded to change your location.

Don't Write Something You Don't Want Everyone to Read

You never know where something you wrote will end up. And don't believe everything you read, either.

Chapter 20

The Ten Most Common Notes Problems

In This Chapter

▶ The ten most common problems you might encounter while using Notes

▶ The ten easy ways to avoid the ten common problems

*H*ey, you can't expect everything to work perfectly all the time, and Notes is no exception. In this chapter, we discuss the ten most common problems — and their ten matching solutions.

Your Laptop Doesn't Connect to Your Server

Problem: Every time you try to use Notes remotely, you get an error message that says *Modem could not connect dial tone.*

Solution: Did you know that two kinds of telephone lines exist? One is called *analog,* and the other is *digital.* You don't need to know the difference between the two — you do need to know, however, that Notes (and any computer program, for that matter) can use only analog lines with its modem. If you get the aforementioned error message as you try to call in, the problem may be that the phone line you've plugged the modem into is digital instead of analog. Most offices (and many hotel rooms) are equipped with digital lines, and that causes all kinds of problems for Notes.

The bottom line is that you must find an analog line to use your modem with Notes. It figures that you can't tell the difference between an analog line and a digital one just by looking at the jack in the wall, doesn't it? You'll probably need to ask someone. If all else fails, you can plug your modem into the phone line being used for the closest fax machine, because fax machines use analog lines, too.

If you are still having problems, check the current location (in the status bar) and make sure the location document in effect has correct information.

To check the contents of the location document currently in effect, click the location section of the status bar and select Edit Current.

You Can't Edit a Field

Problem: You're trying to compose (or perhaps edit) a document, and you can't edit a particular field. You've tried the arrow keys, the Tab key, and even the mouse, but you can't even get the cursor into the field.

Solution: You need to be in edit mode. The easiest way to enter edit mode is to double-click anywhere in the document. Of course you need the proper access to the database and the document to edit. If you don't have the proper access, that's a problem for your administrator (less likely) or the database designer (more likely) to solve. Notes has many security features, and they're all under the control of the designer and administrator. Call one or the other of these folks and explain the problem.

To find out who is the designer or manager of the database, choose File⇨Database⇨Access Control, scroll up and down the list, highlight a name, and then check the access granted to that person in the upper-right corner of the Access Control List dialog box.

You Can't Use a DocLink

Problem: You double-click a DocLink icon, but you can't open the target document.

Solution: Tell the person who composed the document. Most likely, that person created a DocLink to a document that's in a database on a server that you don't have access to.

Your Server Isn't Responding

Problem: You double-click a database icon, but in response you see the error message *Server (servername) is not responding,* or *Network operation did not complete in a reasonable amount of time,* or perhaps *Remote system is no longer responding.*

Solution: Each of these error messages indicates a network problem, over which you have no control. (*Your* job isn't to keep the servers in good working order!) As is often the case, the solution to this problem begins with a call to your administrator.

You Don't Have the Right Certificate

Problem: Whenever you try to access a server, you see the error message *Your ID has not been certified to access the server.* Chapter 14 contains information about certificates.

Solution: Call your administrator and explain the problem.

You Can't Open a Database

Problem: Whenever you try to use a particular database, you see the error message *You are not authorized to access that database.*

Solution: Again, call your administrator and report that the Access Control List is incorrect for the database in question.

Call the Access Control List the "ACL" when you talk to your administrator. That way, you'll sound like you know what you're talking about.

You Can't Use Full-Text Search

Problem: You are trying (unsuccessfully) to create a new full-text index.

Solution: If the database you're trying to index is on a Notes server, the problem is usually that your administrator has set up the server to not allow full-text indexes. Indexes take up lots of disk space, and sometimes administrators get stingy.

You Can't Delete a Document You Composed

Problem: You composed a document in a database, and now you want to delete it — but you can't, no matter how many times you press Delete.

Solution: Call your administrator or the database designer and ask the one you reach to check (1) that the database is properly recording author names in the documents and (2) that the Access Control List enables you to delete documents.

You Can't Launch an Object

Problem: You double-click an embedded object's icon, but you can't get the other program to load.

Solution: To open an embedded object, you must have installed on your computer the program that was used to create the object in the first place. If the object is an embedded Lotus 1-2-3 worksheet, but you don't have 1-2-3 installed on your computer, you *can't* launch or edit that object. (You may also need to install a newer version of Notes; contact your administrator, who knows what to do.) Even if you don't have the program necessary to launch an object, you should be able to view it — just select View instead of Launch in the Object dialog box.

You Don't Know Who Your Administrator Is

Problem: You've read this book, and it seems that every time we discuss a potential problem, we use the "call your administrator" cop-out. The problem is that you don't know who that person is!

Solution: Ask your manager or someone else in your office, or consider changing jobs so that *you're* the administrator — and then call yourself.

Chapter 21

The Ten New Things You Should Know About Notes R5

- -

In This Chapter

▶ The desktop is gone

▶ The Domino Server is no longer needed

▶ Your mail is different

▶ The calendar is different

▶ The server had a name change

▶ Domino Designer sashayed into Notes

▶ Searching is easier

▶ HTML is available

▶ Notes now has subscriptions

▶ You get some groovy new letterheads

- -

*L*otus Notes has been on the market since 1989 — and as the saying goes, "you've come a long way, baby." Here, in no uncertain terms, are the Most Important New Features, which will be of particular interest to people who have upgraded from a previous version. If you're new to Notes — if you haven't used any other releases of this software — some of this chapter may not make any sense.

Desktop, Oh Desktop, Wherefore Art Thou?

Bye, bye, Notes database icons! The first thing you'll notice when you open Notes Release 5 is that the old, familiar desktop is gone — it has been replaced by the Notes Welcome page. (Don't worry, all your database icons are still there, in the Bookmarks bar.) In fact, Notes Release 5 sports a new (and, some would argue, much better) interface. It's prettier and easier to use. The new action bar buttons, the browser-like Forward and Back buttons, and the task bar make Notes easier (and more fun) to use than ever.

Rest assured, though, that you can do everything you're used to doing in previous versions of Notes. And although it may take a day or two to acclimate yourself to the new menus and buttons, it's worth it.

Don't Need No Domino Server

Release 5 is the first version of Notes that does not require a Notes or Domino server. For example, you might use Notes as your program to read e-mail, even though the mail is stored on a Microsoft Exchange server. Or maybe the cool ways you can browse the Web with Notes turns you on — no Domino server required.

Most people will end up mixing and matching, so that some things in your Bookmark bar or Favorites are Notes databases, some are Web pages, and some may even link to USENET newsgroups. The point is that Notes Release 5 now offers one-stop shopping — use Notes to do it all.

This is based on Lotus Notes Release 5's support for what's referred to in polite circles as *Internet standards.* Next time you're at a party, see whether you can work the following phrase into the conversation: "Hey, did you know that Lotus Notes R5 offers full support for POP3, IMAP, HTTP, and even NNTP?" (Aren't you a sparkling conversationalist! You're sure to be a hit, dropping those technological nuggets.)

New Mail

You open your mail — and it looks different. New buttons, new menus, lots of new stuff. The good news is that the basic arrangement of your mail is the same as it ever was. You still have the familiar view, navigation, and document panes. You can still preview documents before opening them. You can send e-mail down the hall or around the world easily.

The better news is that your mail has lots of new features — such as a new and improved memo form, easy-to-use task buttons for managing your messages, and easier-to-set preferences. In addition to a totally revamped look and feel, your mail has two new long-awaited features:

✔ **Automatic spell check.** So how many times have you realized, just after you click the Send button, that you forgot to spell check your memo? That won't happen anymore because Notes now automatically starts to check your memo's spelling before you send it. (You can turn off this automatic feature, if you want.)

✔ **Signatures.** You can also have Notes automatically insert an Internet-style signature at the bottom of every e-mail you write, so you no longer have to type your name, address, phone number, return e-mail address, and shoe size at the bottom of each memo.

New and Improved Calendar

As you poke around in your new Release 5 mail database, sooner or later you'll find the new and improved calendar. Like the mail template, the new calendar is pretty and comes loaded with new features and things you can do. Chief among the new stuff is the ability to see what's known as a *group calendar*. This means that you can view, manage, and print a schedule that includes the appointments and meetings for more than one person — if you have the rights to do so. That's a great feature for a group of people who work together or if you manage the calendars of several people.

The Server Is Now Called Domino

The software used to be called Lotus Notes, but now Lotus makes a distinction between the so-called client (the software that you run on your computer), and the server (the software that runs on the shared server down the hall, in the closet). Henceforth, thou shalt always referrest to the client software as *Lotus Notes* and the server as a *Domino server*. Got it?

New Designer

Did you ever feel the need to poke under the hood of a Notes database? The way you do that in Release 5 is different and involves a brand-new piece of software known as the Domino Designer. The subtleties of same would warrant an entire book of its own, so we purposely didn't include them in this fine tome.

The bottom line: If you are an application designer, make sure you install the Domino Designer program, in addition to the Lotus Notes client software.

Better and Simpler Searching

Did you know that there were at least three ways to search in Lotus Notes? You could search an individual document, an entire view, or through a full-text index. The rub was that each method of searching had its own menu choices, dialog boxes, and things to remember.

Fortunately, all searching in Notes Release 5 happens the same way, through the Search button. So it just doesn't matter if you want to search the document you have open, or the view you're in, or a whole bunch of databases, or even the Web itself — that one Search button does it all!

HTML Mail

In days of yore, sending mail to people who didn't use Lotus Notes was a real problem — especially if you had to send your memo to someone through the Internet.

You could get your mail to that person, of course, but it looked lousy. Although Notes lets you make words bold, or use different fonts, or include something fancy such as a table or a picture, all that jazzy stuff would be lost when you sent mail to someone who didn't use Notes.

But that's a worry of the past. Most people, no matter what mail program they use, will now be able to see the pretty fonts, colors, pictures, and other enhancements in your e-mail messages. (Whoever said that substance was more important than style?)

The capability to send such pretty messages is based on something called HTML mail. (This means that Notes uses the same language to prepare an e-mail that is used to create Web pages on the Internet.) Although most other e-mail programs (such as Microsoft Outlook, Eudora, and America Online) can understand and properly display this type of mail, you may come into contact with somebody who uses a program that still doesn't know how to handle your colors and fonts. Not to worry, though, because such a person will still get your message; it just won't look as nice as you intended.

Subscriptions

Lotus Notes Release 5 includes a new feature, called Subscriptions. When you subscribe to a database or a Web page, Notes will automatically notify you when the database or Web page changes or is edited.

For each subscription, you fill out a profile to determine what triggers the subscription, such as whenever a document is edited, or whenever a document is added by a particular person, or whenever the Web page changes. When such an update happens, Notes can even send you an e-mail that includes a link to the subscribed information.

Cool New Letterhead

Ever since the days of Notes Release 4, you've been able to choose your own letterhead — those cool graphics that appear at the top of the e-mail you send. Life gets better with Notes Release 5 in two ways. First, some new types of letterhead (Lightning Storm is our favorite) have been added. Second, the old ones (such as Pony Express and Wild Confetti) are better than ever. To select the image that appears at the top of the mail you send, open your mail, and then choose Actions⇨Tools⇨Preferences⇨Letterhead.

Glossary

@Function A formula element containing preprogrammed calculations that make writing a formula much easier. Examples are @Sum, @UserName, @Now.

Accelerator key A keystroke combination used to accomplish the same thing as choosing a menu item. Ctrl+Z is the accelerator key for Edit⇨Undo.

Access Control List (ACL) The part of every Notes database that determines who can do what in that database. See also *No Access, depositor, reader, author, editor, designer,* and *manager.*

Actions Tasks that normally involve several keystrokes and that are assigned to buttons or a special menu and then associated with views, forms, and folders so that you can easily perform them. Actions are what happen when you click buttons in the action bar.

Administrator The person who is in charge of running the Notes servers at your company and to whom you should turn if you have questions or problems.

Agent A miniprogram or set of instructions that automates tasks in Notes. (Formerly called a *Macro.*)

Alarm A visual or audible reminder of a scheduled event in your calendar.

Application designer The person at your company who created the database(s) you use. Also known as a *database manager* or an *application manager.*

Application server (1) A Notes server that is only used for application databases — in other words, it does not have anyone's e-mail database on it. (2) A computer application used to create data linked to or embedded in Notes documents.

Archive A special copy of a mail database (or other database) containing documents selected for storage away from current active documents.

Archive log A summary of the documents that have been put in an archive database.

Archive profile A special form used to set the criteria for determining which documents should be put in an archive.

Attachment A file (such as a Lotus 1-2-3 worksheet or a Microsoft Word document) that has been included in a Notes document. You can put attachments only in a rich text field.

Author (1) The person who composed a document and (usually) the only person who can edit it or delete it. (2) A level of access you can have to a database. As an author, you can read documents, compose new documents, edit your own documents, and delete your own documents. (3) Someone like the fine people who wrote this book.

Balloon help The things that show you what each SmartIcon does.

Bookmark A pointer to a Notes item (a search or a database, for instance) or an item on the Web.

Browsing The official, more dignified term for surfing or cruising the Internet. Call it what you want; it means you're looking for information or just wandering around (electronically, of course) to see what there is to see.

Button A rectangular picture resembling a button that launches some action or task when clicked with the mouse.

Calendar A section of your mail database containing time-related documents (such as appointments, meetings, or birthdays).

Category A line in a view that does not represent a document, but rather represents data that is in a given field and is the same in all documents listed below the category. All documents with Nebraska in the state field, for instance, could be listed below a line containing "Nebraska."

cc:Mail Another program from Lotus Development Corporation that's used for e-mail. At many companies, some people use Notes for e-mail and others use cc:Mail.

Certificate A special stamp for your USER.ID that your administrator gives to you. You have to have a certificate specific to your company to use the servers at your company.

Client Another term for *workstation,* the version of Notes installed on computers that people use to do their work. Not to be confused with servers — computers that store information.

Clipboard A section of memory used to hold something you have copied or cut, and plan to paste somewhere else.

Common name The part of your Notes user name that sounds like what your mother calls you. For example, if your User Name is Stephen Londergan/Lotus, your common name is just Stephen Londergan.

Compound document A document containing information from more than one program.

Connection document A document in your personal name and address book that tells your workstation when and how to call the server.

Database In Notes, a collection of Notes documents, folders, views, agents, and other design elements. In general, any organized collection of information.

Database template A shell of a database that you use as a starting point to create your own database. A real time-saver.

DDE Dynamic Data Exchange. A copy of a document created in another application and placed in a Notes document. It retains a link to the original document, so changes to the original are reflected in the copy.

Default A decision about an assumption or preferred value that users can change. The default text color, for instance, is black.

Delivery report A return message that tells you when a message you sent was delivered to the recipient's mail database.

Depositor A level of access that you can have to a database. As a depositor, you can only add documents to a database. You cannot read, edit, or delete them.

Designer A level of access that you can have to a database. In addition to having all the rights that editors have, designers can change a database's forms and views.

Designer client Separate Notes software that allows users and designers to modify database elements.

DESKTOP.DSK The file on your workstation that keeps track of what databases are on your workspace and which documents in them you have already read.

DocLink An icon in one document that you can double-click to quickly go to a different document.

Document (1) An individual item in a Notes database. In other database programs, a document would be called a *record*. (2) A piece of paper with stuff written on it.

Domain (1) All the Notes servers at your company. (2) What a king or queen is in charge of.

Domino Used synonymously with *Notes*. More specifically, the term refers to the aspects of Notes that relate to working with the World Wide Web.

Edit mode The status of an on-screen document in which you are able to change the contents of fields.

Editor A level of access that you can have to a database. Editors can compose documents as well as read and edit documents, even if they didn't compose the documents in the first place.

Electronic signature A special numeric code added to a document to prove that it really was written by the person who sent it.

E-mail An electronic mail message.

Embedded object Information included in a Notes document that came from another program. You can double-click an object to edit it, if you have the originating program on your computer.

Encryption A procedure in which a document or part of a document is scrambled until opened by a person who has the proper decryption key.

Encryption key The numeric code used to scramble and unscramble a document or part of a document.

Error message A dialog box that Notes shows when you make those all-too-frequent mistakes.

Export A way to turn Notes documents into files for use in other programs, such as Lotus 1-2-3 or WordPerfect.

Fax A process of sending a picture of a document over a phone line.

Field A place in a database form for specific individual pieces of information. *First Name* might be a field in a personnel data form.

Folder A database element that lists documents in a database. You put documents in and remove documents from a folder.

Footer Text that appears at the bottom of every printed page.

Form What you use to compose, edit, and read documents.

Frameset A design element of a database containing the rectangles that designers use mainly to display different pieces of information on the Web.

Full-text index Part of a database that locates words and phrases in all documents in a database so that you can later search for text in those documents.

Full-text search Searching for text or phrases in documents in a database.

Fuzzy search A command issued before executing a search in which you tell the Notes search engine to look for variations in or phrases similar to the text you are searching for.

Gateway See *Mail Transfer Agent.*

Group A collection of users' names, defined in either the public directory or your personal name and address book. Using group names saves having to type the individual names of people in a group when sending them e-mail.

Groupware Software that enables several people to work together on computers.

Header (1) Text that appears at the top of every printed page. (2) What you take when you fall over something.

Headlines A database you configure to remind you of the most important new e-mail messages, calendar events, tasks, and modified Web pages.

Help document A special collection of tips about how to use a database.

Hierarchical name A user name that includes not only your common name but also your organization and the level or department in that organization.

Home page (1) See *Welcome page.* (2) A main page on the World Wide Web from which you can navigate to other Web pages.

Home server The one and only Notes server that has *your* e-mail database on it.

Hotspot (1) A place where you shouldn't sit. (2) A location in a form or graphic that, when clicked with the mouse, launches an action.

HTML HyperText Markup Language. The text and code which formats and displays information on WWW pages.

Icon A graphic used to represent a database, a program, or an action.

Import What you do when you want to turn a foreign file, such as a Lotus 1-2-3 worksheet, into a document in a Notes database.

Index Shorter name for the *Full-text index*. Also refers to the background process by which views are updated to be sure that they display current information.

Infobox Now more frequently called *Properties box,* it is a dialog box that usually contains several pages that allow you to change many aspects of the selected item.

Input validation formula A formula included in a form that checks to be sure that you entered data in a field and that it's the right data type.

Install A process or a program that places a usable copy of a program on a hard disk.

Internet A huge collection of computers all connected in a vast global network.

Keyword field A special kind of field that presents you with a list of choices for data input.

LAN Local Area Network. LAN rhymes with "man." It's really just a bunch of wires that connect your computer to other computers.

LAN workstation A computer that has Notes installed on it and is plugged into the network.

Letterhead Fancy graphics you can include in mail database forms.

License A right to use Notes.

Link A graphical representation in one document of another document, database, or view. Click the link to open the other document, database, or view.

LMBCS Lotus Multi-Byte Character Set. A set of characters including standard keyboard characters and characters not found on keyboards.

Location A name and accompanying data that define the places where you use Notes, such as on the LAN at the office, on a modem at home, or not connected at all in the shower. Locations are defined in location documents in your personal N&A book.

Lotus Notes The program that this book is about.

Macro A minicomputer program of Notes commands. This is the old name for what is now called an *Agent.*

MAIL.BOX A special kind of Notes database that holds messages that are pending delivery.

Mail database The database that holds all your incoming and outgoing e-mail messages. No one but you can read the documents in your mail database.

Mail server A Notes server that has mail databases on it.

Mail Transfer Agent MTA. A special program that runs on a Notes server and converts Notes e-mail messages destined for other mail systems, such as the Internet, or even a fax machine.

Manager The highest level of access available for a database.

Modem Hardware that lets you use your Notes workstation to place a phone call to your Notes server. Useful if you need to read your e-mail and other Notes databases when you're at home or on a business trip.

Modem command file A special ASCII file that Notes needs to use a modem. Every brand of modem has its own modem command file.

Mood stamp (Not to be confused with mood rings) a picture that Notes adds at the top of a message so that your reader knows what frame of mind you were in when you sent the message.

Mouse A device that moves a pointer around your screen so you can make selections without using the keyboard.

Mycophile A fungus fancier.

N&A book Name and address book. See *Personal N&A book* and *Public directory*.

Navigation bar See *Universal navigation bar*.

Navigator (1) A program used to find Web pages on the Internet. Notes has a built-in Navigator. Navigators are also available from other companies, including Microsoft, Netscape, and America Online. (2) A database element that substitutes graphics and associated commands for normal menu items, making the use of a database more user-friendly.

NetBIOS The most commonly used protocol for Notes.

Network A collection of computers that are connected by wires and use a network operating system.

Network operating system A type of software used to connect computers. Some common network operating systems include products from Novell, Banyan, and Pathworks. Sometimes called *NOS*.

Newsletter A special memo that is automatically generated to notify users of new documents in a database.

NLM Netware Loadable Module. An operating system that's used only on some Notes servers but never on workstations.

No Access A level of access to a database. If you have No Access to a database, you can't use that database. Period!

NOS See *Network operating system*.

Notes data directory The directory on your computer's hard disk that has your local databases and DESKTOP.DSK.

Notes data folder The folder on your Macintosh that has your local databases and DESKTOP.DSK.

NOTES.INI An ASCII file on every Notes workstation that holds configuration information for that workstation.

Notes log A special Notes database that keeps track of all the phone calls you've made from your remote workstation — if you've made any, that is.

Object See *Embedded object*.

Object Linking and Embedding OLE (pronounced o-lay). The part of the operating system that lets you include information from other programs in a Notes document. See *Embedded object*.

Operating system The program that runs your computer. Notes runs with the Windows, OS/2, UNIX, and Macintosh operating systems.

OS/2 An IBM operating system that you can use on Notes workstations and servers.

Page In Notes, a screen full of database-related information generally used as an opening screen. On the Web, a page is a screen full of information.

Page break A code you insert in a long document that instructs Notes to print subsequent text on a new sheet of paper. Normally, page breaks are not visible.

Pane A section of a Notes window (window pane, get it?). The number, name, and purpose of the pane varies depending on the context.

Password A secret code that you have to enter every time you use your USER.ID.

Permanent Pen (1) A unique font used to make editorial comments in a document. (2) A writing implement specifically designed to stain your clothes.

Person document One type of document in your personal name and address book. The public directory has a Person document for each user at your company. You can also compose a Person document in your *Personal N&A book* to give one of your friends an e-mail nickname or to help you remember someone's complicated e-mail address.

Personal N&A book A database on your computer's hard disk in which you can enter person, group, and connection documents.

Platform Computerese meaning the same as *Operating system*.

Policy document A document that describes the purpose of a database and the rules for its use. (Also called the About This Database document.)

Pop-up A part of a Notes document that has hidden text associated with it. You view this hidden text by clicking the word.

Port The name for the part of your computer where your network or modem is plugged in. Some computers have more than one port; yours might have one port for the network and one port for the modem.

Power tie A knot tied around the neck symbolizing extreme corporate fealty but mistaken for a symbol of corporate authority.

PowerBook A portable Macintosh computer.

Preferences document The Macintosh equivalent of NOTES.INI, which stores system settings.

Private key The part of your user ID that's used to decrypt your encrypted mail messages.

Private view A view that's on only your workstation.

Properties box (1) A place to keep your childhood treasures. (2) In Notes, it is a series of dialog box pages, each represented by a tab, and each relating to features (properties) of a given item. Also called *Infobox*.

Protocol A techie term for the part of your network operating system that is used to connect your Notes workstation with your Notes servers. You may hear about protocols called NetBIOS, SPX, or TCP/IP. Then again, you may never hear protocols mentioned.

Public directory The database on the Notes server that defines all the Notes users, servers, groups, and connections at your company.

Public key The part of your USER.ID that other people use to encrypt mail messages for you.

Query Builder A dialog box you fill out that makes it easy to define criteria for a full-text search.

Query by form A way to enter the criteria for a full-text search, using the same form that was used to enter the document in the first place.

Read Access List A way to control which people can read a document that you compose. You set a document's Read Access List in the Document infobox, on the page with the key tab.

Reader A level of access that you can have to a database. As a Reader, you may read only the documents that other people have composed; you cannot compose your own.

Relational database A database program that allows the full sharing of data between databases and between forms within databases. Notes is not a true relational database.

Remote workstation A Notes workstation that is not connected to a Notes server by a network. Instead, remote workstations often use a modem to talk to the Notes server.

Replica ID A special serial number that every database has that identifies it as the same database, even if there are copies of it on other servers.

Replication The process used to synchronize two copies of a database between two servers or between a server and a workstation.

ResEdit The program you use on a Macintosh to edit your User Preferences document.

Return receipt A special kind of e-mail message that tells you when a recipient opened an e-mail that you sent.

Rich text A special field type that can include more than one font and formatting (such as bold and italics), and can contain embedded objects and attachments.

Ruler The part of the Notes screen that you can use (if you choose to display it) to set margins and tabs in a *Rich text* field.

Search bar The dialog box at the top of the screen (if you choose to display it) that allows you to specify the text to search for and rules for the search.

Section Part of a Notes form or document with its own fields. It may be collapsible, meaning the user can choose to display or conceal its contents, and it may have restricted access, which means only designated people can edit its fields.

Selecting (1) Designating text or data to be deleted, copied, or changed in some way. (2) Choosing documents in a view for such group treatment as categorizing, printing, or deletion.

Selection formula A Notes formula used to designate which documents will be replicated.

Server A shared computer that stores Notes databases.

Server-based mail A setting you use that causes Notes to send off your messages immediately; the opposite of *Workstation-based e-mail.*

Signature Also called an *Electronic signature;* a way for you to guarantee to the recipient of a message that it really, honestly, absolutely came from *you.*

SmartIcon A picture representing an action you can take. Click the SmartIcon to initiate the action.

SmartIcon palette A collection of SmartIcons.

Sort (1) To put items in a list in order. (2) To match your socks.

Spam Junk e-mail, or e-mail sent to too many people. Examples are hysterical notices that you are asked to "send to everyone you know" about Web-based viruses that eat hard disks for lunch and e-mails from Hot Stuff who has a personal message for you at his or her Web site.

SPX A protocol made by Novell.

Static text Text in a form that doesn't change. The title of a form is an example of static text.

Stationery A template of various types of mail messages you might send.

Status bar (1) A line of information at the bottom of the Notes window, part of which you can use to change parts of your document. (2) A drinking establishment on Main Street where they have cold beer and hot tunes. Closed Sundays; shoes and shirt required.

Styles Named collections of paragraph attributes that you can assign to a paragraph all at once.

Subform A section of a form with its own fields, text, graphics, and design, which designers can use in multiple forms.

Subscription An instruction you issue to Notes to send you a memo listing new information in Notes and Web locations you specify.

Tables (1) Small spreadsheets that you can insert into Notes documents. (2) A place to put your cold beer while you're listening to the hot tunes at the status bar.

Task button Oval buttons above the work area of a Notes window; each one represents an open window in Notes and contains a short name of the window plus an X, which you use to close the task.

Template A special kind of Notes database used to create other Notes databases.

TLA Three-letter abbreviation for "three-letter abbreviation." No, it is *not* a three-letter acronym unless you can pronounce the abbreviation as though it were a word. Although you may have heard HTML described as a three-letter acronym, it certainly isn't: Aside from the fact that it has four letters, you can't pronounce HTML.

Typeahead The capability in Notes to start typing the name of an addressee of a memo and have Notes finish it for you.

Universal navigation bar (Have you noticed how many bars are in Notes?) This one is located near the top of the Notes window and contains icons that allow you to perform tasks you associate with the Web — searching, going forward, going back, and stopping a process, for example.

UNIX An operating system that you can use on Notes workstations and servers.

Unread marks Stars or colored text used in views to show you which documents you haven't read yet.

URL Uniform Resource Locator. The address of any particular Web page.

Vacation profile Also called the Out-of-Office agent, a special agent used to reply automatically to messages you receive when you're on vacation.

View A summary of the documents in a database. Most databases have more than one view.

WAN Wide Area Network. A bunch of computers connected in some other way than by network cables. Most frequently used are phone lines, satellites, broadcasts, and tin cans with string.

WARP Release 3 or later versions of *OS/2*.

Web page A document on Web servers that can contain graphics, links to other documents or pages, text, attached files, and multimedia features.

Web server A computer somewhere in the world with Web pages on the Internet.

Welcome page The opening screen in Notes containing tasks you can perform and locations to which you can navigate.

Window One of the *Workspaces* you may have opened in any program. Each Notes window represents a separate Notes document, view, Web page, or other task you have performed. Each Notes window is represented by a task button near the top of the Notes screen.

Windows An operating environment that you can use on Notes workstations and servers. Current versions are Windows 98, Windows 95, Windows NT, Windows 3.1, and Windows for Workgroups.

Workflow Features added to a Notes database that allow users to assign tasks, notify others of assigned responsibilities, and track the completion of tasks.

Workspace (1) The first Notes screen you see, the one containing the tabbed pages and database icons. (2) Any Notes window. (3) The place where your boss lets you work when you're good.

Workstation The computer at your desk or (if you have a laptop) the computer in your briefcase. It's the computer that each person uses to work with Notes.

Workstation-based e-mail A setting that you use when your computer is not connected to a LAN, which causes Notes to queue your outgoing e-mail until you place a phone call (using a modem) to a Notes server.

World Wide Web WWW. A collection of computers on the Internet that have special pages (see *Web page*) you can use.

Index

Notes

Notes